GW00818581

GUIDE TO

B&Bs

OF CHARACTER AND CHARM

IN FRANCE

GUIDE TO
B&Bs
OF CHARACTER AND CHARM
IN FRANCE

Editorial Director Véronique Pettit de Andreis
Translated by Christina Thistlethwayte

RIVAGES

© Copyright 1993 by Editions Rivages SA
106 Boulevard St Germain, 75006 Paris

Editions Rivages is represented in the UK by
Bay View Books Ltd, Bideford, EX39 2QE

ISBN 1 870979 37 0
Printed in Italy

We thank our readers for the new addresses they have proposed
for inclusion in this year's guide.

INTRODUCTION

This guide contains a careful selection of 382 bed-and-breakfast establishments – known as 'maisons d'hôtes – from all over France.

All of them have been visited and their inclusion here is based on their genuineness, charm, surroundings, comfort and quality of welcome. Prices are an important factor too, but don't automatically assume that the cheapest places are the least good. Whether you are looking for independence or good company, somewhere rustic or refined, the descriptions in this guide will help you find what you want.

As a tradition the B&B has long been established in Britain, but in France it is a much more recent development and the number of establishments is growing fast, so very great care has been taken to select only the best for you here. Staying in B&Bs is the exact opposite of mass tourism, and gives you the chance to enjoy your own personalised holiday.

Whether farmhouse or château, the B&Bs we recommend are run by owners for whom a real quality of life is all-important. They take pleasure in sharing with you their love of their house and their region. With this guide, staying in a French B&B ceases to be a possibly disappointing adventure and becomes a pleasant discovery instead.

But don't forget that these are private houses, not hotels. Open the door of any of these houses and you will find a character and a way of life which reflect those of the owner. Before you go in, here are a few words of advice:

- Always book in advance, to avoid disappointment.
- If you are delayed, 'phone to let them know. B&Bs don't have night porters.
- The prices quoted have been given to us for 1993, but owners may revise them during the year.
- Bedmaking and room cleaning are normally done regularly or daily. In some cases they are done on request, or even left to the guests. We have tried to specify what service is available. In addition, some of the bigger houses are difficult to heat in winter, so it's safest to ask about heating arrangements in advance.
- The restaurants named have been recommended by the owners of the B&Bs.
- We have indicated whether there is a lounge or a 'phone for guests' use.

- Ask your hosts about things to do and places to see in the region. They are an excellent source of information and are happy to pass it on.

All you have to do now is follow the guide, and discover the regions and people of France for yourself.

HOW TO USE THE GUIDE

The guide is divided into regions and in each region the *départements* and districts are dealt with in alphabetical order. Maps by Recta Foldex have all the B&Bs flagged on them and will help you find your way. The number on the flag is the same as the number of the text and photo entry about the B&B.

To find a place, you can use either the contents list in the front of the guide, which is arranged by regions, or if you know its name you can find it in the alphabetical index in the back.

TELL US HOW YOU GET ON

To improve the guide, we are always very pleased to hear your reactions and comments on the B&Bs we have selected, as well as your suggestions for new places which you think ought to be in our next edition.

Please write to our UK office: Rivages Guides, c/o Bay View Books Ltd, 13a Bridgeland Street, Bideford, EX39 2QE.

CONTENTS

ALSACE – LORRAINE

AQUITAINE

A U V E R G N E – L I M O U S I N

B O U R G O G N E

C   E   N   T   R   E

CHAMPAGNE ARDENNES

FRANCHE-COMTE

ILE-DE-FRANCE

N O R D - P A S - D E - C A L A I S

N O R M A N D I E

P A Y S   D E   L A   L O I R E

P I C A R D I E

P O I T O U - C H A R E N T E S

P R O V E N C E - C O T E   D ' A Z U R

R H O N E - A L P E S

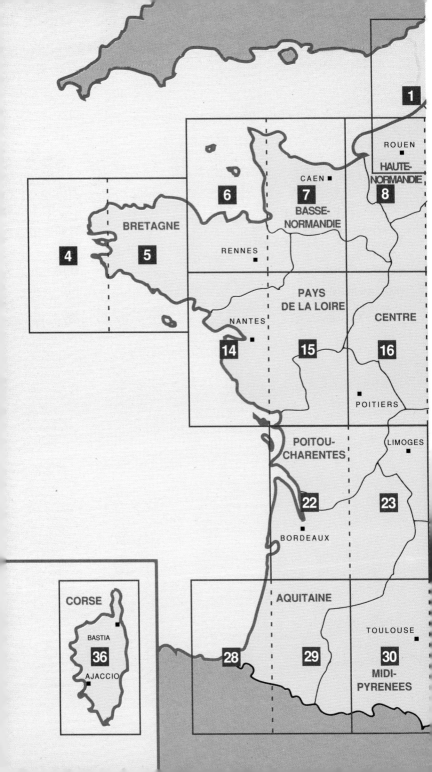

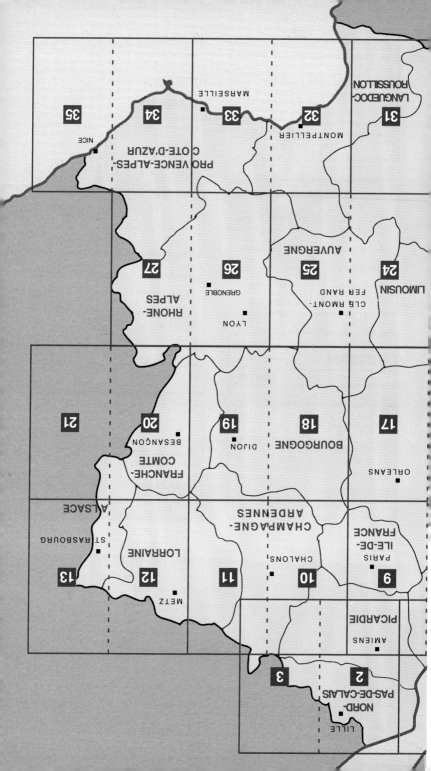

KEY TO THE MAPS

Scale: 1:1,000,000
Maps 30 & 31: scale: 1:1,180,000

MOTORWAYS

❶ Interchange
❷ Half-interchange
❸ Toll-barrier

Kilometre-distance
❶ in total
❷ partial

Motorway
❶ under construction
❷ projected

ROAD CLASSIFICATION

Dual-carriageways

High traffic road

Trunk road

Other road

Road ❶ under construction
❷ projected

TOWNS CLASSIFICATION

❶ by the population

— less than 10,000 inhabitants
— from 10.000 to 30.000
— from 30.000 to 50.000
— from 50.000 to 100.000
— more than 100.000
— towns with over 50.000 inh.

❷ Administrative

— Chief-town of department

TARBES

— Main subdivision of department

CARPENTRAS

— Districts

Combeaufontaine

— Commune, hamlet

Andrézieux-Bouthéon

ROAD WIDTH

4 carriageways

3 lane or
2 wide lane

2 lane

Narrow road
Kilometre-distance
❶ in total
❷ partial

BOUNDARIES

National boundary

County boundary

TOURISM

Picturesque locality — Chenonceaux

Very picturesque locality — **Amboise**✱

Interesting site or natural curiosity — Roches de Ham

Historic castle

Ruins of outstanding beauty

Abbey

National park

DIVERS

Civil Airport
Dam

Canal
Car-ferries

Motorail

Pass

Summit — ▲ 2392

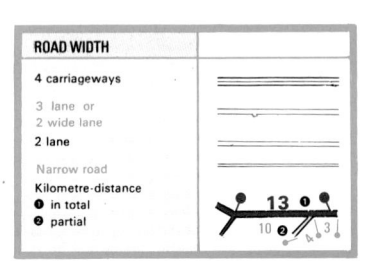

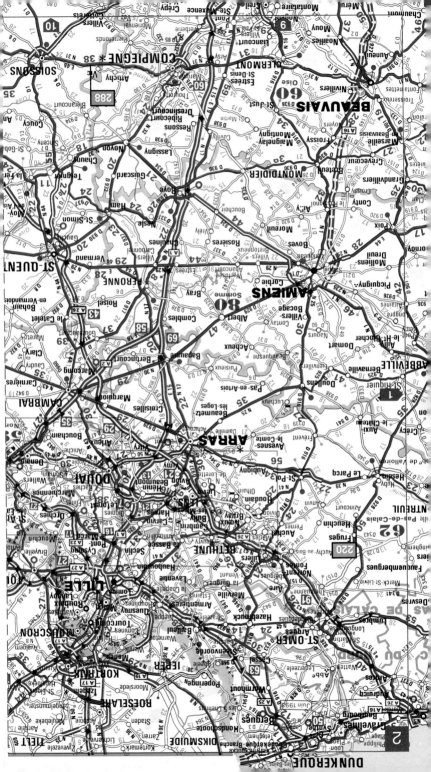

pnte de Penn

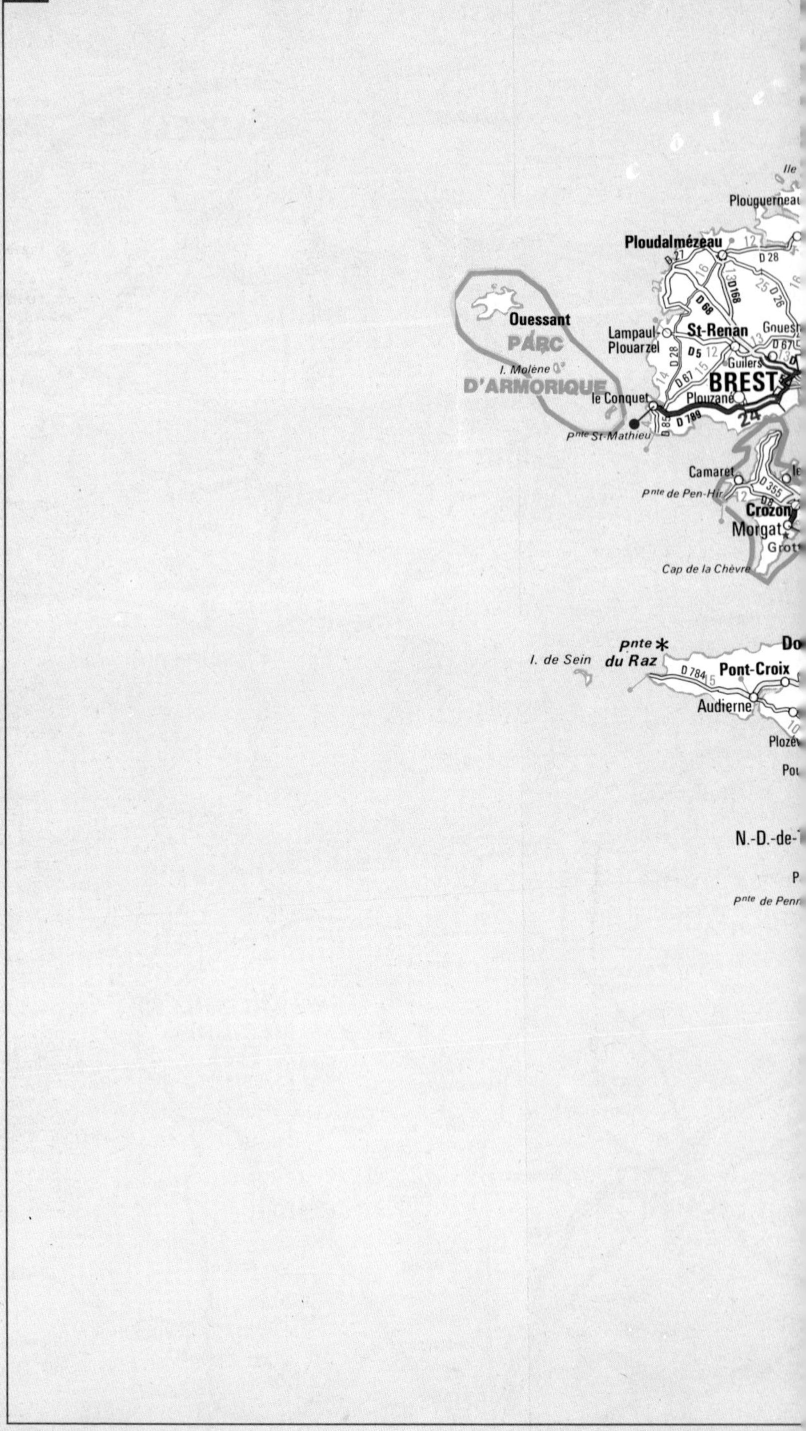

p

N.-D.-de-

Pou

Plozé

Audierne

Pont-Croix

Do D 784 I. de Sein pnte du Raz ✱

Cap de la Chèvre

Gro

Morga

Crozon

pnte de Pen-Hir

Camaret

le

pnte St-Mathieu

le Conquet

D 789

BREST

D'ARMORIQUE

Plouzané

Guilers

D5 12

Lampaul I. Molène ⚓

Plouarzel

PARC

St-Renan

 Goues

Ouessant

D 68

D 168

D 28

Ploudalmézeau

Ploughern eau

île

4

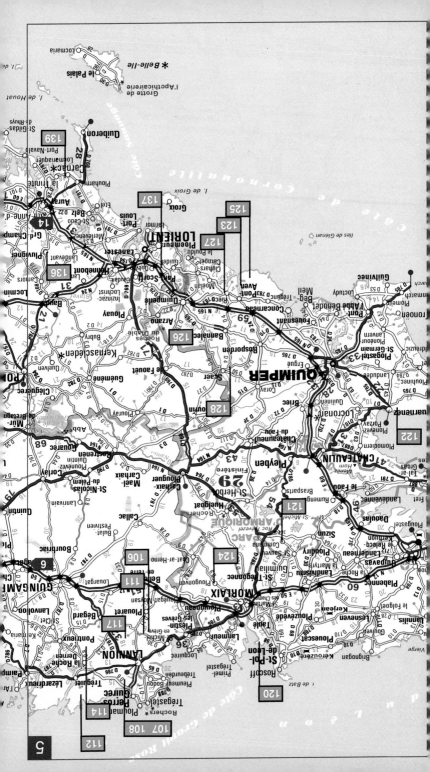

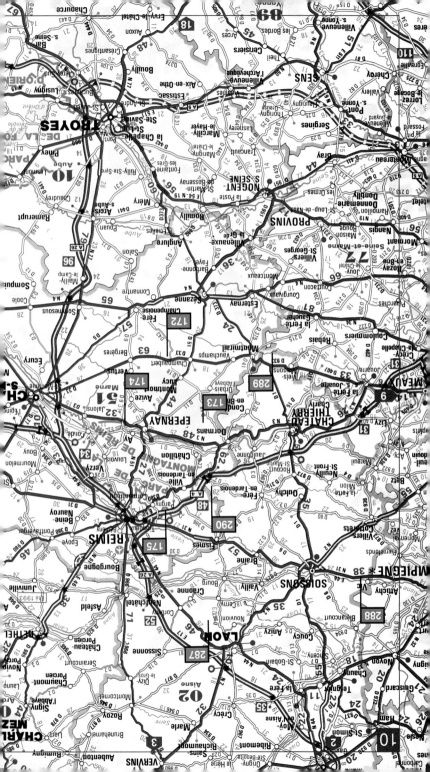

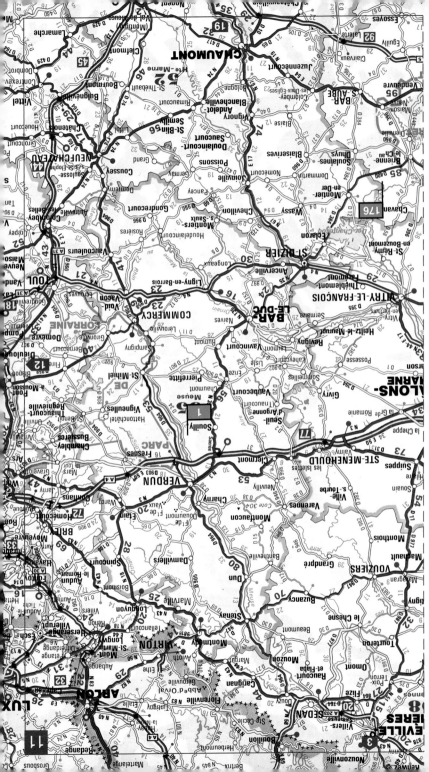

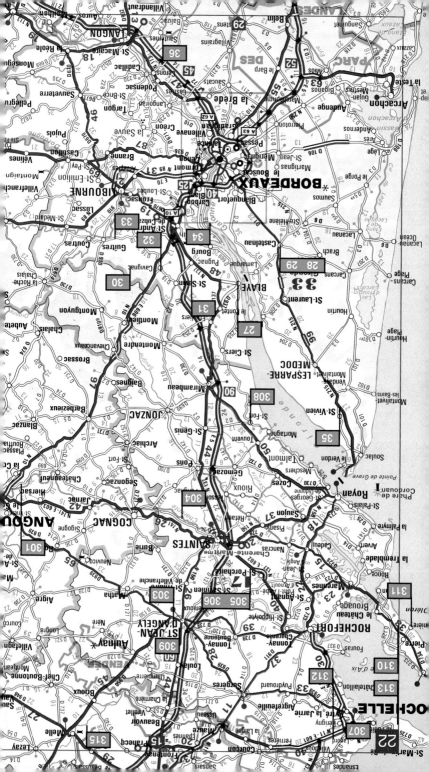

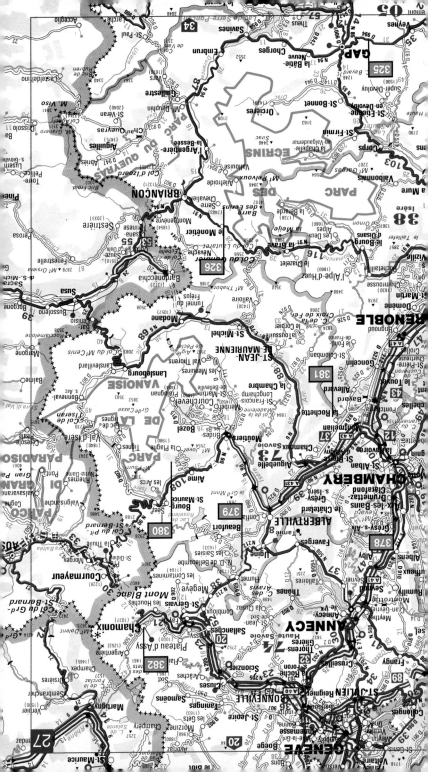

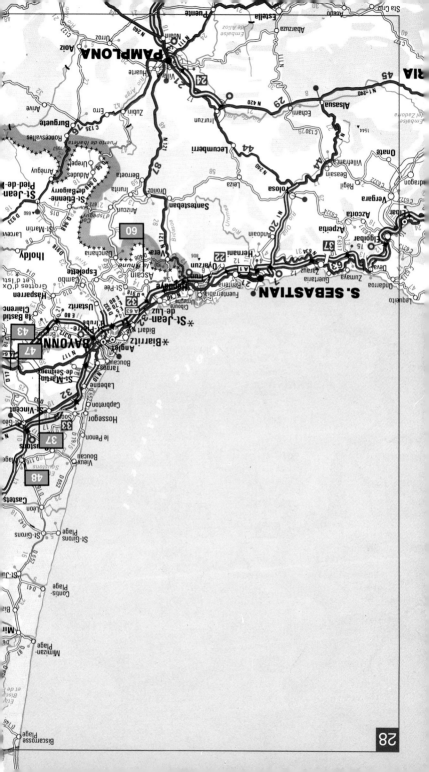

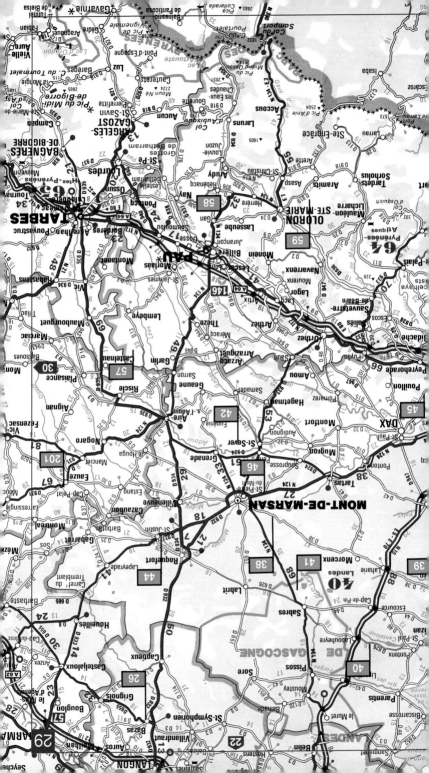

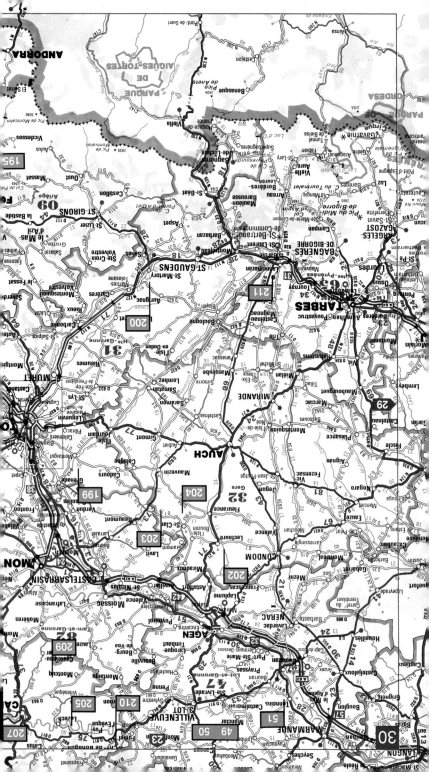

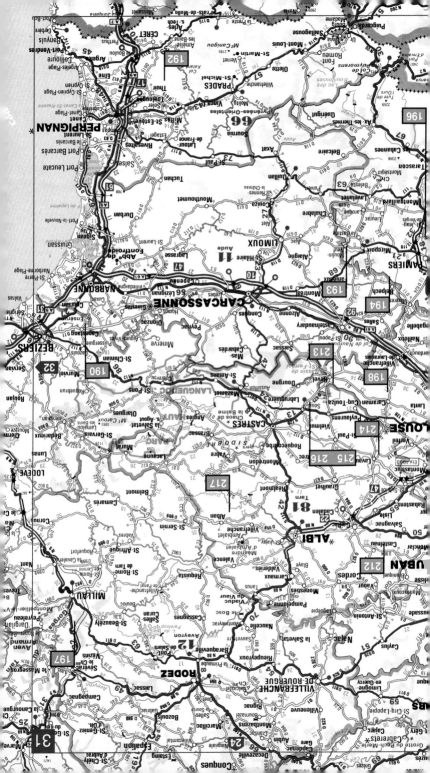

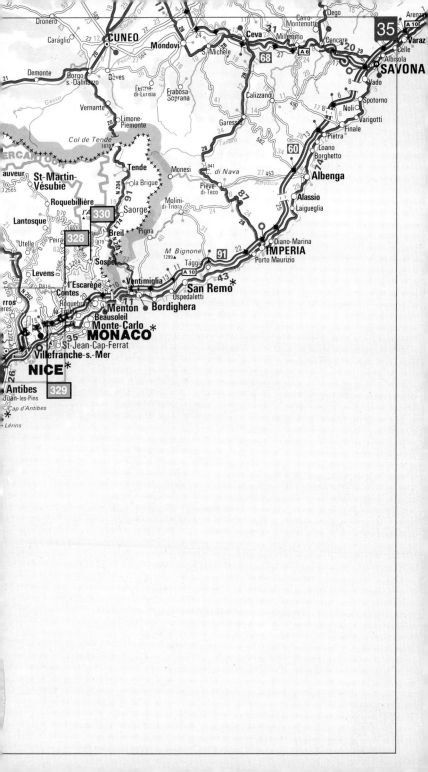

Cap Corse

○ Ile de la Giraglia

○ **Rogliano**
Pino ○
D 180 ○ Sta-Sévera
Luri ○

○ Canari
D 80

Nonza ○ **Brando** ○ Erbalunga

San-Martino-
di-Lota
BASTIA

Désert
des Agriates
St-Florent ○
D 81

l'Ile-Rousse N 197
Santo-Pietro-
di-Tenda
○ Oletta
Ste-Michele

Algajola ○
St-Antonino ○
Belgodère ○ Murato
Borgo
○ la Canonica

✳CALVI
D 151
Muro ○
Lama ○
Campitello
Casamozza

Olmi-Cappella ○
Castifao
Vescovato

Calenzana
Asco ○
Ponte
Leccia
○ Campile
Folelli

Gorges
Popolasca ○
Morosaglia
la Porta
Pero Casevecchie

✳Girolata
PARC
○ Mt Cinto
2707
Francardo
San-
Lorenzo
Piedicroce
○ San-Nicolao

Calacuccia
Omessa ○
2B
HAUTE-CORSE
D 71
Cervione

Col de
Vergio
1464
CORTE
Casamaccioli
Sermano
Valle
d'Alesani
Pietra-di-Verde

✳Girolata
Porto ✳
Evisa
DE
Venaco
Piedicorte
Moita

Piana ✳
Soccia ○
D 23
Guagno-les-
Bains
Vivario ○
Vezzani

Cargèse ○
Vico
Salice ○
Sagone ○
Ghisoni
Aleria

Sari-
d'Orcino
85
Vizzavona
Bocognano

Sarrola-
Carcopino
2A
CORSE-DU-SUD
Bastelica
Prunelli-
di-Fiumorbo

la Punta
AJACCIO
N 196
Frasseto ○
Zicavo
Solenzara

Iles Sanguinaires
Cauro ○
Sta-Maria-
Siché
✳Col de
Bavella

Chiavari ○
Bicchisano ○
Petreto
Aullène ○
Zonza

Acqua Doria ○
Filitosa
Serra-di-
Scopamène
San-Gavino-
di-Garbini

Porto
Pollo
Olmeto
Levie
Ospedale

Propriano ○
Ste-Lucie-
de-Tallano

Campomoro ○
SARTÈNE
Porto-Vecchio

Iles Cerbicale
Cauria ○
N 196

Figari

✳Bonifacio
Ile de Cavallo

Ile de Lavezzi

recta
foldex
Copyright RECTA FOLDEX

S. Teresa
Gallura
C. Testa
Ile Maddalena

CARTES RECTA FOLDEX
POUR VOYAGER EN FRANCE ET DANS LE MONDE ENTIER

RÉALISATIONS ET ÉTUDES CARTOGRAPHIQUES
TOURISTIQUES ET ADMINISTRATIVES
40, 48 rue des Meuniers - 93100 MONTREUIL-SOUS-BOIS (FRANCE)
Tél. (1) 49 88 92 10 - Télex : 234 018 - Télécopie : (1) 49 88 92 09

recta foldex

1
Château de Labessière

55320 Ancemont
(Meuse)
Tel. 29 85 70 21
Fax 29 87 61 60
M. and Mme Eichenauer

Closed for Christmas and New Year. **Rooms** 1 with bath and WC, 1 with shower and WC and 1 suite (5 pers.) with shower room and WC. **Price** 200F (1 pers.), 250-275F (2 pers.), suite 450F (4 pers.) + 60F (extra pers.) **Meals** breakfast incl., evening meal 100-125F. **Facilities** lounge. **Nearby** golf, riding, fishing, Lake La Madine, forest of Argonne, valley of La Saulx. **Spoken** English, German.

Crossing the Meuse before entering the village of Ancemont you find this small château opposite an ancient wash house. The interior has been completely refurbished. You will be made very welcome and sleep in comfortable, well-kept bedrooms with lovely antique wardrobes. The ground floor furniture is less authentic. Breakfast and dinner are served at separate tables in the pleasant dining room. Before leaving be sure to enjoy the garden.

How to get there (Map 11): 10km south of Verdun via D34 or D964 until Dieve.

2
Château d'Alteville

Tarquimpol
57260 Dieuzé
(Moselle)
Tel. 87 86 92 40
Fax 87 86 02 05
M. and Mme L. Barthélémy

Open 1 April-15 Nov. **Rooms** 10 with bath and WC (8 with telephone) and 1 apartment of 2 bedrooms, kitchen and bathroom. **Price** 450-500F (2 pers.), apartment 800F (4 pers.), 900F (5 pers.) + 100F (extra pers.) **Meals** breakfast 40F, evening meals at communal table, on reservation 200F (wine not incl.) **Pets** small dogs allowed on request (+55F). **Nearby** tennis, riding, fishing. **Spoken** English, German.

A very lovely country property close to a number of lakes. You will pass through beautiful rooms: a billiard room/library, a drawing room with antique furniture, a dining room festooned with hunting trophies. The bedrooms have been restored and provide modern comforts while retaining their old-fashioned charm. All have views of the grounds. Good set menus beautifully presented, crystal glasses and silver cutlery. The welcome is refined yet unaffected.

How to get there (Map 12): 54km east of Nancy via N74 and D38 towards Dieuzé, then D999 towards Gelucourt and D199f.

3
La Musardière

57340 Lidrezing
(Moselle)
Tel. 87 86 14 05
Cécile and René Mathis

Open all year. **Rooms** 1 with bath and WC, 2 with shower and WC. **Price** 250-300F (2 pers.)
+50F (extra pers.) **Meals** breakfast incl., evening meal at communal table 100-150F (wine incl.)
Facilities lounge. **Pets** small dogs allowed on request. **Nearby** tennis, riding, Vic sur Seille,
Marsal. **Spoken** English, German.

A small, simple and unpretentious village house where you will find a warm and attentive welcome. The bedrooms are peaceful and delightfully countrified with wide beds like ship's bunks. We recommend those on the ground floor because the others have velux windows. Good set menus in a light room overlooking the garden.

How to get there *(Map 12): 50km south east of Metz via D999 towards Morhange. 10km after Morhange take D199 towards Lidrezing, then follow signs.*

4
Chez M. et Mme Krumeich

23, rue des Potiers
67660 Betschdorf
(Bas-Rhin)
Tel. 88 54 40 56
M. and Mme Krumeich

Open all year. **Rooms** 3 with shower, WC and TV. **Price** 200-290F (2 pers.) + 80F (extra pers.)
Meals breakfast incl., no evening meal. **Restaurant** La Table des Potiers in Betschdorf. **Facilities**
lounge, sheltered parking, pottery courses. **Credit cards** Visa. **Pets** no dogs. **Nearby** swimming
pool, tennis, pottery museum, picturesque villages. **Spoken** English, German.

Betschdorf is a village famous for its potters and you stay in the house of one of them. The different sized bedrooms are comfortable and well decorated and are quiet as they are away from the road. Breakfast is served in a pine-panelled room embellished with pieces of stoneware. The welcome is simple and friendly.

How to get there *(Map 13): 15km north of Haguenau via D263 towards Wissembourg, then D243.*

5
La Maison Fleurie de Colette Geiger

19, route de Neuve-Eglise
67220 Dieffenbach-au-Val
(Bas-Rhin)
Tel. 88 85 60 48
Mme Geiger

Open 1 Feb-31 Dec. **Rooms** 4 with shower and WC, and 1 room for 2 children. **Price** 150F (1 pers.), 190F (2 pers.) + 60F (extra pers.) **Meals** breakfast incl., no evening meal. **Facilities** lounge, telephone. **Pets** small dogs only. **Nearby** tennis, swimming pool – 4km, ski-ing (cross country and ski slopes) – 15km, Haut-Koenigsbourg, Riquewihr, wine route, Mont Ste Odile, swannery, hawking. **Spoken** German.

Situated on a hillside in a small, straggling village, this typically Alsatian house overflows with flowers. Mme Geiger will greet you with a big smile. The small bedrooms are simple and well kept. There is a pleasant garden. Breakfast is served at a large table in the dining room or outside on the terrace. There are many tourist attractions close at hand.

How to get there *(Map 12): 20km west of Sélestat via D424 to Villé, then D697.*

6
Tilly's Bed & Breakfast

28, rue Principale
67140 Le Hohwald
(Bas-Rhin)
Tel. 88 08 30 17
Tilly and Gérard Hazemann

Open all year. **Rooms** 3 studios (2 pers.) with bath, WC and kitchenette (poss. suite 4 pers.) **Price** 395F (2 pers.) – possibility of weekly terms. **Meals** breakfast incl., no evening meal. **Restaurants** in Le Hohwald. **Pets** no dogs. **Nearby** fishing, tennis, riding, archery in summer, ski-ing (cross-country or ski slopes), hiking, wine route, Haut-Koenigsbourg, Mont Ste Odile. **Spoken** English, Italian, German.

Although set in a very pretty mountain village, the approach to the house is not very appealing as it is located on the main street. On the other hand the bedrooms are huge, well arranged, comfortable and cheerful. One of them has a terrace overlooking the countryside. The breakfasts are more than ample and served in the rooms. Friendly welcome.

How to get there *(Map 12): 27km north west of Sélestat via N59 towards St Dié, then D424 towards Villé; after Villé D425 in the direction of Le Hohwald.*

7
Neufeldhof

67280 Oberhaslacht
(Bas-Rhin)
Tel. 88 50 91 48
M. and Mme André

Open all year. **Rooms** 4 with basins (shared shower and WC) and 1 suite (4 pers.) of 2 bedrooms, shower and WC. **Price** 210F-260F (2 pers.) suite 520F (4 pers.) **Meals** breakfast incl., evening meals at communal table, lunch on Saturday, Sunday and national holidays: 75F (wine not incl.). **Facilities** heated swimming pool, equestrian centre, lounge. **Pets** dogs not allowed. **Nearby** tennis, fishing. **Spoken** English, German.

Set in the middle of the countryside this big and very old farm has been converted into an equestrian centre. The interior has character. The bedrooms are comfortable and attractive, and each one has a ceramic stove in working order. The bathrooms are not very special. Excellent meals, very friendly welcome and good views over the countryside.

How to get there *(Map 12): 36km west of Strasbourg via A352. At Molsheim, N420 to Urmatt and D218; in the village, D75 towards Wasselone for 2km; first track on the right.*

8
Le Biblenhof

67120 Soultz-les-Bains
(Bas-Rhin)
Tel. 88 38 21 09
M. and Mme Joseph Schmitt

Open all year except Christmas week. **Rooms** We only recommend the rooms in the annexes. 5 with shower and WC, 1 with shower and shared WC, 3 sharing bathroom and WC, 3 studios (4/5 pers.) with shower and WC. **Price** 190-260F (2 pers.), studio 240-280F (4/5 pers.) **Meals** breakfast 22F, half board possible, evening meal at communal table 60-80F (wine not incl.) **Facilities** lounge, loose boxes. **Pets** dogs not allowed. **Nearby** covered swimming pool, tennis, riding, 18-hole golf course (25km), wine route. **Spoken** English, German.

A gigantic 18th-century farmhouse with a very welcoming façade covered in geraniums. The large entrance hall has great style, with antique furniture and a beautiful wooden staircase leading to the bedrooms. We only recommend the new rooms in the annexes. Very pleasant welcome, good dinners and excellent breakfasts.

How to get there *(Map 12): 20km west of Strasbourg via D45; in the village take D422 towards Irmstett for 500 metres, then follow the signs.*

9
Le Moulin de Huttingue

68480 Oltingue
(Haut-Rhin)
Tel. 89 40 72 91
M. and Mme Thomas

Open all year. **Rooms** 4 with shower and WC and 1 studio (2/3 pers.) with shower and WC. **Price** 220F (1 pers.), 260F (2 pers.), studio 300F (2 pers.) **Meals** breakfast incl., evening meals (separate tables) 100-200F (wine not incl.) **Facilities** lounge, loose boxes, fishing. **Nearby** swimming pool, golf, cross-country ski-ing, Ferrette. **Spoken** English, German.

The Ile flows a few yards from this large and lovely mill. On the ground floor is a welcoming room where breakfast is served in the morning and which becomes a restaurant in the evening. The bedrooms are comfortable and attractive (the blue bedroom is especially nice). Very kind welcome.

How to get there *(Map 20): 20km from Bâle (Switzerland) and 6km south east of Ferrette via D23 towards Kiffis as far as Hippoltskirch, then D21 bis towards Oltingue. It's in the hamlet of Huttingue.*

10
La Maison Bleue

16, rue Saint-Nicolas
68240 Riquewihr
(Haut-Rhin)
Tel. 89 27 53 59/89 27 24 61
Francine and Clément Klur-Graff

Open all year (3 nights min.) **Rooms** 4 studios for 2 pers. and 3 apartments for 4/5 pers. with shower, WC & kitchenette. Rooms cleaned on request. **Price** 220F (2 pers.), 1800F per week for 4 pers. **Meals** breakfast 30F, no evening meals. **Restaurants** nearby **Credit cards** Visa. **Pets** dogs allowed on request. **Nearby** village tour, wine and foie gras tasting, wine route, Haut-Koenigsbourg, old Colmar, golf (3km), swimming pool (5km), tennis. **Spoken** English, German.

This pretty house stands in a very quiet little street in Riquewihr, a perfect Alsatian village. The studios or small apartments have a kitchen area and some have a terrace. There is everything necessary to make a good breakfast for yourself and every morning fresh bread and croissants are delivered to your door in a willow basket. In spite of this somewhat unusual practice, this is one of our best addresses.

How to get there *(Map 12): In Riquewihr.*

11
Chalet des Ayès

Chemin des Ayès
88160 Le Thillot
(Vosges)
Tel. 29 25 00 09
M. and Mme Marsot

Open all year. **Rooms** 1 with bath and WC, 1 with shower and WC, and 12 chalets (4-10 pers.) **Price** 320-380F (2 pers.) +100F (extra bed). **Meals** breakfast 38F, evening meals on reservation, at separate tables 128F (wine not incl.) or at auberge nearby. **Pets** small dogs allowed on request. **Facilities** swimming pool, cross-country ski-ing. **Nearby** ski slopes, villages, mountain walks, wine route, local history museum.

This mountainside chalet is almost on the borders of the Vosges and Alsace. The two comfortable bedrooms are very cosy. One of them has a large bay window with a picture postcard view of the valley. A very friendly welcome, good breakfasts and for those who succumb to the lure of the place there is the possibility of renting one of the charming little chalets by the week.

How to get there *(Map 20): 51km west of Mulhouse via N66 towards Remiremont.*

12
Château de Regagnac

24440 Montferrand-du-Périgord
(Dordogne)
Tel. 53 63 27 02
M. and Mme Pardoux

Open all year. **Children** under 13 not allowed. **Rooms** 2 with bathroom and WC, 3 with shower and WC. **Price** 600F (2 pers.) **Meals** breakfast incl., evening meal at communal table 500F (wine incl.) **Facilities** lounge, telephone, tennis, shooting, walks. **Nearby** golf, equestrian centre, Les Eyzies, Trémolat, Domme, valley of the Dordogne, prehistoric sites. **Spoken** English, Spanish.

The architecture of this old château is elegant and appealing. The bedrooms are very comfortable and all different. The ones in the main body of the building are older, more attractive and bigger. Mme Pardoux is a marvellous cook. Dinners are served in a lovely room with a fireplace. The atmosphere is a little theatrical but this suits the place. Ample breakfast with home-made jams.

How to get there (*Map 23*): *39km east of Bergerac. Take D660 to Beaumont, then D2 to Cadouin Regagnac.*

13
Chez M. et Mme Trickett

La Rigeardie
24310 Bourdeilles
(Dordogne)
Tel. 53 03 78 90
Fax 53 04 56 95
M. and Mme Trickett

Open all year. **Rooms** 4 with shower (2 shared WCs) and 1 suite of 2 bedrooms with shower. Room cleaning every 2-3 days. **Price** 160F (1 pers.), 220F (2 pers.) +40F (extra pers.), suite 420F (2 pers. + 2 children). **Meals** breakfast incl. **Restaurants** nearby. **Facilities** language courses. **Pets** dogs allowed on request. **Nearby** golf. **Spoken** English, German, Italian, Spanish.

A cottage gate opens into the pretty garden of this house, which stands on the roadside in a hamlet. The welcome is kind and discreet. The bedrooms are comfortable and plainly furnished and each one contains an old school desk. The windows overlook the garden. Breakfast with excellent home-made jams is served at a long wooden table.

How to get there (*Map 23*): *27km north of Périgueux via D939 towards Angoulême; at Brantôme D78 to Bourdeilles, then 4km in the direction of Ribérac.*

14
La Bernerie

24320 Bouteilles-Saint-Sébastien
(Dordogne)
Tel. 53 91 51 40
M. and Mme Carruthers

Closed Jan. and Feb. **Rooms** 2 with shower and WC. Room cleaning on request. **Price** 250F (2 pers.) **Meals** in the restaurant 200 metres away: breakfast 25F, lunch or evening meal (closed Wednesday Oct.-May) 60F (set meal, wine incl.) Also Elisabeth at Lusignac and L'Escalier at Verteillac. **Nearby** golf, Romanesque churches, Brantôme, Bourdeilles, St-Jean-de-Côle. **Spoken** English.

L a Bernerie is on the edge of a tiny, well-preserved village which lies in the magnificent green countryside of Périgord. Mr and Mrs Carruthers, a friendly Scottish couple, have created 2 simple guestrooms in their old (slightly over-restored) house. The bedrooms are light and pleasant and overlook the countryside. You are quite independent here and can enjoy breakfast in the auberge-café 'La Bouteille', 200 metres away. An address for fine weather.

How to get there *(Map 23): about 50km south of Angoulême via D939 towards Périgueux, then D708. At La Rochebeaucourt head for Ribérac. In Verteillac turn right before the square towards Bouteilles.*

15
Le Châtenet

24310 Brantôme
(Dordogne)
Tel. 53 05 81 08
Fax 53 05 85 52
M. and Mme Laxton

Open all year. **Rooms** 6 with bath, WC and telephone; 1 studio for longer stays with bath, shower, WC, kitchenette and telephone; 2 suites with bathroom, shower, WC, telephone and TV. Room cleaning, studio, 60F per day. **Price** 470-570F (2 pers.) +60F (extra pers.); suite 750F (2 pers.); studio 650F (4 pers.) **Meals** breakfast 58F, no evening meals. **Restaurants** in Brantôme. **Credit cards** Visa, Eurocard, MasterCard. **Facilities** heated swimming pool, tennis, fishing. **Nearby** golf, Brantôme, Bourdeilles, Puyguilhem, St-Jean-de-Côle. **Spoken** English.

T his is a beautiful and luxurious Périgourdine house. The bedrooms are very well done with pretty furniture and fine fabrics and wallpapers giving an overall impression of affluence. The style is Anglo-French. Breakfasts are more like brunches and may be served on a covered terrace with stone columns supporting the roof.

How to get there *(Map 23): 27km north of Périgueux via D939; at Brantôme D78 for 1.5km to Bourdeilles.*

16
Les Granges

Mauzens-Miremont
24260 Le Bugue
(Dordogne)
Tel. 53 03 25 71
M. and Mme Guy Urvoy

Open all year. **Rooms** 5 with shower and WC. **Price** 250F (2 pers.) +90F (extra pers.) Room cleaning on request. **Meals** breakfast incl., evening meal at communal table 70F (wine incl.), half board 390F (2 pers. in double room). **Facilities** lounge, telephone, swimming pool, tennis. **Pets** dogs allowed on request. **Nearby** 18-hole golf, fishing, shooting, canoeing, riding, lake.

L es Granges is just outside a hamlet and offers the choice of exploring this lovely region or enjoying the facilities on the spot. The panelled bedrooms are identical, functional and comfortable but not very well sound-proofed. Mme Urvoy is very welcoming and prepares excellent meals which are either served in the 'period' dining room or on the lovely flowery terrace overlooking the countryside.

How to get there *(Map 23): 37km south of Périgueux via D710 and D47 towards Sarlat; after St-Félin-de-Reillac.*

17
Domaine du Pinquet

Cussac
24480 Le Buisson-de-Cadouin
(Dordogne)
Tel. 53 22 97 07
Nicole and Daniel Dewitte

Open 15 March-15 Nov. **Rooms** 3 with bath and WC, 1 with shower and WC, and 1 suite (3/4 pers.) with shower and WC. Daily room cleaning except for beds. **Price** 300F (2 pers.) +80F (extra pers.); suite 300F (2 pers.) +150F (extra pers.) **Meals** breakfast included, evening meals at separate tables 110F (wine incl.), half board 260F per pers. in double room. **Facilities** lounge, swimming pool. **Pets** no dogs allowed. **Nearby** tennis, riding, golf, valleys of the Vézère and the Dordogne, châteaux. **Spoken** English.

A house full of character with well kept grounds where all the family join in looking after their guests. The bedrooms are perfect: very comfortable, simple, and decorated in good taste, with decent bathrooms. Good evening meals are served outside in fine weather. A place of quality.

How to get there *(Map 23): 32km east of Bergerac via D660 to Port-de-Couze, then D703 to Lalinde, then D29.*

18
La Daille

Florimont-Gaumiers
24250 Domme
(Dordogne)
Tel. 53 28 40 71
M. and Mme Derek Vaughan
Brown

Open 1 May-2 Nov. (3 nights min.) **Children** under 7 not allowed. **Rooms** 3 with bath, WC and terrace and 1 with shower and WC. **Price** 410F (half board per pers., wine incl.) **Meals** breakfast incl., evening meals at separate tables. **Pets** dogs not allowed. **Nearby** 9-hole golf, canoeing, Domme, Sarlat, L'Abbaye-Nouvelle.

Set in the midst of wild and undulating country this former farm is surrounded by one of the most beautiful gardens imaginable. The comfortable bedrooms are very well decorated in a restrained way, with pieces of English furniture. All have a large bathroom and a private terrace overlooking the flowers and the hills. The constraints of half board are largely made up for by the beauty of the little restaurant (with blue table linen, antiques and a collection of crystal glasses) and the quality of the food. A welcoming place and very British.

How to get there *(Map 23): 35km south of Sarlat via D46 (Domme-St-Martial) and D673. After Salviac, right in Florimont direction.*

19
Le Petit Pey

Monmarvès
24560 Issigeac
(Dordogne)
Tel. 53 58 70 61
Mme Annie de Bosredon

Open Easter – end Oct. (2 nights min.) **Rooms** 2 with shower and WC, and 3 single beds for teenagers in the dovecot. **Price** 240F (2 pers.) +150F (extra pers.) **Meals** breakfast 30F, no evening meal. **Facilities** lounge. **Pets** dogs allowed (+15F). **Nearby** golf (18km), sailing, fishing, riding. **Spoken** English.

This elegant 17th- and 18th-century house has lovely grounds and 2 guest rooms. The most attractive and the 'youngest' is all in pink and occupies the upper floor, under the roof. The other is mainly brown, has a big bed and overlooks the garden, but you have to go down the passage to get to the bathroom. Outside, the old dovecot has been converted, with 3 single beds and is suitable for teenagers. A lovely lounge is available for guests. The welcome is lively and cordial.

How to get there *(Map 23): 2km south of Issigeac towards Castillonnès, then follow the signs.*

20
La Rouquette

24240 Monbazillac
(Dordogne)
Tel. 53 58 30 60/53 58 30 44
M. de Madaillan

Open April – end Oct. (or by request). **Rooms** 4 with bath and WC. **Price** 240-300F (2 pers.)
Meals breakfast incl., no evening meals. **Restaurants** in the village, La Closerie St Jacques and
Château de Monbazillac; in Malfourat (2km) La Tour des Vents and Le Périgord. **Nearby** tennis,
swimming pool, 9-hole golf (7km), vineyards and château of Monbazillac. **Spoken** English.

L a Rouquette is an elegant 17th-century country house overlooking
vineyards and the plain of Bergerac. You will be received with great
kindness. The bedrooms are quiet and comfortable and have good views.
The largest is beautifully decorated and has a private balcony. The smallest
is just as charming, with Venetian painted wood furniture. Breakfast is served
in a big room on the ground floor.

How to get there *(Map 23): 7km south of Bergerac via D13; 150m from the church at
Monbazillac on D14E, take the small road on the right; La Rouquette is 200m further on.*

21
Le Bastit

Saint-Médard-de-Mussidan
24400 Mussidan
(Dordogne)
Tel. 53 81 32 33
M. and Mme Zuidema

Open Easter – All Saints (and by request in winter). **Rooms** 5 with bath and WC (1 on the ground
floor). **Price** 220-245F (1 pers.), 260-290F (2 pers.) **Meals** breakfast incl., no evening meals.
Restaurants Au Velours Rouge in Mussidan (2km). **Facilities** lounge, swimming pool, fishing.
Pets small dogs by request. **Nearby** wine route, châteaux, prehistoric sites, walled towns, 18-
hole golf (35km), riding (6km), canoeing. **Spoken** English.

W e liked this opulent house standing on the banks of the river. The
bedrooms are very comfortable, with pretty English fabrics and some
antique furniture. You will be welcomed as friends. Excellent breakfasts are
served in an elegant dining room or outside in the flowery garden. An
invaluable address between Périgord and the vineyards of Bordeaux.

How to get there *(Map 23): On the N89 coming from Bordeaux, turn left towards St-
Médard just before entering Mussidan; phone for directions.*

22
Doumarias

24800 Saint-Pierre-de-Côle
(Dordogne)
Tel. 53 62 34 37
François and Anita Fargeot

Open 1 April – 15 Oct. **Rooms** 3 with bath and WC, 3 with shower and WC. Room cleaning on request. **Price** 260F (2 pers.) +40F (extra pers.) **Meals** breakfast 20F, half board 420F per day (2 pers. in double room, 4 days min.), evening meal at communal table 75F (wine incl.) **Facilities** swimming pool, fishing in the river. **Pets** dogs not allowed. **Nearby** tennis, riding, golf, caves and château at Villars, Brantôme.

Doumarias stands beneath an old ruined château not far from the lovely village of St-Jean-de-Côle. The bedrooms are charming, with beautiful antique furniture, curios and small paintings. They are comfortable and quiet. Breakfast and dinner are served in a pretty dining room overlooking the garden and the cooking is excellent. A friendly welcome.

How to get there (Map 23): 12km south east of Brantôme via D78 towards Thiviers; 1.5km after St-Pierre-de-Côle.

23
Moulin de la Garrigue

24590 Salignac-Eyvigues
(Dordogne)
Tel. 53 28 84 88
M. and Mme Pierre Vallée

Open all year. **Rooms** 4 with bath, WC and telephone. **Price** 240F (1 pers.), 260F (2 pers.) +70F (extra pers.) **Meals** breakfast incl., no evening meals. **Facilities** swimming pool, fishing. **Nearby** canoeing, mountain-biking, equestrian centre, golf at Gignac (8km).

The Moulin de la Garrigue is in a small wooded valley and has been completely restored to working condition. The bedrooms are in a converted barn and are named after flowers corresponding with their colour schemes. They are comfortable and functional, with two extra beds on a mezzanine. Delicious breakfast, carefully prepared and served in the bedrooms or on the terrace beside the water.

How to get there (Map 23): 32km south west of Brive via N89 to Larche, then D60 towards Salignac, then D62 towards Souillac for 7km; right opposite the mill.

24
Château de Puymartin

24200 Sarlat-la-Canéda
(Dordogne)
Tel. 53 59 29 97
Comte and Comtesse Henri de
Montbron

Open April – All Saints (or by request for weekends). **Rooms** 2 with bath and WC. **Price** 550F (1 pers.), 650F (2 pers.) +150F (child, bed and breakfast). **Meals** breakfast 50F. **Facilities** lounge, private tours of the château. **Pets** dogs allowed by request. **Nearby** swimming pool, tennis, riding.

The evocative, crenellated silhouette of the Château de Puymartin looms over a landscape of hills and forests. The welcome is simple and kind. One of the bedrooms is furnished in medieval style and has two splendid canopied beds. The other is arranged like a sitting room with a collection of mostly Louis XVI marquetry furniture. Both rooms are very large and comfortable and contain some charming objects.

How to get there (Map 23): about 60km south east of Périgueux via D710 to Le Bugue, then D703 towards Les Eyzies and D47 towards Sarlat: it's on the D47 before Sarlat.

25
Manoir de Rochecourbe

24220 Vezac
(Dordogne)
Tel. 53 29 50 79
M. and Mme Albert Roger

Open 1 June – 30 Sept. 3 nights min. **Rooms** 5 with bath and WC (4 with telephone) and 1 suite for 2 pers. **Price** 320-410F (2 pers.) +80F (extra pers.) **Meals** breakfast 32F, no evening meals. **Restaurant** Chez Bonnet. **Facilities** lounge. **Credit cards** Visa. **Pets** dogs allowed on request. **Nearby** tennis, riding, canoeing, flying club, prehistoric sites. **Spoken** English.

A lovely old manor in the heart of the Dordogne, built in the 16th century. The bedrooms are reached by a spiral staircase and are all different, with antique or reproduction furniture, comfortable beds and delightful views. Mme Roger uses flowers from the garden to decorate the breakfast table in the pleasant dining room. A place full of charm.

How to get there (Map 23): 7km south west of Sarlat via D57.

26
Château d'Arbieu

33430 Bazas
(Gironde)
Tel. 56 25 11 18
Fax 56 25 90 52
Comte and Comtesse Philippe de
Chénerilles

Open all year (by request from end Oct. – Easter). **Rooms** 3 with shower and WC, 1 suite with bath, WC and telephone (4 pers.) **Price** 395F (2 pers.) +80F (extra pers.); suite 425F (1 pers.), 450F (2 pers.) +80F (extra pers.) **Meals** breakfast incl., evening meal at communal table, on reservation 150F (wine incl.) **Facilities** lounge, swimming pool. **Credit cards** Visa, Amex. **Spoken** English, German.

A large lounge–cum–billiard room in the Château d'Arbieu serves as the breakfast room and is furnished with antiques of different periods as well as the breakfast tables. All the bedrooms are large and furnished as they were long ago. The bathrooms are a little old-fashioned but each one has a shower cabinet. The evening meal is served in a comfortable room. A relaxed welcome.

How to get there (Map 29): 60km south east of Bordeaux via A62, Langon exit, then D932 towards Mont-de-Marsan, then D655 towards Casteljaloux.

27
Pigou

4, bois de Pigou
Cartelègue
33390 Blaye
(Gironde)
Tel. 57 64 60 68
M. and Mme Heinz Krause

Open April – All Saints. **Rooms** 1 with shower, WC and TV. **Price** 190F (1 pers.), 250F (2 pers.) **Meals** breakfast included, evening meal at communal table by request 90F (wine incl.), half board 280F (1 pers.), 215F (per pers. in double room). **Facilities** lounge. **Pets** dogs allowed on request. **Nearby** fishing, hiking, riding, tennis, châteaux of Medoc, Blaye, St-Emilion. **Spoken** English, German.

S tanding in a landscape of pines, this single–storey house consists of two buildings. The smaller building is kept for guests and has a good sized bedroom with 2 comfortable beds, some pretty green lacquered furniture and a generous library. There is a bathroom and a terrace where breakfast is served. A pleasant, peaceful and welcoming place.

How to get there (Map 22): via A10 Blaye exit, then N137 towards Etauliers and Montendre. 1km from N137: opposite D134 E1.

28
Château du Foulon

Le Foulon
33480 Castelnau-de-Médoc
(Gironde)
Tel. 56 58 20 18 Fax 56 58 23 43
Vicomte and Vicomtesse Jean de
Baritault du Carpia

Open all year. **Rooms** 3, 1 studio (2/3 pers.) and 1 studio (4 pers.) with bath and WC. **Price** 350F (1 pers.), 400F (2 pers.), suite or studio 500F (2 pers.) +150F (extra pers.) **Meals** breakfast incl., no evening meals. **Restaurants** Le Savoye in Margaux, Le Lion d'Or in Arcins. **Facilities** telephone, lounge, tennis, equestrian centre. **Pets** dogs not allowed. **Nearby** 36-hole golf, châteaux of Médoc. **Spoken** English.

Some way from the village, the Château du Foulon was built in 1840. It is a little piece of paradise where you will feel completely at ease. The comfortable bedrooms are very well decorated, with beautiful antique furniture, and all have views of the park. Before leaving taste the great wines of Médoc. Breakfast is served in a lovely dining room. A refined yet welcoming place.

How to get there(Map 22): 28km north west of Bordeaux via D1.

29
Domaine de Carrat

Route de Ste-Hélène
33480 Castelnau-de-Médoc
(Gironde)
Tel. 56 58 24 80
M. and Mme Péry

Open all year. **Rooms** 3 with bath and WC. **Price** 220F (1 pers.), 250-260F (2 pers.), suite 450F (4 pers.) **Meals** breakfast incl., no evening meals. **Restaurants** nearby. **Facilities** lounge, equestrian centre and bathing in the stream in the grounds. **Pets** dogs allowed on request. **Nearby** tennis, lakes, châteaux of Médoc. **Spoken** English, German.

You will find this lovely house in its own grounds in the middle of a forest. M. and Mme Péry have cleverly made the most of the former stables and decorated the rooms with taste. The comfortable bedrooms have family furniture and some can be organised into suites. They all overlook the countryside and are consequently very quiet. Good breakfasts are served in the attractive dining room. Very friendly welcome.

How to get there(Map 22): 28km north west of Bordeaux via D1; at the 2nd set of traffic lights in Castelnau, head towards Ste-Hélène on N215; turn right 200m after leaving Castelnau.

30
La Petite Glaive

33620 Lapouyade
(Gironde)
Tel. 57 49 42 09
M. and Mme Bonnet

Closed 1st week Sep. **Rooms** 1 with bath and WC, 1 with shower and WC. **Price** 195F (2 pers.)
+30-50F (extra pers.) **Meals** breakfast incl., lunch and evening meals 90-100F (wine incl.)
Facilities lounge. Room cleaning on request. **Pets** dogs not allowed. **Nearby** golf, Bordeaux, St-
Emilion, wine route.

This farmhouse auberge is situated on the fringe of an oak and pine forest.
The bedrooms are simple, pleasant and quiet. An agreeable lounge-
library looks onto a small garden where dinner is served in the summer. M.
and Mme Bonnet are very welcoming and use only home–grown farm
produce in their cooking. A good country stop.

*How to get there(Map 23): 27km north of Libourne via D910 towards Montguyon.
In Guîtres take D247 to the left through Bayas; signposted before Lapouyade.*

31
La Bergerie

Les Trias
33920 Saint-Cristoly-de-Blaye
(Gironde)
Tel. 57 42 50 80
M. and Mme de Poncheville

Open all year. **Rooms** 2 houses for 2-6 pers. with lounge, kitchen, bathroom, WC. **Price** 400F
(2 pers.) +150F (extra pers.); room cleaning every four days. **Meals** breakfast incl., no evening
meals. **Restaurants** many in Blaye. **Facilities** lounge, swimming pool, riding on request, boating
on the lake. **Nearby,** wine route, St-Emilion (35km), châteaux and places of historical interest,
golf, tennis (3km).

In the countryside near Blaye and in lovely grounds with a small lake, La
Bergerie is made up of several well renovated old buildings. Each
apartment is large and has a sitting room with fireplace and a kitchen. There
are quarry tiled floors, antique country furniture and attractive fabrics. On
reserving your room you will be offered a choice of breakfast arrangements.
Very kind welcome.

*How to get there(Map 22): 11km south east of Blaye via D22 towards St-Cristoly-
de-Blaye, then St-Urbain; follow signs to Les Trias.*

32
Château de Gourdet

33620 Saint-Mariens
(Gironde)
Tel. 57 58 99 33/57 58 05 37
Yvonne and Daniel Chartier

Closed 1st fortnight of July. **Rooms** 1 with shower and WC, 3 with shower (4 separate WCs). **Price** 150-170F (1 pers.), 175-210F (2 pers.) +75F (extra pers.) **Meals** breakfast incl., evening meals at communal table (book 24h in advance) 75F (wine incl.) **Facilities** lounge, riding in summer. **Nearby** walks, rides, citadels of Blaye and Bourg, St-Emilion. **Spoken** English.

This peaceful gentleman's residence is just outside a small village. The atmosphere is friendly and relaxed. The first floor bedrooms are large and light; unsophisticated but comfortable. Each has its own bathroom though they are not en suite. Good set menus with regional specialities, washed down with a bottle of 'Côte de Blaye'.

How to get there (Map 22): 31km north of Bordeaux via A10, St-André-de-Cubzac exit, then N10 towards Montlieu, then D18 towards St-Savin.

33
Gaudart

33910 Saint-Martin-de-Laye
(Gironde)
Tel. 57 49 41 37
M. and Mme Garret

Closed Easter – All Saints. **Rooms** 2 with bath and WC, 1 with shower and WC, independent entrances. **Price** 170-230F (2 pers.) **Meals** breakfast incl., evening meals on reservation 80f (wine incl.) **Facilities** lounge. **Pets** no dogs allowed. **Nearby** swimming pool, 18-hole golf course, St-Emilion, abbey at Guîtres, vineyards.

A few minutes from the vineyards of St-Emilion, this house is set in quiet pastureland. The vast living room, where breakfast and dinner are served, still has its old regional furniture. The bedrooms are a good size and the beds are comfortable. Two have very nice bathrooms. We preferred the one with the *lit à lange* which is very well furnished. A truly kind welcome.

How to get there (Map 22): 9km north of Libourne via D910 towards Guîtres-Montguyon. In St-Denis-de-Pile, left on D22 for 5km, then follow signs for 1km.

34
Les Lys

Brochard
33440 Saint-Vincent-de-Paul
(Gironde)
Tel. 56 38 91 22/56 77 68 65
Laurence and Pierre Brinboeuf du
Lary

Open all year. **Rooms** 2 with bath and WC, 2 with shower and WC. **Prices** 280F (2 pers.) **Meals** breakfast incl., evening meals at communal table (in the garden) 150 and 250F (wine not incl.), gastronomic meals on request. **Facilities** lounge, lake (planned for 1993). **Nearby** swimming pool, tennis, 18-hole golf, fishing, wine route, old Bordeaux. **Spoken** English, German, Italian.

Forget the road and the closeness of Bordeaux. Pierre du Lary is a very colourful character with a penchant for good food and nice things and with the help of his family he has created something special at Les Lys. In the bedrooms as well as the large lounge, styles have been mixed with a sure touch. Meals are superbly presented festive occasions and not to be missed. An excellent semi-urban stop at good value prices.

How to get there(Map 22): 10km north of Bordeaux. Take A10 exit 32 Ambarès then N10 towards St-André-de-Cubzac. As you come into St-Vincent-de-Paul, beside 'Coficiel'.

35
Mirambeau

50, rue du Général-de-Gaulle
33590 Saint-Vivien-de-Médoc
(Gironde)
Tel. 56 09 51 07
M. and Mme Pierre Lanneau

Open all year. **Children** not allowed. **Rooms** 1 with bath and WC. **Price** 200F (1 pers.), 220F (2 pers.) **Meals** breakfast incl., no evening meal. **Restaurants** Le Grilloir, L'Auberge de Bel Air. **Pets** dogs not allowed. **Nearby** tennis, riding, seaside, châteaux of Médoc, wine route.

Close to the Médoc vineyards, Mirambeau is a pretty house in a flower-filled garden. M. and Mme Lanneau are very welcoming hosts. The house is like a doll's house and has been completely renovated and decorated with pretty fabrics and pale wooden furniture. You will sleep peacefully in comfortable beds. Breakfast with home-made jams, fresh bread, and new laid eggs on request.

How to get there(Map 22): 86km north of Bordeaux via D1 and N215; in St-Vivien-de-Médoc take Grayan road, on corner of 2nd road on right.

36
Domaine du Ciron

Brouquet
33210 Sauternes
(Gironde)
Tel. 56 76 60 17
Fax 56 76 61 74
M. and Mme Peringuey

Open all year. **Children** under 7 not accepted. **Rooms** 1 with bath and WC, 2 with shower and WC, and 1 suite (4 pers.) with bath and WC. **Price** 200F (2 pers.) +60F (extra pers.), suite 350F, **Meals** breakfast incl., no evening meals. **Restaurants** Auberge des Vignes and Le Saprien in Sauternes. **Facilities** swimming pool. **Pets** dogs not allowed. **Nearby** tennis, 18-hole golf, riding (8km), canoeing (8km), Sauternes wine route, châteaux. **Spoken** English.

Sauternes wines are M. and Mme Peringuey's business. They are very welcoming and can give lots of advice on touring the region. The house has four very simple bedrooms which are of a good standard of comfort. The view of the vineyards is all around you. There is a swimming pool in the garden. Breakfast is served beside it or in a pretty dining room.

How to get there(Map 22): 11km west of Langon (A62) on D8 in the direction of Villandraut. Stay on the D8 after Sauternes crossroads; at Brousquet (1km) right by the water tower; signposted.

37
Le Barbé

Place de l'Eglise
40390 Biaudos
(Landes)
Tel. 59 56 73 37
Fax 59 56 75 84
M. and Mme Iriart

Open 1st March – 1st Dec. **Rooms** 1 with shower and WC,. 3 with private shower and shared WC. Room cleaning on request. **Price** 140-150F (1 pers.), 160-185F (2 pers.) +60F (extra pers.) **Meals** breakfast incl., no evening meal. **Restaurant** Chez Pétiole in St-Martin-de-Seignanx. **Facilities** lounge, swimming pool. **Pets** small dogs allowed. **Nearby** golf, Adour valley, walled towns, abbeys, Basque festivals, Basque coast.

Monsieur and Mme Iriart take great pleasure in welcoming and looking after their guests. In the garden of this large village house they have installed a swimming pool surrounded with small tables where breakfast is served in fine weather. The bedrooms are large, very light, and often decorated with souvenirs of their journeys. The general effect is very pleasing.

How to get there(Map 28): 16km east of Bayonne via N117 towards Orthez and Pau.

38
Lamolère

40090 Campet-Lamolère
(Landes)
Tel. 58 06 04 98
Philippe and Béatrice de
Monredon

Open all year. **Rooms** 1 with bath and WC, 2 with bath and shared WC. Room cleaning every three days or on request. **Meals** breakfast incl., evening meal at communal table 75F. **Facilities** lounge, 12th-century chapel, loose boxes, fishing, bicycles. **Pets** dogs allowed in the kennel on request. **Nearby** golf, swimming pool (4km). **Spoken** English, Spanish.

A large gentleman's residence in a 12-hectare park. The bedrooms are aesthetically pleasing, comfortable and harmoniously decorated, and most of the beds are very wide. There are many nice decorative details and some antique furniture. As a rule the excellent evening meals are served outside on a large terrace. Pleasant views, warm welcome and very reasonable prices.

How to get there(Map 29): 5km north west of Mont-de-Marsan via D38; on the Morcenx road.

39
Estounotte

Quartier Naboude
40170 Levignacq
(Landes)
Tel. 58 42 75 97
Mme Lalanne

Open all year. **Rooms** 1 with private bathroom, 3 with private shower (1 shared WC). **Price** 200-260F (2 pers.) depending on season, babies up to 2 years supplement +35F. **Meals** breakfast incl., evening meals at communal table, on reservation (except for one night a week) 85F (wine incl.) **Facilities** lounge, bicycles. **Pets** dogs allowed on request (+50F week). **Nearby** riding, seaside, boat trips, Levignacq church. **Spoken** Spanish.

Nestling among pine trees, this lovely country house has been completely renovated. Good dinners are served at the large table in the dining room, which is decorated in modern country style. The decor in the light and peaceful bedrooms is in the same idiom. The bath/shower rooms are not en suite. Pleasant welcome.

How to get there(Map 29): 30km north of Dax. Leave N10 at Castets, exit 13, and head for Levignacq; signposted.

40
L'Oustau

Quartier Baxentes
40210 Lue
(Landes)
Tel. 58 07 11 58
Fax 58 07 11 97
Guy and Patricia Cassagne

Open Easter – Oct. **Rooms** 5 with private bath, shared WC. **Price** 165F (1 pers.), 175-200F (2 pers.) **Meals** breakfast 20F, no evening meals. **Restaurant** L'Auberge Landaise in Lue. **Pets** dogs not allowed. **Nearby** swimming pool, tennis, golf (35km), village of Pontenx-les-Forges, **Spoken** English, Spanish.

The approach to this old country house is through immensely tall pine trees, giving way to oaks. Some 19th-century furniture, pine-panelled ceilings and good paintings give character to the interior. Mme Cassagne knows how to look after you. The pleasant bedrooms overlook the grounds and are furnished in old-world style. Passing cars on the road about 100m away can disturb the tranquillity.

How to get there *(Map 29): 64km north of Dax via D947, then N10 to Labouheyre, then D626.*

41
Le Bos de Bise

40630 Luglon
(Landes)
Tel. 58 07 50 90
M. and Mme Congoste

Open May – Oct. **Rooms** 2 with shower and WC. Room cleaning on request. **Price** 180-200F (2 pers.) +100F (extra pers.) **Meals** breakfast incl. , evening meals (separate tables) 80F. **Facilities** lounge, bicycles, 2 loose boxes, lake. **Pets** large dogs allowed in kennel only. **Nearby** riding, tennis, golf, canoeing, Napoleon III museum, Marquese museum.

Surrounded completely by pine trees, le Bos de Bise is made up of several buildings connected by a well kept lawn. The two bedrooms are very comfortable and decorated in old-fashioned style. One has an adjoining sitting room and the other is larger with a private terrace. Breakfast and dinner are served in a beamed dining room. Outside, a covered kitchen and a fishing lake are available for your use.

How to get there *(Map 29): 25km north-west of Mont-de-Marsan via N134 towards Sabres, then D14 to the left.*

42
Château Robert

40500 Montgaillard
(Landes)
Tel. 58 45 48 09
M. Clain

Open all year. **Rooms** 3 with bath and WC (1 has an independent entrance). **Price** 300-400F (2 pers.) **Meals** breakfast incl., no evening meal. **Restaurant** farmhouse-auberge (3km). **Facilities** lounge, telephone, swimming pool. **Nearby** riding, golf, walled towns. **Spoken** English, Italian.

In lovely grounds (with a swimming pool), Château Robert has two different façades. The one on the garden side is typically 18th-century, and the other, overlooking the countryside, seems like something out of a Spanish baroque dream. Very pleasant bedrooms, prettily decorated with old furniture made of honey-coloured English pine. Breakfasts are more than ample and are served in a beautiful circular dining room decorated with plants and Louis XV plasterwork.

How to get there (Map 29): 22km south of Mt-de-Marsan via D933 towards St-Sever, then D352 towards Larrivière, then D387 towards Montgaillard and 1st turning left after 1km.

43
Au Masson

Route du Port
40300 Port-de-Lanne
(Landes)
Tel. 58 89 14 57
M. and Mme Duret

Open all year. **Rooms** 3 suites of bedroom and sitting room (2/3 pers.), 2 with bath and WC and 1 with shower and WC. **Price** 190-220F (2 pers.) +70F (extra pers.) **Meals** breakfast incl. in price for 2 pers., no evening meal. **Restaurants** excellent small auberge in the port (100m) and other restaurants (4km) on the banks of the Adour. **Pets** dogs not allowed. **Nearby** tennis, fishing, microlights, water sports, swimming pool, golf in Biarritz, listed sites, bull-fighting.

The luxuriant garden of Au Masson with its ornamental lake and exotic trees is reason enough for a stroll. Breakfasts are served under a wooden canopy in the garden in summer. Ask for the duplex bedroom which is charmingly furnished in 1930s style. The other bedrooms are comfortable but perhaps a little less attractive. Simple and pleasant welcome.

How to get there (Map 28): 29km north east of Bayonne via N117.

44
Betjean

D 933
40240 Saint-Justin
(Landes)
Tel. 58 44 88 42
Marie-Claire Villenave

Open April – Sept. or by request. **Rooms** 1 with bath and WC, 3 with shower and WC. Room cleaning by request. **Price** 220-240F (2 pers.) **Meals** breakfast incl., no evening meals. **Restaurants** in St-Justin, Villeneuve. **Facilities** lounge, telephone, fishing. **Pets** dogs allowed by request. **Nearby** golf, walks, lake, Labastide d'Armagnac. **Spoken** English, Italian.

L ying at the end of a long, sandy track surrounded by pines and ferns, this house is as lovely inside as it is out. You enter through a large room with beams, exposed stonework, rugs and old furniture. The bedrooms are comfortable and well decorated. One of them has a superb bathroom, the others ultra–modern showers. Breakfasts with home-made jams served at a large table... to the sound of music.

How to get there (Map 29): 25km north east of Mont-de-Marsan via D932; it is on D933, the Périgueux road.

45
Château de Monbet

40300 Saint-Lon-les-Mines
(Landes)
Tel. 58 57 80 68
Fax 58 57 89 29
M. and Mme Hubert de Lataillade

Open all year. **Rooms** 1 with bath and WC, 2 with shower and WC, and 2 suites (4 pers.) with shower or bath and WC. **Price** 250-550F (2 pers.), suite 600-900F (4 pers.) **Meals** breakfast incl., evening meal at communal table (minimum 4 pers.); vegetarian 250F, gastronomic 350F. Possibility of half board out of season. **Facilities** lounge. **Pets** dogs allowed on request. **Nearby** 18-hole golf, seaside, abbeys. **Spoken** English.

M onbet is a very pretty little château set on a hill with a wonderful view. The welcome is very pleasant and the bedrooms have an old-fashioned country house atmosphere. The largest, 'des Palombes', is very attractive. Not all bathrooms are en suite, but each is private. In good weather, breakfast is served outside on a patio sheltered from the wind. As we were unable to try an evening meal we cannot, in view of the price, recommend it...

How to get there (Map 29): 13km south west of Dax via D6; from A63 take St-Geours- de-Maremne exit or A64 Peyrehorade exit.

46
Larroque

40090 Saint-Perdon
(Landes)
Tel. 58 75 88 38
Marguerite and Louis Lajus

Open all year. **Rooms** 1 with bath and WC, 1 with shower and WC, and 1 suite (3 pers.) with bath and WC. Room cleaning by request. **Price** 220F (1/2 pers.); suite 220F (2 pers.) +80F (extra pers.) **Meals** breakfast incl., no evening meal. **Facilities** lounge. **Nearby** tennis, golf, St-Sever, St-Girons. **Spoken** English.

This country house has kept its old-fashioned atmosphere. You will be received as if you are part of the family. The interior is full of memories: old furniture, photos of children and ancestral portraits. The bedrooms really are big and have not been changed. You will sleep in superb embroidered sheets. The sound-proofing is only average. Very good breakfast, elegantly served, in a lovely dining room. Pleasant and charmingly old-fashioned lounge.

How to get there (Map 29): 5.5km east of Mont-de-Marsan via N124 in the Dax direction, then D3 left towards St-Perdon-Mugron; signposted as you enter St-Perdon.

47
Marchannau

40390 Sainte-Marie-de-Gosse
(Landes)
Tel. 59 56 35 71
M. and Mme Michel Février

Open all year. **Rooms** 2 with bath, shared WC. Room cleaning on request. **Price** 250F (2 pers.) **Meals** breakfast incl., no evening meals. **Restaurant** Auberge Piet on the Adour. **Facilities** lounge, fishing. **Pets** dogs not allowed. **Nearby** tennis, golf, Basque coast, Basque villages. **Spoken** English, Spanish.

This house almost has its feet in the water. The Adour flowing below its windows gives great serenity to the place. Apart from the tables on the terrace, M. and Mme Février have provided a pleasant breakfast room. The bedrooms are big, comfortable and sensitively renovated and decorated. No evening meals but there are excellent restaurants all along the river Adour.

How to get there (Map 28): 25km from Bayonne via N117. Before the bridge over the Adour, take the towpath for 2km.

48
Le Cassouat

Magescq
40140 Soustons
(Landes)
Tel. 58 47 71 55
M. and Mme Gilbert Desbieys

Open all year. **Rooms** 2 rooms en suite with shared bath and WC, and 2 with shower and WC. **Price** 200-230F (2 pers.) +50F (extra pers.) **Meals** breakfast incl., no evening meals. **Facilities** lounge, telephone. **Nearby** 18-hole golf course, seaside, lake, Landes regional park. **Spoken** a little English.

This very modern house, with its triangular shapes and long roofs, is set in the middle of an oak forest. The atmosphere is pleasant and the bedrooms very comfortable and decorated in contemporary style. A sheltered terrace behind glass allows you to have breakfast while enjoying the landscape.

How to get there (Map 28): 16km north west of Dax via D16.

49
Chanteclair

47290 Cancon
(Lot-et-Garonne)
Tel. 53 01 63 34
Fax 53 41 13 44
Mme Larribeau

Open all year. **Rooms** 3 with shower and WC, 1 suite for 3/4 pers. with 2 bedrooms, bathroom and WC. **Price** 250-290F (2 pers.) suite (2-4 pers.) 250-350F reduced terms for 4 days+ **Meals** breakfast 27.50F, half board 238-258F (per pers.), evening meal on reservation 85F. **Facilities** lounge, swimming pool. **Pets** small dogs allowed. **Nearby** châteaux, golf, tennis (800m), lake fishing, river fishing, riding, mountain bike trips, sailing, canoeing. **Spoken** English, Spanish.

This large country house is on the edge of the Périgord region. Four lovely bedrooms, all comfortable and very pretty, have just been fitted out. You should take advantage of the lovely garden with its swimming pool, or you may prefer a game of billiards. A warm welcome and good regional cooking.

How to get there (Map 23 and 30): 1km west of Cancon, on D124 in Marmande direction.

50
Manoir de Roquegautier

Beaugas
47290 Cancon
(Lot-et-Garonne)
Tel. 53 01 60 75
Christian and Brigitte Vrech

Open April – Oct. **Rooms** 1 with bath and WC, 1 with shower and WC, 2 suites (3/4 pers.) with shower and WC. Room cleaning on request. **Price** 330-350F (2 pers.), suite 590F (4 pers.) **Meals** breakfast incl., evening meal at communal table 78F (wine not incl.) **Facilities** swimming pool. **Pets** no animals allowed. **Nearby** 27-hole golf (3km), equestrian centre, tennis, lake, châteaux of Bonaguil and Biron, Monpazier, Villeréal, Monflanquin.

Between Périgord and the Landes, the manor of Roquegautier dominates a landscape of farmland and copses. M. and Mme Vrech have created a cheerful atmosphere. The recently renovated bedrooms are light and very comfortable, with thick quilts on the beds and pretty pastel coloured curtains. The large bedroom under the eaves has a wonderful arrangement of beams and extends into a round tower. Excellent dinners.

How to get there (Map 23 and 30): 17km north of Villeneuve-sur-Lot via N21 in the Cancon direction.

51
Château de Barry

47320 Clairac
(Lot-et-Garonne)
Tel. 53 84 35 49
Fax 53 84 35 06
M. and Mme Bouet

Open Easter – 15 Oct. **Rooms** 6 with bath, shower and WC (TV on request). **Price** 600-800F (2 pers.) **Meals** breakfast incl., evening meals on reservation, at communal or separate tables 250-350F. **Facilities** telephone, swimming pool. **Nearby** tennis, riding, microlights, golf courses. **Spoken** English.

Built at the end of the 18th century, the Château de Barry is set in a park with flower beds, woods and a swimming pool. The vast bedrooms are luxurious and quiet. The decor is very elaborate, combining mostly late 19th-century furniture with lovely fabrics and carefully chosen objects. The bathrooms are equally comfortable.

How to get there (Map 30): 32km east of Villeneuve-sur-Lot via D911 until Bourran, then D146, then D91 towards Tonneins.

52
Manoir de Barrayre

Le Laussou
47150 Monflanquin
(Lot-et-Garonne)
Tel. 53 36 46 66
Fax 53 36 55 26
Mme Charles

Open all year (by request Oct. – April). **Rooms** 1 with bath and WC, 1 with shower and WC, 1 suite (4 pers.) with 2 bedrooms, bath and WC, 2 apartments (2 pers.) and 1 (4 pers.) with sitting room, kitchen, bath and WC. **Price** 280-330F (2 pers.), suite 480F; apartments 2250-3500F a week. **Meals** breakfast 22F, evening meals on reservation 70-120F. **Facilities** lounge, swimming pool. **Pets** dogs allowed. **Nearby** fishing, riding, golf, walled towns, châteaux, Sarlat, Monbazillac. **Spoken** English.

This 12th-century former priory in the middle of the countryside has kept its medieval character. The bedrooms are huge, with antique furniture and good paintings. The thick stone walls give it great character. The generous bathrooms are well kept. Breakfast is served in the bedrooms.

How to get there *(Map 23): 25km north of Villeneuve-sur-Lot via D676 to Monflanquin, then D272 towards Monpazier; turn left after Laurés; signposted.*

53
Frémauret

Roumagne
47800 Miramont-de-Guyenne
(Lot-et-Garonne)
Tel. 53 93 24 65
M. and Mme Claude Aurélien

Open all year. **Rooms** 1 suite with bath, WC and small sitting room. **Price** 200F (1 pers.), 261F (2 pers.) **Meals** evening meals on reservation, at communal table 90F, gastronomic 170F. **Nearby** swimming pool, lake, tennis, golf, walks, Duras, Pujols, Eymet. **Spoken** Spanish.

The converted dovecot of this elegant farmhouse among the maize fields and pastureland is kept for guests. The two-level suite has a pretty little sitting room and, above, a very pleasant bedroom with old mahogany furniture and pink fabrics. Large modern bathroom. M. and Mme Aurélien will welcome you with great kindness. Excellent seasonal cooking served in the evening.

How to get there *(Map 23): 21km north east of Marmande via D933 towards Miramont, then D668 towards Duras.*

54
Château de Pechgris

Salles
47150 Monflanquin
(Lot-et-Garonne)
Tel. 53 36 53 01
Dr and Mme Xavier Chaussade

Open April – end Oct, 3 nights stay min. in high season. **Rooms** 2 with bath and WC, 1 with private bath and shared WC, and 1 child's bedroom. **Price** 180-230F (2 pers.) **Meals** breakfast 25F, evening meal on request 90F (wine incl.) **Facilities** lounge, telephone, swimming pool, tennis. **Nearby** numerous sporting and cultural activites. **Spoken** English, German.

The knights Templar had the good sense to choose this tranquil, gently undulating spot on which to build their *commanderie*. The house forms a four-sided square and is dominated by an octagonal tower. Good-sized bedrooms, simply decorated, with family furniture and very comfortable beds. Mme Chaussade takes as much care of her cooking as of her guests.

How to get there (Map 23): 23km north of Villeneuve-sur-Lot via D676 to Monflanquin, then D150 towards Salles, then right on the road to Libos, and after 1.2km on the right a drive edged with lime trees: signposted from Salles.

55
Moulin de Majoulassis

Gavaudun
47150 Monflanquin
(Lot-et-Garonne)
Tel. 53 36 41 82
M. and Mme Perreau

Open March – Oct. on request, 2 nights stay min. **Rooms** 2 with bath and WC, and 1 suite (5 pers.) with bath and WC. Room cleaning every 3 days. **Price** 200F (1 pers.), 220F (2 pers.) +120F (extra pers.) **Meals** breakfast incl., half board 190F per pers. in double room (3 nights min.), evening meals at communal table 80F (wine incl.) **Facilities** lounge, fishing in the lake or river. **Pets** dogs not allowed. **Nearby** swimming pools, golf, climbing, châteaux. **Spoken** English.

The bedrooms are not in the main building but very close by, on the first floor of a pretty house. They are large, light and practical with modern furnishings. Each is a different colour and has a small balcony overlooking fields. Pleasant bathrooms. Ample breakfasts are served in the country-style dining room. A friendly atmosphere, enlivened by two young children.

How to get there (Map 23): 25km north of Villeneuve-sur-Lot via D676 to Monflanquin, then D150.

56
L'Ormeraie

47150 Paulhiac
(Lot-et-Garonne)
Tel. 53 36 45 96
Minitel: 11 l'ormeraie 47
Michel de L'Ormeraie

Open 1 April – 15 Nov. **Rooms** 4 with bath or shower and WC, and 1 suite (2 pers.) with bath, WC and sitting room/library. **Price** 275-340F (2 pers.), suite 500F (2 pers.) +85F (extra pers.) **Meals** breakfast incl., evening meals on request 140F (wine incl.) **Facilities** lounge, telephone, swimming pool. **Credit cards** Visa, Eurocard, MasterCard. **Pets** dogs allowed on request (+10F/day). **Nearby** golf (25km), riding, tennis. **Spoken** English, Spanish.

L'Ormeraie is in a raised position backing on to the forest. Every bedroom is different, with antique furniture, but it is a pity that sometimes one detail spoils the harmony. The bathrooms have every modern facility. Breakfast is served in front of the house with a lovely view down the hillside.

How to get there (Map 23): 21km north of Villeneuve-sur-Lot via D676 to Monflanquin, then D272 towards Monpazier; follow the signs.

57
Sauveméa

64350 Arroses
(Pyrénées–Atlantiques)
Tel. 59 68 16 01/59 68 16 08
José and Annie Labat

Open all year. **Rooms** 4 with bath and WC. **Price** 230F (1 pers.), 250F (2 pers.) **Meals** breakfast incl., evening meals 60F (wine incl.) **Facilities** lounge, swimming pool, fishing, loose boxes for horses, riding. **Pets** dogs not allowed. **Nearby** vineyards of Madiran. **Spoken** English.

A farm built around a lovely country house. The bedrooms and their bathrooms are all very spacious, well renovated and have light wood furniture. They are comfortable and quiet. Breakfast is served in a large lounge. For dinner the menus of this farmhouse-auberge are excellent. Swimming pool with view over the countryside and the lake below.

How to get there (Map 29): 44km north of Tarbes via D935 towards Aire-sur-l'Adour, then D248 and D48 to Madiran, and D66 towards Arroses, then D292.

58
Trille

D 934
Route de Rébénacq
64290 Bosdarros-Gan
(Pyrénées-Atlantiques)
Tel. 59 21 79 51 Fax 59 21 66 98
Mme Christiane Bordes

Open all year. **Rooms** 3 with bath and WC, 2 with shower and WC. **Price** 240F (1 pers.), 280F (2 pers.) **Meals** breakfast incl., no evening meals. **Restaurant** Auberge le Tucq (100m). **Facilities** lounge, telephone. **Credit cards** Visa, MasterCard. **Pets** small dogs allowed. **Nearby** 18-hole golf, walks, ski slopes. **Spoken** English, Spanish.

The architecture of Trille is typically Béarnaise. Although the renovation has perhaps gone a little too far, it means the bedrooms have every modern comfort and are equipped with good bathrooms. Mme Bordes is very welcoming and prepares 'made-to-measure' breakfasts served in a large dining/sitting room. When the weather is cold an open fire burns in the fireplace in front of the two comfortable sofas.

How to get there (Map 29): 10km south of Pau via N134 towards Saragosse to Gan; at the 'Cave des Producteurs de Jurançon' in Gan, pass 4 sets of traffic lights, then D934 in the direction Rébénacq, Arudy, Laruns for about 3.5km.

59
Château de Boues

Route d'Arette
La Pierre-Saint-Martin
64570 Féas
(Pyrénées-Atlantiques)
Tel. 59 39 95 49
Mme Monique Domon

Open 1 March – end Oct. or on request. **Rooms** 4 with bath, WC and TV. **Price** 300F (2 pers.) **Meals** breakfast incl., no evening meals. **Restaurant** Lacroutz in Féas. **Facilities** telephone, swimming pool. **Credit cards** Visa. **Pets** dogs allowed on request. **Nearby** tennis, golf at Pau, ski slopes and cross-country ski-ing, la Madeleine, Basque country, Pierre-St-Martin. **Spoken** English.

One of the last châteaux before Spain. The four first-floor bedrooms have a lovely view. Renovated with practicality in mind, they are comfortable and have reproduction furniture. Each one has TV. Outside there is a swimming pool, barbecue and garden furniture. The breakfasts are generous and excellent.

How to get there (Map 29): 42km south west of Pau via N134 to Gan, then D24 to Oloron-Ste-Marie, then D919; before the village of Féas.

60
Olhabidea

64500 Sare
(Pyrénées–Atlantiques)
Tel. 59 54 21 85
Mme Jean Fagoaga

Open all year except Aug. (in winter on request only). **Rooms** 2 with bath and WC, 1 single with private shower and shared WC, and 1 suite for 4 pers. with bath and WC. **Price** 300F (2 pers.), 250F if 2 nights or more. **Meals** breakfast incl., no evening meals. **Restaurants** many close by. **Facilities** lounge. **Pets** dogs allowed on request. **Facilities** lounge, riding. **Nearby** mountains, seaside, Basque villages, Spain (3km), golf (14km), swimming pool, tennis. **Spoken** English.

If you do not know the Basque coast here is a marvellous reason for a visit. The comfort and decor of Olhabidea rival the splendours of the landscape round about. Embroidered sheets, engravings, beams, balustrades and glazed terracotta floors... not one false note. Mme Fagoaga's welcome underlines its success. A place you won't want to leave.

How to get there *(Map 28): 14km south east of St Jean-de-Luz; A63 St Jean-de-Luz Nord exit, then D918 towards Ascain and Sare (D4). Leave Sare in the direction of St-Pée sur Nivelle for 2km. Turn right in front of the old chapel; signposted.*

61
Château de Boussac

Target
03140 Chantelle-de-Boussac
(Allier)
Tel. 70 40 63 20
Fax 70 40 60 03
Marquis and Marquise de Longueil

Open 1 April – 30 Nov. **Rooms** 4 with bath and WC, 1 suite (3 pers.) **Price** 600F (1/2 pers.), suite 900F (1/3 pers.) **Meals** breakfast 50F, half board 900F per pers. in double room (6 days min.), evening meals at communal table, on reservation 260F (wine incl.) **Facilities** lounge. **Credit cards** Visa, MasterCard, Amex. **Pets** dogs allowed on request (+100F per day). **Nearby** tennis, golf; Romanesque churches. **Spoken** English.

A many-facetted building going from medieval austerity to the grace of the 18th century. The rooms are magnificently furnished in traditional style, and the bedrooms are comfortable, well decorated, and contain family mementoes. Evening meals are convivial, and much prized by lovers of game in season. An aristocratic and welcoming place.

How to get there (Map 25): 44km east of Montluçon. From A71, exit 11 Montmarault, then D46 and D42 towards Chantelle.

62
Château de Fragne

03190 Verneix
(Allier)
Tel. 70 07 88 10/70 07 80 87
Fax 70 07 83 73
Comtesse Louis de Montaignac

Open 1 May – 15 Oct. or on request. **Rooms** 4 with bath and WC and 1 suite of 2 bedrooms with bath and WC. **Price** 420F (1 pers.), 600F (2 pers.), suite 600F (3 pers.) **Meals** breakfast 40F, evening meals at communal table (separate tables available) 250F (wine incl.) **Facilities** lounge, fishing in lake. **Pets** dogs allowed on request. **Nearby** equestrian centre, golf. **Spoken** English.

A wide drive leads up to this château set in its beautiful park. All the bedrooms have been restored and are decorated in soft colours with antique furniture, and the bathrooms have not been forgotten. The sitting rooms and dining room overlook a large terrace where it is possible to have breakfast. Everything here very successfully evokes château life in bygone days. Very kind welcome.

How to get there (Map 17): 10km north east of Montluçon. A71 exit Montluçon; D94 towards Montluçon for 2km, then right on D39 towards Verneix; signboard at the junction.

63
Château du Lonzat

Route du Donjon
03220 Jaligny-sur-Besbre
(Allier)
Tel. 70 34 73 39
Fax 70 34 81 31
M. Jacques Advenier

Open 1 March – 23 Dec. **Rooms** 3 with bath, WC and telephone, 2 with shower, WC and telephone, 1 with shower, telephone and shared WC. **Price** 292-630F (2 pers.) +70F (extra pers.) **Meals** breakfast 46F. **Restaurant** in the château in the evening about 140F (wine not incl.) **Credit cards** Visa, Amex. **Nearby** walks, swimming pool, golf. **Spoken** English.

You will be very well received at this small, peaceful château which has a warm atmosphere created by antiques and wood panelling. A lovely restaurant occupies the ground floor rooms. The very pleasant bedrooms have 18th- and 19th-century furniture and good modern bathrooms. One of them has two baths side by side. A young and friendly welcome.

How to get there (Map 18): 20km north of Lapalisse via D480 to Jaligny-sur-Besbre, then D989 towards Le Donjon; it's at Le Lonzat.

64
Château du Riau

03460 Villeneuve-sur-Allier
(Allier)
Tel. 70 43 34 47
Fax 70 43 30 74
M. and Mme Durye

Open all year. **Rooms** 2 with bath and WC, 1 with shower and WC, 2 suites (3-5 pers.) **Price** 600-680F (2 pers.), suite 900F (3/4 pers.), 980F (5 pers.) **Meals** breakfast incl., evening meal at communal table, on reservation. **Facilities** lounge. **Pets** dogs not allowed. **Nearby** swimming pool, tennis, riding, golf, Tronçais forest, Balaine arboretum, châteaux. **Spoken** English.

An exceptional collection of typically Bourbon buildings. Having crossed the moat and passed through the postern gate you reach the main part of the house. The bedrooms are just as guests in past centuries would have found them, with fine 18th-century or Empire furnishings. The bathrooms are a bit old-fashioned. Breakfast is served at the big table in the dining room, which, like the sitting room, is pleasant and well furnished.

How to get there (Map 18): 15km north of Moulins via N7 to Villeneuve-sur-Allier, then D133

65
Le Chalet

Les Ferrons
03160 Ygrande
(Allier)
Tel. 70 66 31 67/70 66 30 72
Mme Vrel

Open all year. **Rooms** 5 with shower and WC. **Price** 150F (1 pers.), 190F (2 pers.) +50F (extra pers.) **Meals** breakfast incl., no evening meals. **Restaurant** Le Pont des Chèvres in Cosne d'Allier (12km). **Facilities** bicycles. **Pets** dogs not allowed. **Nearby** swimming pool, tennis, lake, Tronçais forest, châteaux of the 'Route Jacques Coeur'.

You will be very pleasantly received in this little turn-of-the-century house out in the countryside. The good-sized bedrooms are prettily done, each with its own shower room. The 'grise' bedroom is charmingly romantic. Mme Vrel lives close by and comes every morning to make generous breakfasts, served when you like in a small dining/sitting room.

How to get there *(Map 17): 33km west of Moulins via D953 through Bourbon-l'Archambault; follow the signs.*

66
Château de la Vigne

15700 Ally
(Cantal)
Tel. 71 69 00 20
M. and Mme du Fayet de la Tour

Open Easter – All Saints. **Rooms** 2 with bath and WC and 1 with shower and WC, or possibility of a suite. **Price** 500-600F (2 pers.), suite 650F (4 pers.) **Meals** breakfast 30F, evening meals by request (separate tables) 200F (wine incl.) **Facilities** tennis. **Pets** small dogs permitted by special request. **Nearby** fishing, 9-hole golf in Mauriac, lake, beach. **Spoken** English.

In the middle of the countryside lies the very ancient Château de la Vigne. The owners will welcome you like old friends. Each room is enhanced by beautiful family furniture. The sitting room is superb and the bedrooms comfortable; some are elegant, others rather grand. Your breakfast will be served the minute you get out of bed. Before leaving ask for a tour of the château.

How to get there *(Map 24): 52km north of Aurillac via D922, then D680 to Ally and D681 towards Mauriac.*

67
Château de Bassignac

Bassignac
15240 Saignes
(Cantal)
Tel. 71 40 82 82
M. and Mme Besson

Open Easter – All Saints (on request in winter). **Rooms** 3 with bath and WC, 1 apartment (3/4 pers.) of 2 bedrooms, lobby, bathroom and WC. **Price** 390-480F (2 pers.) +50F (extra pers.); apartment 620F (4 pers.) **Meals** breakfast incl., half board 780-830F (2 pers., 3 days min.), evening meal at communal table 250F (wine incl.) **Facilities** lounge, fishing. **Pets** dogs allowed on request. **Nearby** golf, cross country ski-ing, villages, Romanesque churches, châteaux. **Spoken** English.

A fortified house of great character in an undulating, wooded setting. An immediately welcoming impression is given by the two ground floor rooms. Lovely bedrooms with 19th-century furniture, curios and nice fabrics. A log fire adds atmosphere to the excellent evening meals. The younger generation of the family run a farmhouse-auberge at the entrance to the park.

How to get there (Map 24): 67km north of Aurillac via D922; 12km from Bort-les-Orgues take D312 in the Brousse direction.

68
Chez M. et Mme Prudent

Rue des Nobles
15410 Salers
(Cantal)
Tel. 71 40 75 36
M. Philippe Prudent

Open all year. **Rooms** 6 with bath and WC. **Price** 171-181F (1 pers.), 192-202F (2 pers.) **Meals** breakfast incl., no evening meals. **Restaurants** nearby. **Credit cards** Visa. **Nearby** swimming pool, cross-country and piste ski-ing. **Spoken** English, German.

Entirely built of volcanic basalt, Salers is a small medieval town miraculously spared by the passage of time. In this attractive house the bedrooms are small, simple and not all well soundproofed, but they are comfortable and well kept. Choose those overlooking the volcanos. Good breakfast served with a smile in the bedrooms or in a pretty garden with a magnificent view. Inexpensive and welcoming.

How to get there (Map 24): 47km north of Aurillac. From Clermont-Ferrand D922 to Mauriac, then D122 and D22; in centre of Salers go to Place Tyssendier d'Escous and take 1st small street on left.

69
Domaine des Tilleuls

La Seiglière
23200 Aubusson
(Creuse)
Tel. 55 83 88 76
M. and Mme Sheridan

Open all year. **Rooms** 3 with shower and WC, 1 with basin and WC. **Price** 175F (1 pers.), 225F (2 pers.) **Meals** breakfast incl., evening meal 100F. **Restaurants** Le Lion d'Or and Les Lissiers in Aubusson (2km). **Facilities** lounge. **Pets** dogs not allowed. **Nearby** tapestry museum in Aubusson, workshops of Lissiers, Vassivière lake, golf (35km), equestrian centre (7km).

Mark Sheridan, an Englishman, has renovated this welcoming country-house and opened it for guests. The well-proportioned bedrooms have 19th-century furniture and floral wallpapers. They are all comfortable and quiet, though the invisible and distant road sometimes reminds one of its presence. Elegant lounge/dining room done in English style with beautiful wallpaper, pictures, and deep chesterfields. Good value for money.

How to get there *(Map 24): 2km east of Aubusson, at the entrance to La Seiglière.*

70
Les Bastides du Mézenc

43550 Saint-Front
(Haute-Loire)
Tel. 71 59 51 57
Paul and Nadège Coffy

Open all year. **Rooms** 2 bedrooms, 2 suites for 3 pers. with shower and WC. Room cleaning available on request. **Price** 120F (per pers.) **Meals** breakfast 30F, half board 270F or 300F per pers. (3 days min.), lunch (60F) and dinner (150F) at communal table (wine incl.) **Facilities** lounge, fishing, riding, loose boxes, dog sledging, cross-country ski-ing trips, ski slopes. **Pets** dogs allowed on request. **Nearby** lake St-Front, summit of the Mézenc, Puy-en-Velay (30km), golf (25km), climbing, hang-gliding. **Spoken** English, Spanish.

The little road leading to this isolated house crosses a wide plateau of grassland and broom. Inside, a large and magnificent sitting room has antique furniture, exotic and unusual objects, paintings, and comfortable sitting areas. The bedrooms are equally attractive. The countryside and the on-the-spot activities (horse and dog sledging) make Les Bastides unique.

How to get there *(Map 25): about 30km south east of Le Puy; at Le Puy head for Valence, at Les Pandraux take D36, then D500 towards Fay; signposted.*

71
Château de la Roche

La Roche-Chaptuzat
63260 Aigueperse
(Puy-de-Dôme)
Tel. 73 63 65 81
(1) 45 74 18 50 (winter)
Compte and Comtesse de Torcy

Open end May – end Oct. **Rooms** 1 with bath and WC and 2 suites (2/3 pers.) of 2 bedrooms, bath and WC. **Price** 500F (1 pers.), 700F (2 pers.), suite 600-800F (2 pers.) **Meals** breakfast incl., no evening meals. **Restaurants** Le Grillon in Chaptuzat (400m) and Le Marché (4km). **Facilities** lounge, tour of the château. **Nearby** swimming pool, riding, golf, gorges of La Sioule, Riom, Vichy. **Spoken** English.

On arrival at the village this medieval château is immediately noticeable, standing on a green hill. The rooms have their original windows and the furniture is equally antique. The bedrooms are comfortable, warm and hung with beautiful fabrics. Generous breakfasts are served on china hand-painted by the lady of the house and her daughter. Natural and friendly welcome.

How to get there (Map 25): 35km north of Clermont-Ferrand. On the Orléans motorway take Gannat exit, then Aigueperse, Chaptuzat, La Roche; signposted.

72
Chez M. Gebrillat

Chemin de Siorac
63500 Perrier
(Puy-de-Dôme)
Tel. 73 89 15 02
Fax 73 55 08 85
Paul Gebrillat and Mireille de St. Aubain

Open all year. **Rooms** 3 with bath and WC, 1 with shower and WC. **Price** 250F (2 pers.) +75F (extra pers.) **Meals** breakfast 25F, evening meals on request 80F (wine not included). **Restaurants** Le Relais and Le Parc at Issoire. **Facilities** fishing. **Pets** dogs not allowed. **Nearby** Volcano park, châteaux, forests, golf (40km), swimming and riding centre, ski slopes and cross-country ski-ing. **Spoken** English.

This very old village house is situated close to the volcanos. It has been tastefully restored and made comfortable. The bedrooms have a good blend of old regional furniture, unusual objects and very pretty fabrics. Pleasant bathrooms. Breakfast is served in a vaulted room, or under a wooden canopy overlooking the garden. Excellent welcome and very reasonable prices. What more could one ask for?

How to get there (Map 25): 3km west of Issoire in the Champeix direction (D996), in the middle of the village.

73
Les Ourgeaux

Pageas
87230 Châlus
(Haute-Vienne)
Tel. 55 78 50 97
Fax 55 78 54 76
M. and Mme McKeand

Open all year (on request Nov. – Easter). **Children** under 7 not accepted. **No smoking. Rooms** 1 with bath and WC, 2 with shower and WC, dovecot (2/4 pers.) with shower, WC, sitting room, kitchen. **Price** 260-310F (2 pers.), dovecot 400F (2 pers.) +100F (extra pers.) **Meals** breakfast 30F. **Restaurant** in the house for lunch and evening meal 130F (wine not incl.) **Facilities** lounge. **Credit cards** Visa (+2%) **Pets** dogs not allowed. **Nearby** tennis, golf, lake. **Spoken** English.

This house is buried among fields and woods. It is utterly peaceful. The owners have decorated each bedroom with equal care; they are light, with soft, toning colour schemes, pretty quilts, and some pieces of antique furniture. Equally successful is the comfortable music room, one part arranged as a small and cosy restaurant. An irresistible place.

How to get there (Map 23): 25km south west of Limoges via N21 towards Périgueux. In Châlus, turn right on D901 towards Rochechouart; signposted after 2.5km.

74
Château de Brie

87150 Champagnac-la-Rivière
(Haute-Vienne)
Tel. 55 78 17 52
Comte and Comtesse du Manoir
de Juaye

Open 1 April – 1 Nov. (or on request). **Rooms** 4 with bath and WC. **Price** 500-600F (2 pers.), possibility of a suite 800F (3 pers.) **Meals** breakfast incl., evening meals on reservation or at nearby restaurants. **Facilities** lounge. **Pets** dogs allowed on request. **Nearby** riding, sailing, fishing, walks, mountain biking, lake St-Mathieu. **Spoken** English.

Built in the 15th century on medieval foundations, the Château de Brie has superb views over the countryside. Each huge bedroom has a style of its own, with antiques and excellent decor. You wander through the ages from the 16th century to the Empire before meeting the 20th century in the small and impeccable modern bathrooms. A very elegant lounge is available. Breakfasts are served in the library. Warm and natural welcome.

How to get there (Map 23): 45km south west of Limoges via N21 to Châlus, then D42; it's between Châlus and Cussac.

75
Les Hauts de Boscartus

87520 Cieux
(Haute–Vienne)
Tel. 55 03 30 63
M. and Mme Hennebel

Open all year. **Non-smokers** preferred. **Rooms** 2 with shower and shared WC. Rooms cleaned, beds made at guests' expense. **Price** 170F (1 pers.), 220F (2 pers.) **Meals** breakfast incl. **Restaurants** auberges nearby. **Facilities** lounge, telephone. **Pets** dogs not allowed. **Nearby** tennis, lake, golf, Montemart (listed village), Monts de Blond.

Standing on a hillside, this house is surrounded by fir trees. The pleasant sitting room is arranged around two features: the fireplace and the large picture window. The attractive and comfortable bedrooms have lovely views and are totally quiet. On the breakfast table you will find croissants, white cheese and excellent home produce (honey, jams, spicy bread). Good quality.

How to get there *(Map 23): 30km north west of Limoges via N147 towards Bellac to Chamboret, then D711 to Cieux, then D204 and D95.*

76
Fougeolles

87120 Eymoutiers
(Haute–Vienne)
Tel. 55 69 11 44/55 69 18 50
Mme Jacques Du Montant

Open all year. **Rooms** 3 with bath and WC (1 not en suite), 1 with shower and shared WC. **Price** 250-300F (2 pers.) +30F (child). **Meals** breakfast incl. , lunch and dinner at weekends and every day except Sunday evening and Monday from 1 July-31 Aug. 80-150F (wine not incl.) **Facilities** lounge, fishing. **Pets** dogs not allowed. **Nearby** golf, tennis, swimming pool, marine sports, plateau des Millevaches, lake Vassivière, Aubusson. **Spoken** English.

In the heart of an agricultural estate specialising in sheep rearing, this 17th-century house has pleasant, comfortable bedrooms furnished with antiques and brightened with lovely fabrics. The lounge and dining room have their original furnishings and some unusual objects on display. In good weather breakfast is served outside (dinners are in the pretty farmhouse–auberge belonging to the children of the family). Excellent welcome and a truly genuine place.

How to get there *(Map 24): 45km south east of Limoges via D979 towards Eymoutiers; signposted 500m before entering the village, on the left.*

77
Laucournet

Glanges
87380 Saint-Germain-les-Belles
(Haute-Vienne)
Tel: 55 00 81 27
M. and Mme Desmaison

Open May – Sept. **Rooms** 1 suite (up to 5 pers.) of 2 bedrooms with bath, shower and WC. Room cleaning at guests' expense. **Price** 170F (1 pers.), 200F (2 pers.), 260F (4 pers.) **Meals** breakfast incl., no evening meals. **Restaurants** available in Fressange (5km). **Facilities** lounge, loose boxes. **Nearby** tennis, rivers, lakes, riding, golf. **Spoken** English.

Even if only two of you come here, this delightfully typically Limousin small house will be reserved for you alone. On the ground floor is a lounge with some regional furniture, a more modern bathroom and a covered terrace for breakfast. On the first floor two comfortable and pleasantly decorated bedrooms have lovely views over the fields. Peace, independence and an excellent welcome.

How to get there *(Map 23): 36km south east of Limoges via N20 to Magnac, then D82 for 2km, then D120 to Lascaux, then 1km on the St-Meard road.*

78
Le Repaire

87140 Vaulry
(Haute-Vienne)
Tel. 55 53 33 66
M. and Mme Richard Hartz

Open all year. **Rooms** 5 with shower and shared WC (3 heated in winter). **Price** 160F (2 pers.), 200F (3 pers.) **Meals** breakfast incl., half board 900F per pers. in double room (7 days min.), evening meal at communal or separate table 60F (wine incl.) **Pets** animals not allowed. **Facilities** loose boxes, river fishing. **Nearby** lake, tennis, walks. **Spoken** English.

An old renovated farmhouse in the heart of the Blond mountains, near forests and lakes. The bedrooms are simple, with pine beds. The walls have been plastered to leave some of the stonework showing, and the floors are in the Limousin fashion, with wide boards. The ambience is half old, half new. There is often local trout or lamb for dinner. Friendly and discreet welcome.

How to get there *(Map 23): 30km north west of Limoges via N147. At 'Le Chatain' take D72 to Breuilaufa, then Le Repaire.*

79
Tarperon

Quemigny-sur-Seine
21510 Aignay-le-Duc
(Côte-d'Or)
Tel. 80 93 83 74
Mme de Champsavin

Open 15 March – All Saints, 2 nights minimum stay. **Rooms** 3 with bath and WC, 1 with shower and WC, and 1 suite (3 pers.) with shower and WC. **Price** 330F (2 pers.), suite 500F (3 pers.) **Meals** breakfast incl., half board 315F per pers. in double room, evening meals at communal table 150F (aperitif, wine and coffee incl.) **Facilities** lounge, telephone, loose boxes, fly fishing. **Pets** dogs allowed on request. **Nearby** golf, riding, walks. **Spoken** English, German.

You will discover this isolated Burgundian manor a little way off the road. Inside, each ravishing bedroom is a concert of bright colours. There are also paintings, antique terracottas, and frescoes of the seaside in the bathrooms. The small lounge has extraordinary Chinese furniture. Beside it is the dining room, its walls hung with portraits of ancestors, and it is under their gaze that breakfast is served.

How to get there (Map 19): 28km south of Châtillon-sur-Seine via N71 and D32 towards Aignay. At Cosne, take D954 towards Aignay.

80
Château de Chorey-les-Beaune

Rue Jacques Germain
21200 Chorey-les-Beaune
(Côte-d'Or)
Tel. 80 22 06 05 Fax 80 24 03 93
M. and Mme François Germain

Open 1 March – 30 Nov. **Rooms** 5 with bath and WC and 1 suite (4 pers.) with bath and WC. **Price** 520-570F +100F (extra pers.), suite 780F. **Meals** breakfast 60F, no evening meals. **Restaurants** nearby. **Facilities** lounge, wine tasting in the cellars. **Credit cards** Visa. **Nearby** 18-hole golf, Hôtel-Dieu in Beaune, wine growing area of Burgundy, Romanesque churches, abbeys. **Spoken** English, German.

The Château de Chorey-les-Beaune is very close to Beaune, in a wine-growing village. It has belonged to the Germain family for many generations and has been sensitively and carefully renovated by them. The main building is 12th-century, the towers are 13th-century and the garden is encircled by a moat. The bedrooms have been tastefully and simply decorated. M. and Mme Germain are charming hosts and will take you to visit their cellars so that you can taste their wines, which are known throughout the region for their quality.

How to get there (Map 19): 3km north of Beaune, at the entrance to the village.

81
Le Relais de Chasse

Chambœuf
21220 Gevrey-Chambertin
(Côte-d'Or)
Tel. 80 51 81 60
Fax 80 34 15 96
Michelle and Hubert Girard

Open all year, 2 nights min. **No smoking. Rooms** 4 with bath and WC. **Price** 320-350 (2 pers.) **Meals** breakfast incl., no evening meal. **Restaurants** many nearby. **Facilities** lounge, telephone. **Pets** dogs not allowed. **Nearby** Beaune, Dijon. **Spoken** English.

Le Relais de Chasse is a fine house overlooking a beautiful park. It is in a charming little village close to the greatest vineyards of Burgundy. Most of the bedrooms are large and decorated in regional style with antique furniture. At a big table in the country-style dining room excellent breakfasts are served: fruit, spicy bread, boiled eggs, home-made jams. In good weather they are served outside on the terrace facing the garden. Warm welcome.

How to get there (Map 19): 18km south west of Dijon via A31 exit Nuits-St-Georges, then N74 to Gevrey-Chambertin, then left on D31 towards Chamboeuf; 1st private drive on the left after the church.

82
Château de Longecourt

21110 Longecourt-en-Plaine
(Côte-d'Or)
Tel. 80 39 88 76
Comtesse Bertrand de Saint-Seine

Open all year. **Rooms** 3 with bath and WC, 2 with bath and shared WC. **Price** 700F (1-2 pers.), +150F (extra pers.) **Meals** breakfast included, evening meal at communal table 250F (wine incl.) **Facilities** lounge, loose boxes, fishing. **Pets** dogs allowed. **Nearby** riding, 18-hole golf, wine route. **Spoken** English.

Longecourt is a 17th-century jewel in pink brick, surrounded by water. Mme de Saint-Seine will welcome you simply and with kindness. Some of the rooms are very sumptuous, others easier to live in. The lounge-library and the pink dining room are very refined. All the bedrooms are different, peaceful, comfortable and furnished with antiques. The placid waters of the moat can be seen from the bedroom windows. We preferred the 'Catherine de Medici' room.

How to get there (Map 19): 18km south east of Dijon via D996 and D968 towards St-Jean-de-Losne; it's on the Place de la Mairie in Longecourt.

83
L'Enclos

Arrans
21500 Montbard
(Côte-d'Or)
Tel. 80 92 16 12
Mireille and Marcel Clerget

Open 1 March – 30 Nov. **Rooms** 1 with shower and WC, 1 with bath and shared WC, 2 sharing shower and WC. Room cleaning on request. **Price** 200-250F (2 pers.) +100F (extra pers.) **Meals** breakfast incl., no evening meals. **Restaurants** 4km away and in Montbard. **Facilities** lounge, telephone. **Nearby** swimming pool, tennis, golf, Fontenay abbey (5km), Burgundy canals, Ancy le Franc.

A pretty village house in a flowery garden recommended for families because it has two large bedrooms with several beds. One is split-level and very big, but its bathroom is rather far away. The other, under the eaves, has 3 wide beds, a sweet shower room and a pretty view of the countryside. Very rural style. Spontaneous and very kind welcome.

How to get there (Map 18): 42km south west of Châtillon-sur-Seine via D980. In Montbard take D5 towards Laignes for 9km.

84
Domaine de Loisy

28, rue Général-de-Gaulle
21700 Nuits-Saint-Georges
(Côte-d'Or)
Tel. 80 61 02 72
Fax 80 61 36 14
Comtesse Michel de Loisy

Open all year. **Rooms** 4 with bath and WC, 2 without bath or shower. **Prices** 550-850F (2 pers.) **Meals** breakfast incl., evening meals at communal table 270F (wine incl.) **Facilities** lounge, telephone, visit to the wine cellars and wine tasting 300F (2 pers.) **Credit cards** Amex. **Pets** dogs allowed on request. **Nearby** swimming pool, tennis, riding, Dijon, Beaune, château of Clos de Vougeot. **Spoken,** English, Italian.

M me Loisy is a wine expert and wine lovers will especially appreciate this house and its refined ambience. Two rather exotic gardens encircle the building. The bedrooms are very comfortable and furnished in old-fashioned style. Double-glazing insulates them from the busy road. There is a lovely lounge, and breakfast and sometimes dinner are served in the large dining room.

How to get there (Map 19): 22km south of Dijon via N74; it's on the edge of town on the Beaune road.

85
Château de Chanteloup

Guipy
58420 Brinon-sur-Beuvron
(Nièvre)
Tel. 86 29 01 26
M. Mainguet

Open all year. **Rooms** 2 with bath and WC. **Price** 210F (1 pers.), 250F (2 pers.) **Meals** breakfast incl., no evening meals but there are cooking facilities. **Facilities** lounges, equestrian centre. **Nearby** tennis, fishing, golf, Gallo-Roman excavations, Romanesque church. **Spoken** English.

Chanteloup enjoys an isolated position in the middle of the countryside. The equestrian centre in the outbuildings does not mar the beauty of the surroundings. You will be pleasantly greeted and will have the choice of two comfortable bedrooms with reproduction furniture. The lounge is quiet and a good place for reading. Breakfast is served in an attractive dining room. Very reasonably priced.

How to get there *(Map 18): 22km south of Clamecy via D23. In Brinon-sur-Beunon take D5 left towards Corbigny. After Dompierre-sur-Hery turn right on D274.*

86
Le Marais

Gimouille
58470 Magny-Cours
(Nièvre)
Tel. 86 21 00 55
Fax 86 21 05 05
Comtesse Christian de Montrichard

Closed 1 Nov. – 1 April. **Rooms** 4 suites. **Price** 800-1400F (2 pers.) **Meals** breakfast incl., evening meals at communal table 400F. **Facilities** lounges. **Credit cards** accepted. **Pets** dogs not allowed. **Nearby** golf (15km), boating on the canal. **Spoken** English, Italian.

The severe military architecture of the Château de Marais makes a marvellous contrast with the comfort and beauty of its interior. The three lounges as well as the bedrooms are full of period furniture, antiques, tapestries and ancestral portraits, tracing the rich history of the château. It is a veritable museum where you will be very pleasantly received, and a very peaceful place. It is a pity the prices are so high.

How to get there *(Map 18): 8km south west of Nevers via N7, then D976 towards Bourges; signposted.*

87
Château de Lesvault

58370 Onlay
(Nièvre)
Tel. 86 84 32 91
Fax 86 84 32 91
Mme Lee and M. Simonds

Open all year. **Rooms** 1 with bath and WC, 5 with shower and WC, 4 with bath and shared WC. **Prices** 250-400F (1 pers.), 350-475F (2 pers.) **Meals** breakfast incl., evening meals at communal table, or not as preferred, 130F (wine not incl.) **Facilities** telephone, loose boxes, fly fishing. **Credit cards** Visa, Amex. **Pets** dogs allowed in the kennel on request. **Nearby** swimming pool, tennis. **Spoken** English.

From lovely sloping grounds, le Château de Lesvault overlooks a green landscape. The welcome is charming, the atmosphere artistic. Painters and sculptors from all over the world come here and their work is scattered about the rooms. We recommend the bedrooms with bathrooms. All of them are quiet, comfortable and well decorated. Breakfast is served at separate tables in a small dining room, and candlelit dinners in a vaulted room.

How to get there (Map 18): 5km west of Château-Chinon via D978, then D37 to Moulins-Engilbert, then 5km towards Onlay on D18.

88
La Rêverie

6, rue Joyeuse
58150 Pouilly-sur-Loire
(Nièvre)
Tel. 86 39 07 87
M. and Mme Lapeyrade

Open all year (on request in winter). **Rooms** 5 with bath and WC, telephone and TV, of which 1 with spa bath. **Price** 250-420F (2 pers.) **Meals** breakfast 35F, no evening meals. **Restaurants** in village. **Facilities** lounge, art gallery. **Pets** no animals allowed. **Nearby** tennis, golf, Sancerre. **Spoken** English.

Set in the peace of the charming village of Pouilly-sur-Loire, La Rêverie (the dream) well deserves its name. The care and kindness of M. and Mme Lapeyrade are worthy of special mention. All the comfortable bedrooms have been lovingly decorated, with well-matched fabrics, wallpapers and carpets. The lounge decoration is in 19th-century style, and breakfast is enjoyed in the art gallery to the accompaniment of music.

How to get there (Map 17): 40km from Nevers and Bourges; 15km south of Cosne-sur-Loire via N7.

89
Château du Vieil Azy

Le Vieil Azy
58270 Saint-Benin-d'Azy
(Nièvre)
Tel. 86 58 47 93
Vicomtesse Benoist d'Azy le Noan

Open 15 March – 1st Dec. **Rooms** 2 with bath and WC, 4 suites with bath, WC and telephone. **Price** 300F (1/2 pers.), suite 600F. **Meals** breakfast 40F, evening meals on reservation 100-120F. **Restaurants** Auberge de Sauvigny and Moulin de L'Etang (15km). **Facilities** lounge, riding, fishing. **Nearby** 18-hole golf, swimming pool, tennis, château d'Azy, château of the dukes of Nevers, Apremont.

This château stands in the middle of a park with ancient trees, close to a large lake. There is a beautiful wooden staircase in the entrance hall and the large sitting room has a library and an impressive fireplace. The lovely bedrooms are a little dark, with an atmosphere of days gone by. You will be welcomed not by the owners, but by the manager's wife. A good departure point for various excursions.

How to get there (Map 18): 16km east of Nevers via N81 towards Decize, then D978 to St-Benin-d'Azy, then D9 after the municipal swimming pool.

90
Baudrières

Le Bourg
71370 Baudrières
(Saône-et-Loire)
Tel. 85 47 32 18
Mme Vachet

Open March - Nov. (on request out of season). **Rooms** 1 with bath and WC, 1 with shower and WC. Room cleaning on request. **Price** 250F (1 pers.), 300F (2 pers.) +80F (extra pers.) **Meals** breakfast incl., no evening meals. **Facilities** lounge, tennis (+supl.) **Nearby** riding, swimming pool, lake, fishing, 18-hole golf. **Spoken** English, Italian.

A very pretty house covered in Virginia creeper in a peaceful little village. The welcome is relaxed and the bedrooms, tastefully arranged, are comfortable and welcoming. The decor is equally successful in the lounge which has old regional furniture. Excellent breakfasts served outside under a wooden canopy in good weather.

How to get there (Map 19): 17km north east of Tournus via N6 towards Sennecey-le-Grand, then right to Gigny on D18. Cross the river into Baudrières.

91
La Ferme

71460 Bissy-sous-Uxelles
(Saône-et-Loire)
Tel. 85 50 15 03
M. and Mme de La Bussière

Open all year. **Rooms** 2 with shower and WC, 2 with shower and shared WC, 2 with basin sharing 1 shower and 2 WCs. **Price** 110-150F (1 pers.), 150-260F (2 pers.) **Meals** breakfast incl., no evening meals. **Restaurants** close by. **Facilities** loose boxes. **Nearby** lake, fishing, golf, Cluny, Cormatin. **Spoken** English, German.

In this delightful little village, close to the church, you will find the courtyard of this character farmhouse. The welcome here is very friendly and lively. The bedrooms have been well restored and are impeccable, with pretty quilts on the beds. The biggest have a kitchenette. Excellent and generous breakfast served at a large table. A good rural stop.

How to get there (Map 19): 17km west of Tournus via D215 towards Mancey and left on D314 towards Chapaize. In Bissy beside the church.

92
Château de Sassangy

Sassangy
71390 Buxy
(Saône-et-Loire)
Tel. 85 96 12 40
Fax 85 96 11 44
M. and Mme Marceau

Open March – Oct. **Rooms** 6 with bath or shower, WC and telephone, and 1 suite (4/6 pers.) with 2 bedrooms, sitting room, bath and WC. **Price** 400-500F (1 pers.), 500-600F (2 pers.), 600-900F (3/6 pers.) **Meals** breakfast incl., evening meals on reservation (except Sunday) 100-150F. **Facilities** lounge. **Credit cards** Visa. **Pets** dogs not allowed. **Nearby** golf, cellar visits, châteaux, Romanesque churches, Beaune, Cluny. **Spoken** English.

This elegant 18th-century château has been sensitively and tastefully restored. Standing against a small hill, it enjoys panoramic views over a lovely park, an ornamental lake, and pastures. The bedrooms are large and very comfortable. You will dine in a huge, light, vaulted kitchen, which is well equipped and tastefully decorated. Mme Marceau does the cooking and will welcome you warmly.

How to get there (Map 19): 6km west of Buxy via A6 Chalon Sud exit, then towards Monchanin on N80, exit Sassangy after 15km.

93
Ferme-Auberge de Lavaux

Chatenay
71800 La Clayette
(Saône-et-Loire)
Tel. 85 28 08 48
M. Paul Gélin

Open Easter - 11 Nov. **Rooms** 2 with bath and WC, 2 with shower and WC. **Price** 240-260F (2 pers.) **Meals** breakfast incl., meals at the farm restaurant 80-100F (wine not incl.) **Facilities** fishing. **Pets** dogs not allowed. **Nearby** Romanesque churches, Cluny, Paray-le-Monial.

This is a green and hilly part of Burgundy. This lovely farmhouse inn stands on a hillside and has well tended grounds. The bedrooms open off an external wooden gallery. They are simple, quite large, and decorated in rural style but a bit dark. The former stables have been turned into a pleasant inn, with beams and exposed stonework. Tempting local cooking at very good prices. Pleasant welcome.

How to get there *(Map 18): about 40km south east of Paray-le-Monial via N79 towards Charolles, then D985 towards La Clayette and D987 towards Mâcon for 5km, then left on D300 towards Chatenay.*

94
Château de la Fredière

Céron
71110 Marcigny
(Saône-et-Loire)
Tel. 85 25 19 67
Fax 85 25 35 01
Mme Edith Charlier

Open 10 Jan. – 20 Dec. **Rooms** 6 and 2 suites with bath, WC and telephone, 3 with shower, WC and telephone. **Price** 200-520F (1/2 pers.), suite 840-950F. **Meals** breakfast 55F, evening meals on reservation (except Wednesday) 100-150F (wine not incl.) **Facilities** lounge, swimming pool, 18-hole golf course. **Pets** dogs allowed on request. **Nearby** Romanesque churches. **Spoken** English.

Château de la Fredière is surrounded by a lovely golf course. Thanks to Mme Charlier's kind welcome the atmosphere is friendly. The pleasant bedrooms are well decorated and elegantly furnished. We particularly recommend the ones in the château. There is a lounge, and an intimate dining room for breakfasts. Dinner is served at the golf club.

How to get there *(Map 25): 40km north of Roanne via D482 and D982 to Marcigny, then D990 towards Le Donjon-Lapalisse; signposted golf.*

95
Les Récollets

Place du Champ-de-Foire
71110 Marcigny
(Saône-et-Loire)
Tel. 85 25 03 34
Fax 85 25 06 91
Mme Badin

Open all year. **Rooms** 7 with bath and WC, 2 suites (4/6 pers.) with 2 bedrooms, bath and WC. **Price** 300F (1 pers.), 420-450F (2 pers.) +120F (extra pers.) **Meals** breakfast incl., evening meals on reservation (separate tables) 200F (wine incl.) **Facilities** lounge. **Credit cards** Visa, Amex. **Nearby** golf, Roman tour.

Built on the edge of the small village of Marcigny, this former convent has extensive views and a pretty garden. The bedrooms are comfortable and have 19th-century furniture, like the rest of the house. They are quiet. Mme Badin greets her guests with kindness and thoughtfulness. She prepares good breakfasts, which are served in a bright room with flowery decor and flower-painted furniture. An elegant place, though a bit expensive.

How to get there (Map 25): 30km north of Roanne via D482 and D982 in the Digoin direction to Marcigny.

96
Château de Poujux

Saint-Aubin-en-Charollais
71430 Palinges
(Saône-et-Loire)
Tel. 85 70 43 64
M. and Mme Céali

Open all year. **Rooms** 5 with bath and WC, 2 with shower and WC. **Price** 350-500F (2 pers.) +50F (extra pers.); children under 6 free. **Meals** breakfast 30F, evening meal at communal table, on reservation 160F (wine incl.) **Facilities** lounge. **Nearby** Cluny abbey, Romanesque churches, villages of Berzé-le-Châtel and Martailly-les-Briançon. **Spoken** English, German.

Apart from looking after its guests, this château breeds racing thoroughbreds. The bedrooms are large, pleasant, but rather basically furnished, with some 19th-century pieces and comfortable beds. There is a lounge and a dining room where generous breakfasts are served. It is very peaceful. You will be well received but the prices are a little high.

How to get there (Map 18): 14km north of Paray-le-Monial via Paris-Châlon autoroute, then N80 to Le Creusot, then 'route express' towards Paray-le-Monial, exit Charolles; it's before St-Aubin.

97
Château de Martigny

Poisson
71600 Paray-le-Monial
(Saône-et-Loire)
Tel. 85 81 53 21
Mme Edith Dor

Open Easter – All Saints. **Rooms** 3 with bath and WC, 1 with bath and shared WC, 2 with shared bath and WC, 1 studio (4 pers.) and 1 suite (3 pers.) with bath and WC. **Price** 350-500F (1/2 pers.), suite 450F (3 pers.), 550F (4 pers.) **Meals** breakfast 50F, lunch and evening meal at communal table, or not as preferred, 160F (wine not incl.) **Facilities** lounge, swimming pool, bicycles, drama courses. **Pets** dogs allowed on request. **Nearby** riding, tennis, fishing, golf (25km), Romanesque churches. **Spoken** English.

The château faces a superb panorama. Everything has been arranged for your comfort by Mme Dor with exceptionally good taste. Lovely bedrooms, with good furniture and delicate colours. Even the bathrooms are beautiful. Excellent, unforgettable meals served either in the dining room or outside.

How to get there *(Map 18): 8km south of Paray-le-Monial via D34.*

98
Château de Maizières

BP 19
71133 Saint-Loup-de-la-Salle
(Saône-et-Loire)
Tel. 85 49 45 79
M. and Mme Ryaux

Open all year. **Rooms** 5 with bath and WC, of which one has access for the handicapped. **Prices** 400-600F (2 pers.) +100F (extra pers.) **Meals** breakfast incl., evening meal on request 120F. **Restaurants:** in Beaune (10km). **Facilities** lounge, fishing, riding and loose boxes (on request). **Pets** dogs allowed on request. **Nearby** 18-hole golf (6km), tennis, Beaune. **Spoken** English, Spanish.

In a park with lakes, waterways and meadows where horses graze, you will find the Château de Maizières, a former monastery which has been sensitively restored. The very light bedrooms have high ceilings and contain furniture painted by a young English artist. They and the bathrooms are tastefully decorated. Mme Ryaux is a delightful young woman and an attentive hostess.

How to get there *(Map 19): about 12km south east of Beaune via D970; at St-Loup-de-la-Salle, take D62 towards Demigny for 1.5km.*

99
Château de Beaufer
Route d'Ozenay
71700 Tournus
(Saône-et-Loire)
Tel. 85 51 18 24
Fax 85 51 25 04
M. and Mme Roggen

Open 15 March – All Saints (on request out of season, 3 days min.) **Rooms** 6 with bath and WC, of which 1 is a single with shower. **Price** 380F (1 pers.), 450-550F (2 pers.), 710F (3 pers.), suite 680F (2 pers.) **Meals** breakfast incl., no evening meal. **Restaurants** in Tournus. **Facilities** lounge, swimming pool. **Credit cards** Visa. **Pets** dogs allowed on request (+40F). **Nearby** golf, polo. **Spoken** English, Italian, German.

This small château backs on to a hill and faces a rural, wooded landscape. It is beautifully arranged for the comfort and peace of its guests. The high-beamed lounge opens on to the swimming pool. The bedrooms are in several buildings. They are big, well kept, and decorated with prints and pretty furniture. The beds are huge and the bathrooms excellent.

How to get there *(Map 19): 25km south of Chalon-sur-Saône via N6 and A6 to Tournus, then D14 towards Ozenay; signposted 3km from Tournus.*

100
Château de Prunoy
Prunoy
89120 Charny
(Yonne)
Tel. 86 63 66 91
Fax 86 63 77 79
Mme Roumilhac

Closed 3 Jan. – 15 Feb. **Rooms** 13 with bath, WC and telephone, 6 suites (4/5 pers.) of 2 bedrooms, bath, WC and telephone. **Price** 600F (2 pers.), suite 840F (4 pers.) **Meals** breakfast 45F, half board 525F per pers. in double room, (5 days min.), lunch and dinner 180F (wine not incl.) **Facilities** lounge, swimming pool, tennis, spa bath, boating on the lake. **Credit cards** accepted. **Nearby** riding, golf, wine route.

Standing in superb grounds with a lake, this château is full of surprises. The extremely comfortable bedrooms contain an amazing accumulation of old furniture, objects and ceramics. Even the bathrooms are unusual. Generous breakfasts are served whenever you like. There is an excellent restaurant in the château, with simple but refined cooking. Mme Roumilhac's warm welcome completes the picture.

How to get there *(Map 18): 23km west of Joigny via A6, exit Joigny towards Montargis, Charny (D943 and D16).*

101
La Coudre

La Coudre
89120 Perreux
(Yonne)
Tel 86 91 61 42/86 91 62 91
M. and Mme Lusardi

Open all year. **Rooms** 4 with bath and WC. **Price** 430-520F (2 pers.) **Meals** breakfast incl.,
evening meals at communal table, on reservation 180F (wine incl.) **Restaurant** Le Cheval Blanc
in Charny. **Facilities** lounge, telephone, potter's studio on the property. **Pets** dogs not allowed.
Nearby 18-hole golf, tennis, riding, château de St Fargeau. **Spoken** English, Italian.

This large, well-restored house stands beside a small country road with
its pretty garden around it. Inside there are well-proportioned rooms
and fine antiques. The large bedrooms, plush and comfortable, are prettily
decorated. Each has a good bathroom. Breakfast is served at a long wooden
table. Dinners feature good regional produce and are accompanied by
excellent wines.

How to get there *(Map 18): 15km from A6 Joigny exit. Head towards Montargis,
then D3 towards Toucy to Sommecaise and D57 towards Perreux; 1km before the village.*

102
La Chasseuserie

Lavau
89170 Saint-Fargeau
(Yonne)
Tel 86 74 16 09
Mme Anne-Marie Marty

Open all year, on written reservation. **Rooms** 1 with bath and WC, 1 suite of 2 bedrooms with
bath and WC. Room cleaning, if required, on payment of supplement. **Price** 200F 1st night,
160F 2nd and 3rd nights (2 pers.), suite (4 pers.) 360F 1st night, 290F 2nd and 3rd nights.
Meals breakfast incl., no evening meal. **Restaurant** Ferme-auberge de la Cour Buisson close by.
Facilities lounge, tennis, bicycles. **Pets** small dogs allowed on request. **Nearby** canals, shooting,
fishing, St-Fargeau, Ratilly. **Spoken** English.

Standing in the middle of the countryside, surrounded by flowers, this is
a most alluring house. The comfortable bedrooms are peaceful, pleasantly
decorated, and have a pretty view. Breakfast is served in an attractive lounge-
dining room or in the garden. Good prices.

How to get there *(Map 17): 52km south west of Auxerre via D965 to Lavau, then
D74 towards Bléneau for 3km; signposted.*

103
Chez Mme Defrance

4, place de la Liberté
89710 Senan
(Yonne)
Tel. 86 91 59 89
Mme Defrance

Open all year. **Rooms** 1 with shower and WC, 2 sharing bath and WC (possible suite). **Price** 160-250F (1 pers.), 220-310F (2 pers.) **Meals** breakfast incl., evening meals at communal table, on reservation 90F (wine incl.) **Facilities** lounge. **Pets** dogs not allowed. **Nearby** tennis, golf. **Spoken** English.

A character house in a village, a little set back from a grass-covered walk planted with lime trees. It is very tranquil. The interior is simple and well kept with some antique furniture. We recommend the large bedroom with floral wallpaper, waxed wood floor and a comfortable double bed. Mme Defrance, a cheerful and witty woman, will ask you to choose where you would like to have breakfast: bedroom, garden or dining room.

How to get there (Map 18): 26km north west of Auxerre via A6 exit Auxerre Nord, then N6 towards Joigny and D14. In Bassou turn left for Neuilly and D153 to Senan. From Paris, A6 exit Joigny, then D89.

104
Les Lammes

89210 Venizy
(Yonne)
Tel. 86 43 44 42
Mme Antoinette Puissant

Closed end Oct. – Easter, in Aug. for week or weekend only. **Rooms** 8 suites (2/4 pers.) with kitchen, sitting room, bath and WC. **Price** 380F (2 pers.) +100F (extra pers.) **Meals** breakfast incl., no evening meals. **Restaurants** close by. **Facilities** swimming pool, fishing. **Nearby** tennis, wine route, Fontenay abbey. **Spoken** English, German, Italian.

This large farm is made up of several buildings. The bedrooms are all suites with a sitting area and a kitchen area. Patchwork bedcovers and antique furniture make for a pleasant atmosphere, and many rooms have a view of the large swimming pool. Breakfast is served in a huge well-decorated room or outside under a canopy. Enthusiastic welcome.

How to get there (Map 18): 30km north east of Auxerre via N77. Go through St-Florentin and take D30 towards Venizy; 300m after l'auberge de Pommerats on the left.

105
Ferme de Malido

Saint-Alban
22400 Lamballe
(Côtes d'Armor)
Tel. 96 32 94 74
M. and Mme Robert Legrand

Open all year. **Rooms** 5 with shower and WC. **Price** 180F (1 pers.), 200-250F (2 pers.) +70F (extra pers.) **Meals** breakfast incl., no evening meals; barbecue in the garden. **Restaurants** close by. **Facilities** lounge, telephone. **Pets** dogs allowed on request (+20F). **Nearby** swimming pool, tennis, fishing, riding, sailing, golf, walks. **Spoken** English, German.

In the heartland of France, the road which leads to Malido goes past many farms. When you arrive in its pretty, flowery courtyard you will be received with great kindness. The bedrooms are simple and clean, decorated in soft colours and with modern pale-wood furniture. There is a lounge and a dining room. Many tourist attractions are nearby and the seaside is only 4km away.

How to get there (Map 6): 21km north east of St Brieuc. Take N12 to Lamballe, then D791 north from Lamballe towards Le Val André. At St-Alban, take the St-Brieuc road for 2km.

106
Manoir de Kerguéréon

Ploubezre
22300 Lannion
(Côtes d'Armor)
Tel. 96 38 91 46
M. and Mme de Bellefon

Open Easter – All Saints. **Rooms** 2 with bath and WC. **Price** 480F (2 pers.) + 100F (extra pers.) **Meals** breakfast incl., no evening meal. **Restaurants** 8km away, and Les Côtes d'Armor in Plestin-les-Grèves (10km). **Facilities** lounge. **Pets** dogs allowed on request. **Nearby** water sports, tennis, riding, golf, châteaux of Rosanbo, Kergrist and Tonquedec, chapels, Lannion, Tréguier, Morlaix, pink granite coast, concerts and folklore festivals. **Spoken** English.

Standing in the middle of the countryside beside a small stud farm, this is the archetypal Breton manor, with a tower and Gothic–arched doorways. The interior contains lovely furniture and pottery and has kept its old character. The lounge, dining room, and the two very beautiful bedrooms are totally charming. Excellent breakfasts (hot pancakes and home-made jams), and a very warm welcome.

How to get there (Map 5): 10km south of Lannion via D11, then at Kerauzern D30 towards Ploumillau; 4th road on the left after the railway line.

107
Le Colombier

Coat Gourhant
22700 Louannec
(Côtes d'Armor)
Tel. 96 23 29 30
M. and Mme Fajolles

Open all year. **Rooms** 4 with shower and WC. **Price** 220-250F (2 pers.) **Meals** breakfast incl., no evening meals. **Restaurants** Le Surois and Le Sphinx. **Facilities** lounge. **Pets** dogs allowed on request. **Nearby** seaside, golf, tennis, riding, sea fishing, golden gorse route, Port Blanc, Tonquedec. **Spoken** English.

This is an old, well-renovated farmhouse in the middle of the countryside, yet only a few minutes from the sea. You will be warmly greeted and will like the bedrooms with their sloping ceilings. They are light, comfortable and pretty, each with its own colour scheme. In the small sitting room there is a mass of tourist information. Excellent breakfast, served in a large countrified room with subtle and inviting decor. A good, economical address.

How to get there (Map 5): 2km from Perros-Guirec in the Lannion direction, at the large roundabout take Louannec road, then 1st small road on the right uphill; signposted.

108
Rosmapamon

Louannec
22700 Perros-Guirec
(Côtes-d'Armor)
Tel. 96 23 00 87
Mme Annick Sillard

Open 1 April – 30 Sept. **Rooms** 2 with bath and WC, 2 with shower and WC. **Price** 230-300F (1 pers.), 280-350F (2 pers.) +70F (extra pers.) **Meals** breakfast incl., no evening meals. **Facilities** lounge, telephone. **Pets** dogs allowed on request. **Nearby** 18-hole golf, seaside, water sports, seawater therapy, bird watching, pink granite coast. **Spoken** English.

A few hundred metres from the sea and the port of Perros-Guirec, Rosmapamon stands on a hillside in wooded grounds. The house belonged to Ernest Renan and is simple and elegant. You will be very pleasantly greeted. The peaceful first floor bedrooms are charming and overlook the garden. When you awake, a good breakfast with fresh orange juice will be served at the large table in the dining room.

How to get there: (Map 5) 2km east of Perros-Guirec on D6.

109
La Pastourelle

Saint-Lormel
22130 Plancoët
(Côtes-d'Armor)
Tel. 96 84 03 77
Mme Ledé

Open 1 March – 15 Nov. **Rooms** 1 with bath and WC, 4 with shower and WC. **Price** 210F (2 pers.) +60F (extra pers.) **Meals** breakfast incl., half board 160F per pers. in double room (5 nights min.), evening meals at separate tables, on reservation 70F (wine not incl.) **Facilities** lounge. **Pets** small dogs allowed on request. **Nearby** tennis, sailing, golf, Dinan. **Spoken** English.

L a Pastourelle lies deep in the country, protected by a pretty garden which slopes towards it. It is a cheerful, bright place, the interior full of charm. The bedrooms are cosy and well-kept and overlook the grounds. Excellent dinners served at separate tables in a large dining room prettily decorated in local style.

How to get there *(Map 6): 4km north of Plancoët via D768 towards Dinard and St-Lormel; 1st road on the left leaving Plancoët.*

110
Le Char à Bancs

22170 Plélo
(Côtes d'Armor)
Tel. 96 74 13 63
Famille Jean-Paul Lamour

Open all year (on request out of season). **Rooms** 4 with bath or shower and WC. **Price** 320F (2 pers.) **Meals** breakfast incl., no evening meal. **Restaurant** auberge, 400m (light meals only), restaurants close by. **Facilities** lounge, farm museum, pedalos on the river, ponies. **Nearby** seaside , Chatelaudren, Paimpol, golf (10km), tennis.

L e Char à Bancs is a good farmhouse inn with a waterway and nearby 'La Ferme des Aïeux' – farm of our forefathers – which has been in the family since 1400 and has now been converted into a small museum. The bedrooms are on the first floor and each has its own theme: 'chapelière' (hatter), 'oiseaux' (birds), 'horloge' (clock) and 'musique' (music)... All are comfortable and warm, with beams and thick quilts. Really generous breakfasts and excellent welcome.

How to get there *(Map 6): between St-Brieuc (20km to the west) and Guingamp. 4km north of the Paris-Brest dual carriageway, exit Plélo; signposted.*

111
Le Presbytère

Tregrom
22420 Plouaret
(Côtes d'Armor)
Tel. 96 47 94 15
Nicole de Morchoven

Open all year. **Rooms** 1 with bath and WC, 2 with shower and WC, 2 suites (3/4 pers.) **Price** 250-320F (2 pers.), suite 320-430F. **Meals** breakfast incl., evening meals on request. **Restaurants** 7km away in Belle-Isle-en-Terre and Plouaret. **Facilities** lounge. **Pets** dogs allowed on request (suppl.) **Nearby** fishing, riding, tennis, golf, walks, seaside (20km). **Spoken** English.

This beautiful rectory opposite the church hides a charming interior. Each room is a perfect blend of carefully chosen wallpapers, fabrics and antique furniture. Bedrooms and bathrooms are very comfortable and the breakfast room is really enchanting. You will feel quite at home. Excellent welcome.

How to get there (Map 5): 20km south of Lannion. On N12 between St-Brieuc and Morlaix turn off at Louargat, then signposted Tregrom.

112
Manoir de Kergrec'h

22820 Plougrescant
(Côtes d'Armor)
Tel. 96 92 59 13/96 92 56 06
Vicomte and Vicomtesse de Roquefeuil

Open all year. **Rooms** 3 rooms and 2 suites with bath and WC. **Price** 500F (2 pers.), suite 700f (3 pers.), 800F (4 pers.) **Meals** breakfast incl., no evening meal. **Restaurants** in Tréguier. **Facilities** telephone, coastal walks. **Pets** dogs allowed on request. **Nearby** beach, windsurfing, sea fishing, tennis, golf, pink granite coast, golden gorse coast. **Spoken** English.

With grounds stretching along the pink granite coast, the Manoir de Kergrec'h retains all its charm. Guests are well looked after. The bedrooms have recently been renovated in perfect taste; each has antique furniture and a character of its own. Breakfast is served around the dining room table or in the bedrooms: crêpes, far breton (a flan with prunes), fruit, home-made jams. A lovely place.

How to get there (Map 5): Between Perros-Guirec and Paimpol; 7km north of Tréguier. From Guingamp take D8, signposted.

113
Château de Pontgamp

22150 Plouguenast
(Côtes d'Armor)
Tel. 96 28 71 99
M. Pourdieu Le Coz

Open all year. **Rooms** 2 suites of one bedroom and sitting room (2 pers.) with bath and WC. **Price** 250-300F (2 pers.) +150F (extra room). **Meals** breakfast incl., no evening meals. **Restaurant** L'Auberge du Cheval Blanc in Loudéac. **Facilities** lounge, Breton crêpe cookery courses. **Dogs** not allowed. **Nearby** fishing, seaside, tennis, monuments and manors, village of Moncontour, guided or unaccompanied tours of the area, guided tours of antique shops. **Spoken** English.

In spite of its position in the village of Plouguenast, Pontgamp is a quiet place, surrounded by greenery. The bedrooms are large, comfortable and nicely furnished. A very large room on the ground floor acts as both lounge and dining room and has exceptional 1950s furniture designed by Le Corbusier. You will be received as friends. Ample breakfasts and good value prices.

How to get there *(Map 6): 12km north of Loudéac via D768; it's in the village.*

114
Château de Kermezen

22450 Pommerit-Jaudy
(Côtes d'Armor)
Tel. 96 91 35 75
Compte and Comtesse de Kermel

Open all year. **Rooms** 4 bedrooms and 1 suite (4 pers.) with bath and WC. **Price** 450-520F (2 pers.) +100F (extra pers.), suite 780F (4 pers.) **Meals** breakfast incl., no evening meals. **Restaurants** nearby. **Facilities** lounge, fishing and Kermezen path. **Credit cards** Visa. **Nearby** riding, tennis, golf, seaside, isle of Bréhat, pink granite coast. **Spoken** English.

Kermezen stands in beautiful green, undulating Breton countryside. You will receive a marvellous welcome from the owners, whose family has lived here for 500 years. Inside there is a large, light lounge which is very well-furnished. The bedrooms are also elegant (the 'aux coqs' is a little masterpiece). Breakfast can be served in the bedrooms but it would be a pity not to use the lovely 17th-century dining room. A very beautiful place.

How to get there *(Map 5): 10km south of Tréguier via D8 to La Roche-Derrien and Pommerit-Jaudy; signposted.*

115
Château du Val d'Arguenon

Notre-Dame-du-Guildo
22380 Saint-Cast
(Côtes-d'Armor)
Tel. 96 41 07 03 Fax 96 41 02 67
M. and Mme de La Blanchardière

Open all year, (on request in winter). **Rooms** 2 with bath and WC, 2 with shower and WC, 1 suite (2 pers. +1 child) with bath and WC. **Price** 370-530F (2 pers.), suite 660F (2 pers.) +60F (child). **Meals** breakfast incl., no evening meals. **Restaurants** 3 within 400 metres. **Facilities** lounge, tennis, fishing, loose boxes, beach. **Pets** small dogs allowed on request. **Nearby** golf courses, riding, sailing club, Emerald coast, Channel Islands. **Spoken** English.

The château is by the sea and offers very beautiful coastal walks. The welcome is relaxed and warm. The rooms are very beautiful and full of their original furniture. The lounge and dining room are open to guests. The bedrooms are large, well equipped, comfortable and quiet. Very close to Dinard, St Malo, Dinan, Lamballe and Mont-St-Michel.

How to get there (Map 6): 16km west of Dinard via D786; just after Guildo bridge.

116
La Corbinais

22980 Saint-Michel-de-Plelan
(Côtes-d'Armor)
Tel. 96 27 64 81
M. Beaupère

Open all year. **Rooms** 1 with bath and WC, 3 with shower and WC (of which 1 has external WC). **Price** 200F (2 pers.) +50F (extra pers.) **Meals** breakfast incl, evening meals at communal table, on reservation 70F (wine not incl.) **Facilities** lounge, loose boxes, 9-hole golf (planned for '93). **Nearby** riding, golf. **Spoken** English.

A small Breton granite house in a flower garden. There is a warm, country-style room with a tall fireplace, antique furniture and ornaments, and a long wooden table where very good dinners are served. The five charming bedrooms upstairs have pretty pale fabrics and pleasant, small bathrooms. Add to this the possibility of practising your golf (even without your own clubs) and a particularly kind welcome.

How to get there (Map 6): 17km west of Dinan via N176 towards Plélan, then right on to D19 for 3km towards Plancoët through Plélan-le-Petit.

117
Le Queffiou

Route du Château
22140 Tonquédec
(Côtes-d'Armor)
Tel. 96 35 84 50
Mme Sadoc

Closed 20Sept. – 15 Jan. **Rooms** 2 with bath and WC, 3 with shower and WC. **Price** 300-350F (2 pers.) +100F (extra pers.) **Meals** breakfast incl., evening meals at separate tables, on reservation 150F (wine not incl.) **Facilities** lounge. **Pets** no dogs allowed. **Nearby** tennis, riding, fishing, golf, pink granite coast. **Spoken** English.

This is a very welcoming house a few hundred metres from the fortress of Tonquédec. The bedrooms are large, light, and very comfortable. Each has a style of its own, classical or modern, and all have excellent bathrooms. Madame Sadoc is a marvellous cook; if you book in time you will have a truly gastronomic dinner.

How to get there (Map 5): 10km south east of Lannion via D767 towards Guingamp to Cavan, then right towards Tonquédec. Once in the village, it's 500m on the road to the château.

118
Château de la Ville-Guérif

22650 Trégon
(Côtes d'Armor)
Tel. 96 27 24 93
Vicomte S. de Pontbriand

Open June – Sept. **Rooms** 3 with bath and WC, 2 with shower and WC. **Price** 350-400F +100F (extra pers.) **Meals** breakfast incl., no evening meals. **Facilities** lounge. **Pets** dogs allowed on request. **Nearby** swimming pool, tennis, fishing, riding centre, golf, Mont-St-Michel, St-Malo, Dinan, Dinard, Cap Fréhel. **Spoken** English, German.

This astonishing little 19th-century folly has something of an Italian villa about it. The interior is very authentic, with antique furniture, panelling, paintings and ornaments. The walls are newly and tastefully papered or painted. An incredible double staircase leads to vast bedrooms which are light, full of charm and well-equipped, as are the bathrooms. And finally, the welcome is so energetic and full of fun that you forget the closeness of the road. An engaging place.

How to get there (Map 6): 16km west of Dinard towards St-Brieuc (3km after Ploubalay); at Trégon head for the beaches.

119
La Ferme du Breil

22650 Trégon
(Côtes d'Armor)
Tel. 96 27 30 55
Comtesse de Blacas

Open all year. **Rooms** 4 with bath and WC. **Prices** 340-390F (2 pers.) +100F (extra pers.) +50F (child). If you stay 7 days, 1 day is free. **Meals** breakfast incl., no evening meals. **Restaurants** at 2km. **Facilities** lounge. **Pets** dogs allowed on request. **Nearby** golf, riding (10km), tennis, seaside, sailing school, Mont-St-Michel, St-Malo, Dinan, pink granite coast, Cap Fréhel. **Spoken** English, Spanish.

This charming farmhouse with its well kept grounds is very close to the sea... and to the road, but this does not disturb the peace of the bedrooms under the sloping roof. These lovely rooms are very cosy with their floral fabrics, engravings and antique furniture. All have good modern bathrooms. There is an elegant lounge with deep, green leather chairs for the use of guests, and breakfast is served there at separate tables. A welcoming place, and of good quality.

How to get there (Map 6): 13km west of Dinard towards St-Brieuc through Ploubalay; after 2km turn left towards Plessix-Balisson.

120
Manoir de Kervezec

29660 Carantec
(Finistère)
Tel. 98 67 00 26
Mme Bohic

Open Easter – end Oct. **Rooms** 3 with bath and WC, 3 with shower and WC. **Price** 180-240F (1 pers.), 250-300F (2 pers.) +60F (extra pers.) **Meals** breakfast incl., no evening meal. **Facilities** lounge. **Nearby** tennis, riding, sailing, footpaths, 18-hole golf, châteaux.

In the middle of a market gardening area, this 19th-century house has an exceptional position. From its south facing terrace there is a splendid panoramic view of the coastline and the sea. Small or large, the bedrooms are quiet, very attractive, light and well kept. Generous breakfasts are served on the terrace or in a room embellished with antique regional furniture.

How to get there (Map 5): 12km north of Morlaix. In Morlaix D58 towards Roscoff and turn off for Carantec. Signboard before Carantec on the left.

121
Kerfornedic

29450 Commana
(Finistère)
Tel. 98 78 06 26
M. and Mme Le Signor

Open all year. **Rooms** 2 with shower and WC. **Price** 220 (1 pers.), 250F (2 pers.) **Meals** breakfast incl., no evening meal. **Restaurant** Les Voyageurs in Sizun. **Pets** no dogs allowed. **Nearby** riding, tennis, golf, walks, lake, bathing, windsurfing, fishing (200m), local history museums.

This very old rambling house, surrounded by flowers, is set in the superb landscape of the Arré hills. Once over the threshold, you will be captivated by the beauty of the simple interior: everywhere, whitewashed walls, beams, dried flowers and well-chosen ornaments. The bedrooms have the same atmosphere and the welcome is warm too. A charming place.

How to get there (Map 5): 41km south west of Morlaix via N12 to Landivisiau, then D30 and D764 to Sizun, then D30 after Sizun to St-Cadou, then towards Commana; it's on the right after 2km.

122
Manoir de Kervent

29100 Douarnenez
(Finistère)
Tel. 98 92 04 90
Mme Lefloch

Open all year. **Rooms** 2 with shower and WC, 1 suite (4 pers.) with shower and WC. **Price** 220-240F (2 pers.), suite 350-400F (4 pers.) Weekend rates (Friday and Saturday incl. evening meals) 700F for 2 pers.; applies from 15 Sept. – 15 June. **Meals** breakfast incl. **Restaurants** in Douarnenez. **Facilities** lounge. **Pets** dogs allowed on request. **Nearby** beach, tennis, golf, pointe du Raz, Locronan.

Kervent is on the outskirts of Douarnenez but in the countryside. With flowers both inside and out, this house will quickly charm you. The good-sized bedrooms are well furnished and very pleasant. Breakfast is served at a big table in the light and elegant dining room. Madame Lefloch is full of humour and kindness and has prepared a veritable tourists' bible to help you enjoy the region.

How to get there (Map 5): 2km south west of Douarnenez via D765 towards Audierne; it's on the right 500m after the traffic lights.

123
Pen Ker Dagorn

Chemin des Vieux-Fours
29920 Kerdruc
(Finistère)
Tel. 98 06 85 01
Mme Brossier-Publier

Open 1 April – 30 Oct. (2 days min.) **Rooms** 1 with bath and WC, 2 with shower and WC. **Price** 240F (2 pers.) **Meals** breakfast 30F, no evening meal. **Restaurants** in Port-Manech, Pont-Aven, Riec and Nevez. **Facilities** lounge. **Pets** dogs not allowed. **Nearby** beaches, bicycle and boat hire, tennis, riding, golf, Belon, Pont-Aven.

A very attractive country house set amid lush greenery. Each bedroom has a style of its own, with carefully chosen decorations in which wood predominates. All are large, comfortable and light, and the bathrooms may amuse you. Excellent breakfasts are served at separate tables. M. and Mme Publier are charmingly attentive. A real success.

How to get there (Map 5): 5km south of Pont-Aven via D70 towards Concarneau, then immediately left towards Le Henant-Kerdruc; signposted.

124
La Grange de Coatelan

29640 Plougonven
(Finistère)
Tel. 98 72 60 16
Charlick and Yolande de Ternay

Open Easter – All Saints (2 days min.) **Rooms** 2 with bath and WC. **Price** 150F (1 pers.), 200F (2 pers.) + 80F (extra pers.) **Meals** breakfast incl., crêperie in the evenings (not Wednesday). **Pets** no dogs allowed. **Nearby** riding, seaside, Arrée hills, wayside cross of Plougonven. **Spoken** English.

L ying close to the Arrée hills, La Grange was once a weaver's farm. On the ground floor there is a small auberge done out in pale wood with an open fireplace, and a bar area in the shape of a boat's hull. The cooking is excellent and the atmosphere just as successful. The two bedrooms are tastefully decorated and have unusual bathrooms. A magical place.

How to get there (Map 5): 7km south of Morlaix via D109 towards Plourin-lès-Morlaix, then Plougonven; signposted.

125
Kerambris

29920 Port-Manech
(Finistère)
Tel. 98 06 83 82
Mme Gourlaouen

Open all year. **Rooms** 4 with shower and WC. **Price** 180F (1 pers.), 210F (2 pers.) **Meals** breakfast incl., no evening meals. **Restaurants** in Pont-Aven and Port-Manech. **Facilities** coastal path. **Pets** dogs not allowed. **Nearby** sailing, tennis, riding, golf, Pont-Aven. **Spoken** English.

A long and ancient Breton house in grey granite 300m from the sea. A coastal path offers superb walks. Inside, the small bedrooms are simple but very well-kept. Friendly and discreet, Mme Gourlaouen will look after you well. She makes generous breakfasts and will advise you on where to eat for dinner. The garden and the closeness of Pont-Aven make up for the lack of a lounge.

How to get there *(Map 5): 10km south of Pont-Aven via D77; turn right before the village then left; signposted.*

126
La Clarté

25, La Clarté
29310 Querrien
(Finistère)
Tel. 98 71 31 61
Jean and Lucie Guillou

Open all year. No smoking. 2 nights min. **Rooms** 2 with bath and WC, 2 with shower and WC, one of which is a family room (3 pers.) Room cleaning on request. **Price** 230F (2 pers.), 330F (3 pers.) **Meals** breakfast incl., no evening meals. **Restaurants** auberge on the farm and farmhouse-auberges 4km and 10km away. **Facilities** lounge, telephone. **Pets** no dogs allowed. **Nearby** beaches, footpaths, tennis, river fishing, hacking, golf (25km), chapels of Ste-Barbe, St-Fiacre, Kerasquet.

N ear a charming Breton village, La Clarté stands in the middle of a superb garden, full of flowers and different varieties of trees. Inside it is comfortable and pleasant. The decoration combines the modern with the quaint. The bedrooms are bright and cheerful, with a lovely view. Gourmet breakfasts include pancakes, honey, wholemeal organic bread and other home-made treats. Marvellous welcome.

How to get there *(Map 5): 15km north east of Quimperlé via D970 towards Le Faouët; signposted from Querrien.*

127
Le Chatel

29124 Riec-sur-Belon
(Finistère)
Tel. 98 06 00 04
M. Gourlaouen

Open all year. **Rooms** 2 with bath and WC, 3 with shower and WC. Room cleaning on request. **Price** 170F (2 pers.) +50F (extra pers.) **Meals** breakfast 30F, no evening meals. **Facilities** deer farm, bicycles. **Nearby** tennis, riding, 18-hole golf, seaside, Pont-Aven. **Spoken** English

A few minutes from Pont-Aven, this lovely farm is made up of a number of buildings which are all very charming. There are flowers everywhere. The bedrooms are pleasant, comfortable and pretty, with white walls and country-style decorations. The welcome is very kind and excellent breakfasts are served in an attractive room containing antique country furniture. Before leaving ask to see the deer farm.

How to get there (Map 5): 1km east of Pont-Aven via D783 towards Riec-sur-Belon for 800m, then signed to the right.

128
Kerloaï

29390 Scaër
(Finistère)
Tel. 98 59 42 60
M. and Mme Penn

Open all year. **Rooms** 4 with shower and WC. **Price** 190F (1 pers.), 240F (2 pers.) **Meals** breakfast incl., evening meals sometimes (winter only) at communal table. **Restaurants** 4km, and a farmhouse auberge. **Facilities** lounge. **Pets** dogs allowed on request. **Nearby** swimming pool, tennis, seaside. **Spoken** English, German.

When booking a room in advance in Kerloaï you will be given the choice between two comfortable and pretty, old-fashioned bedrooms and two others, also comfortable but more modern. The whole place is peaceful and welcoming. The dining room furniture is typically Breton but the deep chairs in the sitting room make some concessions to comfort. On waking, and before a stroll in the garden, enjoy a generous breakfast in the dining room, which is decorated with flower arrangements.

How to get there (Map 5): 32km east of Quimper via D15. Leaving Scaër go 3km towards Coray-Briec on D50, then turn left at the place called Ty-Ru-Bar, signposted, and 1st left towards Kerloaï.

129
Manoir de la Duchée

La Duchée
Saint-Briac-sur-Mer
35800 Dinard
(Ille-et-Vilaine)
Tel. 99 88 00 02
Jean-François Stenou

Open 1 March – 1 Nov. and during school holidays (and on reservation). **Rooms** 5 with bath, WC and TV, of which 1 is a duplex. **Price** 290F (1 pers.), 340F (2 pers.), 450F (3 pers.), 500F (4 pers.) +50F (extra pers.) **Meals** breakfast incl., no evening meals. **Restaurants** nearby. **Facilities** lounges, riding, mountain bikes on the property. **Pets** no dogs allowed. **Nearby** sea, sailing, tennis, swimming pool, golf (3km); Mont-St-Michel, St-Malo, Dinan, Dinard, Cap Fréhel.

This small manor lies deep in the countryside and backs on to a farm. The very comfortable bedrooms are full of character and, for the most part, have late 19th-century furniture painted with floral motifs. On the ground floor, a beautiful room with beams and exposed stonework serves as a slightly theatrical background for good breakfasts: a log fire, a big chandelier, antique furniture and ornaments, music... Take care, the staircase to some of the bedrooms will call on your mountaineering skills.

How to get there (Map 6): *9km east of Dinard and 3km from Saint-Briac.*

130
La Forêt

5, chemin du Pâtis
35300 Fougères
(Ille-et-Vilaine)
Tel. 99 99 00 52
M. and Mme Juban

Open all year. **Rooms** 1 with shower and WC, 2 with basin and shared bath and WC. **Price** 210-230F (2 pers.) **Meals** breakfast incl., evening meals at communal table, on reservation 100F (wine incl.) **Facilities** lounge, forest trail, jogging course, bicycles. **Pets** dogs allowed on request. **Nearby** swimming pool, tennis, riding, fishing lake, golf, Mont-St-Michel, old Fougères, St-Malo, Cancale. **Spoken** English.

Sheltered by a beautiful flower-filled garden, this modern house is on the edge of Fougères, not far from a superb forest. It is very peaceful and the welcome is spontaneous and warm. The arrangement of the house and the bedrooms is very pleasant and full of thoughtful details – antiques, pretty fabrics, books and ornaments. One feels quite at home. Exceptionally good breakfast. Well priced.

How to get there (Map 7): *In Fougères on the Flers road in the direction of the forest of Fougères.*

131
Château de Léauville

35369 Landujan
(Ille-et-Vilaine)
Tel. 99 07 21 14
Fax 99 07 21 80
Marie-Pierre and Patrick
Gicquiaux

Open 15 March – 15 Nov. **Rooms** 7 with bath, WC and telephone (of which 6 have fireplace and sitting area) and 1 small bedroom with shower, WC and telephone. **Price** 570-720F (2 pers.) +100F (extra pers.) **Meals** breakfast 56F, half board 476-600F (per pers.), evening meal on reservation (separate tables) 185F (wine not incl.) **Facilities** lounge, heated swimming pool, equestrian centre. **Pets** dogs allowed on request. **Nearby** golf. **Spoken** English.

The Château de Leauville is a mixture of 16th and 17th century architecture. Set in beautiful grounds with a swimming pool, it is built on a human scale, quiet and full of charm. The comfortable bedrooms are well decorated and have large bathrooms (often in the towers). Breakfast and evening meals are served in a rustic yet pleasant dining room. Very good welcome. Prices a bit high.

How to get there (Map 6): In the Brest direction on RN12; 30km after Rennes take exit Bécherel Landujan; signposted

132
Château des Blosses

35406 Saint-Ouen-de-la-Rouërie
(Ille-et-Vilaine)
Tel. 99 98 36 16
Fax 99 98 39 32
M. and Mme Jacques Barbier

Open 15 Feb. – 15 Nov. **Rooms** 7 with bath and WC. **Price** 520-800F (2 pers.) **Meals** breakfast incl., half board 480-580F per pers. in double room (3 nights min.), evening meals on reservation (separate tables) 225F (wine incl.) **Facilities** lounge, golf range. **Credit cards** Visa, Amex. **Pets** no dogs allowed. **Nearby** golf, swimming pool, Mont-St-Michel. **Spoken** English.

Built in the 19th century, the château stands in a very large wooded park, partly occupied by a golf range. The interior is authentically rural, with hunting trophies, old furniture and many keepsakes. The comfortable bedrooms are charmingly arranged. Excellent evening meals, which M. and Mme Barbier sometimes attend.

How to get there (Map 7): 28km north west of Fougères via D155 to Antrain, then D296 for 4km; signed. Coming from Pontorson-Mont-St-Michel, take N175 towards Rennes for 9km, then D97; signposted.

133
Le Petit Moulin du Rouvre

35720 Sainte-Pierre-de-Plesguen
(Ille-et-Vilaine)
Tel. 99 73 85 84
Mme Annie Michel-Québriac

Open all year. **Rooms** 4 with bath and WC. **Price** 190F (1 pers.), 270F (2 pers.) +100F (extra pers.) **Meals** breakfast incl., half board 230F per pers. in double room, evening meals at communal table from 95F (wine not incl.) **Facilities** lounge, fishing. **Pets** small dogs allowed on request (+50F). **Nearby** golf, Mont-St-Michel, old Dinan. **Spoken** English.

It would be hard not to be attracted by this small mill standing alone on the edge of the millpond. If you arrive at the end of a fine afternoon you will see the sunlight glittering on the water and dappling the pretty furniture in the lounge. The bedrooms are small but pleasant. The east wall of one of them is all glass. Do not miss the evening meals with Breton specialities. Charming welcome.

How to get there (Map 6): 13km east of Dinan via D794, then N137 and D10; follow signs in the village.

134
La Carrière

8, rue de la Carrière
56120 Josselin
(Morbihan)
Tel. 97 22 22 62
M. and Mme Bignon

Open all year. **Rooms** 4 with bath and WC, 2 with shower and WC, and 2 for children without bath or shower. **Price** 280-315F (2 pers.) +80F (extra pers.), childrens room 160F. **Meals** breakfast incl., evening meals (separate tables) 190F (wine and aperitif incl.) **Facilities** lounge. **Pets** dogs allowed on request. **Nearby** Josselin, Rochefort-en-Terre. **Spoken** English, German.

La Carrière stands on a hill just outside the small town of Josselin, with its famous medieval château. It is a very refined large house built in a classic architectural style. The dining room is bright and overlooks the terrace. The lounge lends itself to reading. The bedrooms are comfortable and have good furniture. A superb house, as welcoming as its owners.

How to get there (Map 6): 54km north of Vannes via N166 to Roc-St-André, then D4; it's behind the château.

135
Chaumière de Kérizac

56390 Locqueltas
(Morbihan)
Tel. 97 66 60 13
Fax 97 66 66 73
M. and Mme Cheilletz-Maignan

Open all year. **Rooms** 1 with shower and WC, 2 with bath and shared WC. **Price** 200F (1 pers.), 300F (2 pers.) **Meals** breakfast incl., no evening meal. **Restaurants** in Locqueltas and Vannes. **Facilities** lounge, pond, jogging course. **Pets** no dogs allowed. **Nearby** swimming pool, tennis, riding, golf, Gulf of Morbihan. **Spoken** English.

A Breton hamlet, some farms, and then a little further on these two charming thatched cottages. There are two big and very comfortable bedrooms under the sloping roof; the third is smaller but has a private garden. Everything inside is marvellous: antique furniture, lace, small pictures, souvenirs from all over the world, pretty colours. Good breakfasts served inside or in the garden depending on the weather. Pleasant reception.

How to get there (Map 14): 10km north east of Vannes via D767 towards Locminé. At Locmaria Grd-Champ take D133 to the right towards Locqueltas; signposted.

136
Le Cosquer-Trélécan

56330 Pluvigner
(Morbihan)
Tel. 97 24 72 69
Bernard and Françoise Menut

Open all year. **Rooms** 1 suite (4 pers.) with bath and WC (+ basin in each bedroom). **Price** 150F (1 pers.), 190F (2 pers.), 250F (3 pers.), 310F (4 pers.) **Meals** breakfast incl., no evening meal. **Restaurants** close by. **Facilities** lounge. **Pets** no dogs allowed. **Nearby** seaside, riding, Camors forest, Gulf of Morbihan, St-Goustan. **Spoken** English.

S he is an antique dealer, he a beekeeper. Their thatched cottage is set in peaceful green countryside. The pretty little suite is perfect for a family. Breakfast is a treat served in a lovely room decorated with well-chosen antiques; sometimes there is an open fire, and sometimes music. Very good welcome.

How to get there (Map 5): 32km north west of Vannes via N165 to Auray and D768 towards Pontivy. At Pluvigner take D102 towards Languidic, then signs to 'Brocante'.

137
Manoir de Kerlebert

56530 Quéven
(Morbihan)
Tel. 97 05 06 80
Pol and Cathy Chenailler

Open all year. **Rooms** 2 with bath and WC, 2 with shower and WC. Room cleaning every 5/6 days. **Price** 185F (1 pers.), 210F (2 pers.) **Meals** breakfast incl., no evening meal. **Restaurants** in Lorient. **Facilities** lounge, equestrian centre, loose boxes. **Pets** dogs allowed on request. **Nearby** sea, golf.

The manor of Kerlebert is outside the small town of Quéven and is surrounded by copses and large trees. It is a peaceful, unspoilt place. The comfortable bedrooms overlook the grounds and one of them is decorated in Art Nouveau style. Breakfast is served in the dining room, and there is a simply furnished but comfortable lounge. Your hosts are young and informal.

How to get there (Map 5): 3km north west of Lorient via N165, exit Quéven; signposted from Quéven; it's 1km from the village.

138
Château de Talhouët

56220 Rochefort-en-Terre
(Morbihan)
Tel. 97 43 34 72
M. Jean-Pol Soulaine

Closed 15 Jan. – 15 Feb. **Rooms** 8 with bath and WC, 1 with shower, telephone and TV. **Price** 550-950F (2 pers.) **Meals** breakfast incl., half board 505-705F per pers. in double room, evening meal (separate tables) 230F (wine not incl.) **Facilities** lounge. **Credit cards** Visa, Amex. **Pets** dogs allowed (+30F). **Nearby** tennis, fishing, golf. **Spoken** English.

On the tranquil edge of the forest stands Talhouët, a château in true Breton style. The rooms are enormous and have been entirely restored in excellent taste to preserve the character of the place. Light colours enliven the bedrooms, which otherwise could have been a bit austere. The bathrooms are superb, with high quality fittings. The hospitality is attentive and professional, and guests feel quite at ease.

How to get there (Map 14): 33km north west of Redon via D775 towards Vannes, then D774; turn right towards Rochefort-en-Terre. Go through Rochefort and take D774 towards Malestroit for 4km, then left to Chateau de Talhoüet.

139
La Maison du Latz

56470 La Trinité-sur-Mer
(Morbihan)
Tel. 97 55 80 91
Nicole Le Rouzic

Open all year. **Rooms** 3 and 1 suite (4 pers.) with bath and WC. **Price** 260-300F (2 pers.), suite 450F (4 pers.) **Meals** breakfast incl., evening meals at communal or separate tables (reservation the evening before) 80-120F (wine not incl.) **Facilities** lounge, telephone, fishing. **Nearby** golf, tennis, riding, sailing, sea fishing, Quiberon, Belle-Ile, Carnac, Gulf of Morbihan. **Spoken** English.

The view from this house is typical of the Gulf of Morbihan. Here fresh water meets salt and there are many little islands and white boats. To make the most of this view there is a verandah overlooking the bay and breakfast is served there from daybreak onwards. The bedrooms are quiet, comfortable and plain. The 'verte' has the best view but all overlook the sea. Mme Le Rouzic makes one feel quite at home.

How to get there *(Map 5): 11km south of Auray via D28 and D781 towards La Trinité-sur-Mer until the bridge, then towards Le Latz.*

140
Château de la Verrerie

Oizon
18700 Aubigny-sur-Nère
(Cher)
Tel. 48 58 06 91
Fax 48 58 21 25
Comte and Comtesse A. de Vogüé

Open 1 March – 1 Nov. **Rooms** 10 with bath, WC and telephone (of which 1 with shower and WC) and 1 suite (2 pers.) with bath and WC. **Price** 880-1100F (2 pers.) +150F (extra pers.), suite 1300F (2 pers.) **Meals** breakfast 55F, evening meals at communal table, on reservation (15 days in advance) 450F (wine incl.), or restaurant in the park. **Facilities** lounge, tennis, riding, fishing, loose boxes, lake. **Credit cards** Visa. **Pets** small dogs allowed on request. **Nearby** 18-hole golf, village of la Borne (pottery), route Jacques-Coeur (châteaux). **Spoken** English, German.

Standing on the edge of the water and the forest, this ducal château was built just after the 100 Years War. The interior is absolute perfection: vast, sumptuous, comfortable, authentic. You can either have dinner with the owners, or in the small restaurant in the park which has an excellent menu.

How to get there (Map 17): 40km south of Gien via D940 to Aubigny-sur-Nère; it's at 'La Verrerie'.

141
Domaine de Vilotte

Ardenais
18170 Le Châtelet-en-Berry
(Cher)
Tel. 48 96 04 96 (Fax the same)
M. Jacques de Boisgrollier

Open 1 May – 15 Sept. **Rooms** 5 with bath and WC. **Price** 300-330F (1 pers.), 350-380F (2 pers.) +60-80F (extra pers.) **Meals** breakfast incl., evening meals at communal table 80-140F (wine incl.) **Facilities** lounge, fishing, bicycles. **Nearby** equestrian centre, 18-hole golf, Tronçais forest, route Jacques-Coeur, George Sand's house, Alain-Fournier's school. **Spoken** English.

This ancient Roman site is utterly tranquil. M. and Mme Boisgrollier, friends of the owner, will offer you tastefully furnished bedrooms overlooking a large garden. The decor is on the whole a success, and there are interesting collections of old tools, radio sets and ceramic stoves. Friendly welcome and very peaceful surroundings.

How to get there (Map 17): 8km east of Le Châtelet via D951, towards St-Amand; turn right 500m after the village; signposted.

142
Manoir d'Estiveaux

Estiveaux
18170 Le Châtelet-en-Berry
(Cher)
Tel. 48 56 22 64
Mme de Faverges

Open all year. **Rooms** 2 with bath, WC and TV, 2 with shower, WC and TV, and 1 suite of 2 bedrooms with bath and WC. **Price** 300-450F (1/2 pers.) +65F (extra pers.), suite 500F. **Meals** breakfast incl., evening meals at communal or separate table from 150F (wine incl.) **Facilities** lounge, telephone, fishing. **Pets** dogs allowed on request. **Nearby** swimming pool, 18-hole golf, tennis, riding, Romanesque churches, châteaux.

This country house stands in its own park with a lake and lies close to the route Jacques-Coeur and its many châteaux. The house is beautifully preserved and the huge bedrooms are perfectly decorated. Mme de Faverges' welcome is warm and unaffected. Ask her advice on touring the area – she knows a great deal about it.

How to get there (Map 17): 46km north of Montluçon via D943 to Culan, then D65 to Le Châtelet; then D951 for 1.5km.

143
La Rongère

18110 Saint-Eloy-de-Gy
(Cher)
Tel. 48 25 41 53
Florence and Philippe Atger-Rochefort

Open all year. **Rooms** 1 with bath and WC, 2 with shower and WC, 1 suite of 2 bedrooms with bath and WC. **Price** 240F (1/2 pers.) +60F (extra pers.), suite 400F (4 pers.) **Meals** breakfast incl. **Restaurant** for lunch and evening meals 75-98F + à la carte (wine not incl.) **Facilities** lounge. **Nearby** tennis, riding, Bourges. **Spoken** English, German.

This is a pleasant house, built at the beginning of the century, and set in the peaceful surroundings of a large park. The façade may be in need of rejuvenation but the interior is charming. The small dining room is pretty and has interesting windows; the large bedrooms are furnished with antiques and have good bathrooms. There is an attractive restaurant in the adjoining building. The welcome is young and relaxed.

How to get there (Map 17): 8km north west of Bourges via N76 towards Mehun-sur-Yèvre, then right on D104 towards Vouzeron.

144
Château de Quantilly

Quantilly
18110 Saint-Martin-d'Auxigny
(Cher)
Tel. 48 64 51 21
M. de Botmiliau

Open 1 May – 31 Oct., 2 nights min. **Rooms** 3 with shower and WC (poss. suite), TV on request. **Price** 300F (2 pers.) **Meals** breakfast incl., no evening meals. **Restaurants** close by. **Pets** no dogs allowed. **Facilities** loose boxes. **Nearby** 18-hole golf, lake bathing, châteaux, village of La Borne (pottery), Bourges, Menetou vineyards. **Spoken** English.

Château de Quantilly has a real old country house atmosphere. The entrance hall is a touch bohemian and on 'return from the hunt' lines. The lovely old furniture in the three large bedrooms seems as if it has always been there. It is a pity that the shower rooms are rather cramped (they are in the turrets). Generous breakfasts are served in the fine dining room overlooking the park. The welcome is as natural as the place itself.

How to get there *(Map 17): 15km north of Bourges via D940 towards Gien, then D59 towards Quantilly; signposted.*

145
Château de Maillebois

28170 Maillebois
(Eure-et-Loir)
Tel. 37 48 17 01
M. Armand-Delille

Open 15 April – 15 Oct. **Rooms** 1 with bath and WC, 1 with bath and WC not en suite. **Price** 700F. **Meals** breakfast incl., no evening meals. **Facilities** tennis. **Pets** dogs allowed in the kennels. **Nearby** swimming pool, riding, Chartres cathedral, Verneuil-sur-Avre, Senonches forest.

This magnificent 17th-century château reigns over a 300-hectare park. M. Armand-Delille will greet you unaffectedly and leave you to do your own thing. The interior is very appealing. The bedrooms all have antique furniture, functioning bathrooms and a superb view. A majestic corridor hung with old tapestries leads to them. Breakfast is served in a room furnished in Directoire style.

How to get there *(Map 8): 34km north west of Chartres via D939 towards Verneuil-sur-Avre; it's 9.5km after Châteauneuf-en-Thymerais at the crossroads with D20 (the Dreux-Senonches road).*

146
Château de Boisrenault

36500 Buzançais
(Indre)
Tel. 54 84 03 01
M. and Mme Y. du Manoir

Closed January. **Rooms** 4 with bath and WC, 2 with shower and WC, 2 sharing shower and WC, 1 suite (4 pers.) with bath and WC. **Price** 300-400F (1 pers.), 350-450F (2 pers.), suite 750F (4 pers.) **Meals** breakfast incl., evening meals at communal table 130F (wine not incl.) **Facilities** lounge, swimming pool. **Credit cards** Visa, Amex. **Nearby** golf, Brenne (lake), châteaux of the Loire. **Spoken** English.

A neo-Gothic château in a park. Its huge bedrooms are luxuriously classical, like the 'aux faisans', or more exotic, like the 'tahitienne'. The studied elegance of the decor includes details such as the motifs painted on the bathroom tiles, which echo the fabrics in each bedroom. The library/TV room is for guests' use, as is an enormous sitting room. Very pleasant welcome.

How to get there (Map 16): 25km north west of Châteauroux via N143 towards Buzançais, then D926 towards Levroux; turn right 3km from the village.

147
Moulin de Chézeaux

Rivarennes
36800 Saint-Gaultier
(Indre)
Tel. 54 47 01 84
Fax 54 47 10 93
Ren Rijpstra

Open all year. **No smoking. Children** under 10 not admitted. **Rooms** 2 with bath and WC, 1 with shower and WC. **Price** 325-350F (1 pers.) **Meals** breakfast incl., evening meals 120F. **Facilities** lounge, fishing. **Pets** no animals allowed. **Nearby** 18-hole golf, swimming pool, tennis, canoeing, riding, la Brenne (lake). **Spoken** English.

This small white mill with blue shutters is surrounded by masses of geraniums and close to a lake. It has been restored by Ren Rijsptra, an interior designer. The lounge is furnished in English style with a fireplace. The bedrooms are enchanting: antique furniture, lovely curtains, embroidered sheets, flower arrangements. In good weather the excellent breakfasts are served outside. The welcome is discreetly attentive, and every detail is taken care of. A very good place.

How to get there (Map 16): 10km west of Argenton-sur-Creuse; D927 and N151 towards Le Blanc; 2km after St-Gaultier turn left; signposted.

148
Château du Gerfaut

37190 Azay-le-Rideau
(Indre-et-Loire)
Tel. 47 45 40 16/47 45 26 07
Fax 47 45 20 15
Marquis de Chenerilles

Open all year (in winter on request). **Rooms** 4 with bath and WC, 1 with bath and external WC, 2 with shower and WC. **Price** 295-450F (1 pers.), 395-550F (2 pers.) **Meals** breakfast incl., evening meals at communal table, on reservation 200F (all incl.) **Facilities** lounge, tennis, lake, telephone. **Credit cards** accepted. **Pets** no dogs allowed. **Nearby** golf, châteaux, wine cellars. **Spoken** English.

The falcons of Louis XI were bred and reared here but the château itself was only built in the last century. A majestic staircase leads to the huge bedrooms. Breakfast is served in a large room with exceptional Empire furniture which once belonged to Jérôme Bonaparte. The château stands in lands and forests extending to Villandry and Azay-le-Rideau. Courteous reception.

How to get there *(Map 16): 18km north east of Chinon via D751 towards Tours, then leaving Azay-le-Rideau take the Villandry road; signposted.*

149
Manoir de Montour

37420 Beaumont-en-Véron
(Indre-et-Loire)
Tel. 47 58 43 76
Mme M. Krebs

Open Easter – All Saints. **Rooms** 3 (of which 1 for 4 pers.) with bath and WC, and 2 studios (3/4 pers.) with bath, shower and WC. **Price** 340F (2 pers.), 450F (4 pers.), studio 400F (2 pers.) **Meals** breakfast incl., no evening meals. **Facilities** lounge, telephone. **Pets** small dogs allowed. **Nearby** swimming pool, tennis, riding, fishing, golf, Azay-le-Rideau, Fontevraud.

It is rare to find so much character even in a very old house: lots of wood, terracotta, old fireplaces... Here time has stood still – except in the bathrooms, which are modern. The bedrooms are very large and quiet and the pleasant lounge has pale blue panelling. Breakfast is served in the dining room or the very pretty garden. Marion Krebs will greet you as if you were old friends.

How to get there *(Map 16): 5km north west of Chinon via D749 towards Avoine and Bourgueil until Coulaine, then towards Savigny en Véron.*

150
Domaine de Pallus

Cravant-les-Côteaux
37500 Chinon
(Indre-et-Loire)
Tel. 47 93 08 94
Fax 47 98 43 00
M. and Mme B. Chauveau

Open all year. **Rooms** 2 rooms and 1 suite with bath and WC. **Price** 450-500F (2 pers.), suite +150F (extra pers.) **Meals** breakfast incl., no evening meals. **Restaurants** L'Océanic in Chinon and Château de Marçay. **Facilities** lounge, telephone, swimming pool. **Pets** no dogs allowed. **Nearby** fishing, golf, riding, châteaux of the Loire. **Spoken** English, German.

Located 2km from a village, this gorgeous Touraine house has lovely rooms, where antique furniture of different eras blend happily together. Each bedroom has a style of its own, with many good decorative details. The bathrooms are superb and guests may enjoy the lounges as well as the garden. The welcome is agreeable and breakfast is excellent.

How to get there (Map 16): 8km east of Chinon on D21 to Cravant-les-Côteaux; leaving the village, Pallus is on the right after 1.5km.

151
La Butte de L'Epine

37340 Continvoir
(Indre-et-Loire)
Tel. 47 96 62 25
M. Michel Bodet

Open 1 April – 1 Nov. **Rooms** 2 with bath and WC. **Price** 240-260F (1 pers.), 260-280F (2 pers.) +60F (extra pers.) **Meals** breakfast incl., no evening meals. **Restaurants** 6km. **Facilities** lounge, bicycles. **Pets** no dogs allowed. **Nearby** 18-hole golf, riding (3km), lake, tennis, walks, vineyards, châteaux, museums. **Spoken** English.

In Les Landes de la Gâtine Tourangelle M. and Mme Bodet have realised their dream: to build a 17th–century–style house using materials of the period. In the centre is a large and prettily decorated beamed room which serves as both lounge and dining room. The two comfortable bedrooms are simple and dainty, with floral wallpaper. Breakfast is served at a communal table inside or outside depending on the weather. Friendly welcome.

How to get there (Map 16): 13km north of Bourgueil via D749 towards Château-la-Vallière, then right on D15 to Continvoir. In Continvoir take D64.

152
Manoir du Grand Martigny

Vallières, 37230 Fondettes
(Indre-et-Loire)
Tel. 47 42 29 87
Fax 47 42 24 44
Henri and Monique Desmarais

Open end March – 12 Nov. **Rooms** 5 and 2 suites (3/4 pers.) with bath and WC. **Price** 450-690F (2 pers.) +150F (extra pers.), suite 950F (3/4 pers.) **Meals** breakfast incl., no evening meals. **Restaurants** Pont de la Motte in Fondette, La Poële d'Or in St Cyr-sur-Loire. **Facilities** lounge, loose boxes, park. **Pets** no dogs allowed. **Nearby** riding, tennis, golf, Loire châteaux. **Spoken** English.

This elegant building stands on the banks of the Loire in peaceful well-kept grounds. Inside, the unostentatious luxury of the lounge is echoed in all the bedrooms and bathrooms. We particularly liked the bedroom called 'Jouy', which is a real success. The closeness of Tours compensates for the lack of evening meals at the Manoir. Efficient and discreet service.

How to get there (Map 16): 5km west of Tours via N152 towards Luynes; signposted.

153
La Huberdière

37530 Nazelles
(Indre-et-Loire)
Tel. 47 57 39 32
Fax 47 23 15 79
Mme Sandrier

Open all year. **Rooms** 6 with bath and WC. **Price** 330F (1 pers.), 375-540 (2 pers.) +85F (extra pers.) **Meals** breakfast incl., evening meals at communal table 150-210F (wine incl.) **Facilities** lounge, fishing. **Nearby** tennis, riding, 18-hole golf, swimming pool, canoeing, cave dwellings, Loire châteaux, Touraine wine route. **Spoken** English.

Standing in a prominent position among undulating and wooded hills this former hunting lodge has been much altered over the years. The bedrooms contain some beautiful old furniture. Among them, 'Pompadour' is a masterpiece. Mme Sandrier loves cooking and takes particular care with the evening meals. She leaves you to eat without her, so as not to run the risk of spoiling her sauces. The château is sometimes hired out for receptions, and if you arrive after one of these the ground floor will seem a little bare.

How to get there (Map 16): 17km north of Ambroise via D79 towards Chançay, then follow signs to 'vallée de Vaugadeland'.

154
Domaine de Beauséjours

37220 Panzoult
(Indre-et-Loire)
Tel. 47 58 64 64
Mme Marie-Claude Chauveau

Open all year. **Rooms** 1 with bath and WC, 2 with shower and WC, 2 suites of 2 bedrooms with bath and WC. Room cleaning on request. **Price** 400F (2 pers.), suite 550-600F (4 pers.) **Meals** breakfast incl., no evening meals. **Restaurants** close by. **Facilities** lounge, swimming pool. **Pets** dogs allowed on request. **Nearby** tennis, golf, fishing, Loire châteaux. **Spoken** English.

Beauséjours has an excellent atmosphere. The simple bedrooms are comfortable, with beautiful views over vineyards and the distant plain. The lounge, terrace and swimming pool are all easily accessible. If you are interested in wine, a member of the family will invite you to a tasting. No evening meals but plenty of restaurants nearby.

How to get there (Map 16): 12km east of Chinon via D21 to Panzoult; on the left before the village.

155
Le Clos Saint-Clair

Départementale 18
37800 Pussigny
(Indre-et-Loire)
Tel. 47 65 01 27
Fax 47 65 04 21
Mme Anne-Marie Liné

Open all year. **Rooms** 4 with shower and WC (2/4 pers.); independent entrances. Room cleaning twice weekly or on request. **Price** 200F (1 pers.), 250F (2 pers.) +60F (extra pers.) **Meals** breakfast incl., evening meals at communal table, on reservation (except national holidays and Sunday) 90F (wine incl.) **Facilities** lounge, tennis, fishing, bicycle hire. **Pets** no dogs allowed. **Nearby** golf, swimming pool, Romanesque churches, châteaux.

At the entrance to a pretty Touraine village stand these two old houses in a flowery and well-kept garden. The charming bedrooms are countrified and elegant, with some antique pieces of furniture, colourful fabrics and many little details to make them welcoming. Breakfast is served on an irresistible verandah overlooking the garden; evening meals are made with produce from the farm.

How to get there (Map 16): 50km south of Tours via A10, exit Ste-Maure, then right on RN10 to Port-de-Piles, then right on D5 towards Marigny Marmande for 2km, turn left on D18 towards Pussigny for 1km.

156
La Maison de Louis Le Barbier

15, Grande Rue
37120 Richelieu
(Indre-et-Loire)
Tel. 47 58 19 23
Mme Leroy

Open May – Oct. **Rooms** 1 with bath and WC, 2 with shower and WC. **Price** 300F (1 pers.), 350F (2 pers.) **Meals** breakfast incl., no evening meals. **Restaurants** Le Petit Jardin and L'Hôtel de la Place de l'Eglise (500m). **Nearby** riding, swimming pool, tennis, fishing, Chinon, Loire châteaux. **Spoken** English, Dutch.

L ouis XIII's secretary built this house. The sumptuous bedrooms will take you right back to the days of the great Cardinal Richelieu. Two overlook the garden and the other the street (it is a bit noisy in the early mornings). Small, delightful bathrooms, excellent breakfasts and a very kind welcome.

How to get there (Map 16): 29km north west of Châtellerault via A10 then D749; it's in the main street of Richelieu.

157
Les Religeuses

24, place des Religieuses
37120 Richelieu
(Indre-et-Loire)
Tel. 47 58 10 42
Mme Marie-Josèphe Le Platre

Closed 15 Dec. – 15 Jan. **Rooms** 1 with bath and WC, 3 with shower and WC, 1 suite (3 pers.) with washroom and WC. **Price** 200-250F (1 pers.), 220-270F (2 pers.), suite 380F (3 pers.) **Meals** breakfast incl., no evening meals. **Restaurants** Le Roy Doré in Richelieu, Relais des 2 Provinces in Pouant. **Facilities** lounge. **Pets** small dogs sometimes allowed. **Nearby** swimming pool, tennis, golf, châteaux of the Loire, Chinon, Azay-le-Rideau.

W ithin the walls of the town of Richelieu, this house is certain to please. Mme Le Platre is charming and will show you round the house, which is full of antiques and curios. Everything is clean and shiny and smells of fresh polish, and the comfortable bedrooms are as well kept as the rest. The house is reasonably quiet, although in the town. In summer, breakfast is served in the sunlit garden.

How to get there (Map 16): 29km north west of Châtellerault via A10 then D749; signposted in Richelieu.

158
Manoir de Becheron

37190 Saché
(Indre-et-Loire)
Tel. 47 26 86 26
Mme Martine Jacquet

Open April to Oct. (on request in winter). **Rooms** 2 with bath and WC, 1 with shower and WC. **Price** 360-410F (2 pers.) +60F (extra pers.) **Meals** breakfast incl., occasional evening meals. **Restaurants** nearby. **Facilities** lounge, loose boxes, bicycle hire. **Pets** dogs allowed on request. **Nearby** tennis, riding, golf. **Spoken** English.

This elegantly proportioned manor was built between the 14th and 17th centuries and stands above a pretty garden. The reception rooms have retained their character. Beautiful, well decorated bedrooms, old furniture, panelling, books, ornaments. Large and comfortable bathrooms. Breakfast is served at a table in the dining room. Very friendly welcome.

How to get there *(Map 16): 5.5km east of Azay-le-Rideau via A10 exit Tours-Sud, then D751 and D8; left after Ballan towards Saché and D84 to the right before the Indre river.*

159
Le Prieuré Sainte Anne

10, rue Chaude
37510 Savonnières
(Indre-et-Loire)
Tel. 47 50 03 26
Mme Caré

Open March – Nov. **Rooms** 1 suite (2 pers.) with shower and WC. **Price** 220F (1 pers.), 275F (2 pers.) +80F (extra pers.) **Meals** breakfast incl., no evening meals. **Restaurants** in the town. **Facilities** lounge. **Pets** no dogs allowed. **Nearby** 18-hole golf, châteaux.

This 15th–century house is in an almost rural setting a little set back from a quiet village street. Old polished furniture, antique plates hanging on the wall, immense fireplaces, comfortable wool mattresses: it is a simple, cared-for place, which leaves a fond impression. There is no evening meal but a small restaurant is only a few minutes walk away. Madame Caré is very kind.

How to get there *(Map 16): 13km west of Tours via D7 towards Villandry; in the village, on the Druye road, take "rue du Paradis" before the Mairie, then turn right.*

160
La Ferme des Berthiers

37800 Sepmes
(Indre-et-Loire)
Tel. 47 65 50 61
Mme Ane-Marie Vergnaud

Open all year. **Rooms** 1 with bath and WC, 2 with shower and WC and 1 child's room. Room cleaning every 3 days. **Price** 160F (1 pers.), 220F (2 pers.) **Meals** breakfast incl., evening meals at communal or separate tables 80F (wine incl.) **Facilities** lounge. **Pets** dogs allowed on request. **Nearby** fishing and bathing in a lake, golf, Loire châteaux, wine cellars. **Spoken** English, Dutch, German.

There are stables next to the house but these are not a problem. The bedrooms are very simple but their bathrooms are modern. The evening meal is served in a room with a big fireplace. It would be a real shame to miss Anne-Marie Vergnauds's talented cooking; her meals are an excellent way of sampling the region. Children are welcome.

How to get there (Map 16): 40km south of Tours via A10 exit Ste-Maure-de-Touraine, then D59 towards Ligueil; signposted as you leave the village.

161
Manoir de Foncher

37510 Villandry
(Indre-et-Loire)
Tel. 47 50 02 40
M. and Mme Salles

Open April to Sept. **Rooms** 1 with bath and WC, possibility of a suite. **Price** 550F (2 pers.), suite 750F (3 pers.), 850F (4 pers.) **Meals** breakfast incl., no evening meals. **Restaurants** close by. **Facilities** lounge. **Nearby** riding, golf. **Spoken** English.

At the tip of a spit of land between the Loire and the Cher, this manor looks the same as it did in the 16th century, with mullioned windows, external gallery and an exceptional spiral staircase. Breakfast is served on an immense convent table in a room dominated by a huge fireplace. The very comfortable bedrooms are beautiful and authentic. Charming bathroom. Ideal for visiting the châteaux of the Loire. Warm welcome.

How to get there (Map 16): 15km west of Tours via D7 towards Villandry. At Savonières, cross the bridge and turn left along the right bank of the Cher for 3km.

162
Château de Jallanges

Vernou-sur-Brenne
37210 Vouvray
(Indre-et-Loire)
Tel. 47 52 01 71
Mme Danièle Ferry-Balin

Open all year. **Rooms** 4 with bath and WC, 2 suites (2/5 pers.) with lounge, dressing room, bath and WC. **Price** 650-800F (2/3 pers.), suite 800-850F (2 pers.) +150F (extra pers.) **Meals** breakfast incl., evening meals at communal table, on reservation 250F (wine incl.) **Facilities** lounge, telephone, billiards, bicycles, helicopter trips, carriage trips, antique shop. **Pets** dogs allowed on request (+50F). **Nearby** golf, fishing, riding. **Spoken** English, German.

With its brick-and-stone Renaissance façade and grand courtyard this Château is a fine sight. It is being lovingly restored by the family, who will look after you with efficiency and kindness. The bedrooms are prettily decorated, with views over the park or the small French garden. Some of them are suites; the one on the first floor is very attractive. Good evening meals.

How to get there (Map 16): 15km east of Tours via N152 towards Amboise, then at Vouvray take D46 towards Vernou-sur-Brenne.

163
La Rabouillère

Chemin de Marçon
41700 Contres
(Loir-et-Cher)
Tel. 54 79 05 14
Mme Thimonnier

Open 1 March – 30 Nov. **Rooms** 5 with bath, WC and TV. **Price** 300F (1 pers.), 350-500F (2 pers.), 600F (3 pers.), 650F (4 pers.) **Meals** breakfast incl., no evening meals. **Restaurants** in Court-Cheverny and Contres. **Facilities** lounge, telephone. **Pets** no dogs allowed. **Nearby** tennis, riding, fishing, 18-hole golf, Loire châteaux. **Spoken** a little English.

Recently built using old materials, this long house is surrounded by 5 hectares of woods and meadows. The bedrooms are named after flowers. They are simple and comfortable and the bathrooms are very pleasant. Mme Thimonnier loves her house and enjoys opening it to guests. When the weather is cold an open fire burns in the sitting room fireplace.

How to get there (Map 16): 19km south of Blois via D765. At Cheverny take D102 towards Contres for 6km; signposted 'Chambres d'hôtes'.

164
La Borde

41160 Danzé
(Loir-et-Cher)
Tel. 54 80 68 42
M. and Mme Kamette

Open all year. **Rooms** 3 with shower and WC, 1 suite of 2 bedrooms with bath and WC, 1 suite with shower and WC. **Price** 120-160F (1 pers.), 170-220F (2 pers.), suite 300-350 (3 pers.), 350-400F (4 pers.) – reduction after the 2nd night. **Meals** breakfast incl., no evening meals. **Restaurants** Le Marmiton in Danzé (2km) and Le Manoir de la Forêt in La Ville-aux-Clercs (3km). **Facilities** lounge, telephone, fishing. **Pets** dogs allowed on request. **Nearby** swimming pools, tennis, riding, golf, Loire châteaux, Loir valley.

L a Borde is a beautiful 1930s house in a large park. Guests are very well looked after. All the bedrooms overlook the grounds; they are large, comfortable, and are fitted out with 1950s light oak furniture. One room serves as both TV-lounge and dining room, where generous breakfasts are served. Good value.

How to get there (Map 16): 15km north of Vendôme via D36 to Danzé, then D24 towards La Ville-aux-Clercs.

165
Manoir de Clénord

Route de Clénord
41250 Mont-près-Chambord
(Loir-et-Cher)
Tel. 54 70 41 62
Fax 54 70 33 99
Mme Renauld

Open all year. **Rooms** 4 with bath and WC and 2 suites (2/4 pers.) **Price** 320-550F (2 pers.), suites 650-950F. **Meals** breakfast incl., half board on request, evening meals at communal table, on reservation 140F. **Facilities** lounge, swimming pool, tennis, bicycles, canoes, French language course. **Credit cards** Visa. **Pets** no dogs allowed. **Nearby** 18-hole golf, forest, Loire châteaux, wine cellars. **Spoken** English, Spanish.

T o get to this small 18th-century manor house you drive through woods. Mme Renauld will greet you very warmly and show you the bedrooms, prettily arranged with antique furniture and overlooking the French gardens. In the morning breakfast is served in a countrified dining room or on a terrace, weather permitting. Very pleasant and restful atmosphere.

How to get there (Map 16): 9km east of Blois via D765 towards Romorantin, then left on D923 towards Bracieux. In the village, to the right before the church; signposted.

166
Château de Colliers

41500 Muides-sur-Loire
(Loir-et-Cher)
Tel. 54 87 50 75
Fax 54 87 03 64
M. and Mme de Gélis

Open 1 March – 15 Nov. **Rooms** 4 with bath and WC, 1 suite (4 pers.) of 2 bedrooms with bath and WC. **Price** 550-650F (2 pers.), suite 750F. **Meals** breakfast incl., evening meals at communal table, on reservation 200F. **Restaurants** Le Relais de B. Robin in Bracieux (18km) and Les Calanques in Mer (5km). **Facilities** lounge, telephone, swimming pool. **Nearby** 18-hole golf, equestrian centre, watersports, Loire châteaux. **Spoken** English, Spanish.

A small 18th-century house overlooking the Loire with superbly light classical architecture. A pleasure to look at. The lounge has arched windows, the dining room is covered with original frescos reaching to the ceiling and there are views directly over the Loire. The pretty bedrooms are sometimes a bit small (one has a terrace). A really pleasant welcome.

How to get there *(Map 16): 16km north east of Blois via D951 and 5km north of Mer via D152; it's before the village on the edge of the river.*

167
En Val de Loire

46, rue de Meuves
41150 Onzain
(Loir-et-Cher)
Tel. 54 20 78 82
Fax 54 20 78 82
Mme Langlais

Open April – end Dec. **Rooms** 2 with bath and WC, 3 with shower and WC. **Price** 320F (2 pers.) **Meals** breakfast incl., evening meals (some days) at communal or separate table 100-250F. **Facilities** lounge. **Pets** dogs not allowed. **Nearby** swimming pool, tennis, riding, golf. **Spoken** English.

A long garden with, at the end of it, a house surrounded by flowers. It is small and welcoming and has been decorated by M. and Mme Langlais themselves: a model of good taste and comfort. In the bedrooms there are matching soft furnishings and lampshades, and antique furniture. Cosy lounge-dining room with deep armchairs in front of the fire. Breakfast with 21 different types of jam...

How to get there *(Map 16): 15km south west of Blois via N152 towards Amboise, then right on D58 at Chouzy towards Monteaux as far as Onzain.*

168
La Villa Médicis

Macé
41000 Saint-Denis-sur-Loire
(Loir-et-Cher)
Tel. 54 74 46 38 Fax 54 78 20 27
Baronne Baxin de Caix de
Rembures

Open all year. **Rooms** 1 with bath and WC, 4 with shower and WC, 1 suite (2 pers.) **Price** 300F (1 pers.), 350F (2 pers.), suite 450F. **Meals** breakfast incl., evening meals, on reservation, at communal or separate tables 200F. Assiette anglaise 80F. **Facilities** lounges. **Pets** dogs not allowed. **Nearby** riding, canoeing, rowing, windsurfing, fishing, Loire châteaux. **Spoken** English, German, Italian, Spanish.

Marie de Medici loved to bathe in the three springs in this park, which borders the Loire. If the bathrooms are rather on the small side (except the one on the ground floor), the bedrooms, dining room and lounge are large, light, welcoming rooms and prettily arranged. Madame de Caix's care and kindness make this a friendly place.

How to get there *(Map 16): 3km north of Blois via N152 towards Orléans, then Macé; 500m on the right before the church.*

169
Château de la Voûte

41800 Troo
(Loir-et-Cher)
Tel. 54 72 52 52
MM. Clays and Venon

Open all year. **Rooms** 2 with bath and WC, 1 with shower and WC, 2 suites with bath and WC. **Price** 370-470F (2 pers.), suite 550F (2 pers.) **Meals** breakfast incl., no evening meals. **Restaurants** Le Cheval Blanc, La Grotte, La Paix (200m). **Facilities** fishing. **Pets** dogs not allowed. **Nearby** riding, tennis, golf, Loir valley, Ronsard's birthplace. **Spoken** English.

The gardens of the Château de la Voûte are on two terraces. The owners will look after you well. In each bedroom they have expressed their taste for decoration and antiques. All have their own style, established by the pictures, furniture and carpets: Pompadour, Empire, Louis XIII. They are all comfortable and quiet. Breakfast is served in the bedrooms or on the terrace.

How to get there *(Map 16): 25km west of Vendôme via D917 and 5km from Montoire; signposted in the village.*

170
Château de la Giraudière

41220 Villeny
(Loir-et-Cher)
Tel. 54 83 72 38
Mme Anne Giordano-Orsini

Open Easter – All Saints. **Rooms** 2 with bath and WC, 3 with bath and shared WC. **Price** 350F
(2 pers.) **Meals** breakfast incl., evening meals, on reservation, at communal or separate tables
75F (wine not incl.) **Facilities** lounge, tennis. **Pets** no dogs allowed. **Nearby** fishing, riding, golf.
Spoken English.

This attractive Louis XIII château has beautifully kept grounds and lies in mid-forest. The interior is very pleasing. Light streams in through the large sitting room windows, illuminating the elegant furniture. The bedrooms are very refined and have a lovely view over the grounds. An excellent place to stay while visiting the Sologne. You will be made very welcome.

How to get there (Map 17): 39km east of Blois via D951 to Muides-sur-Loire, then D103. At La Ferté-St-Cyr take D925 towards La Marolle-en-Sologne; it's 800m from the road.

171
Sainte Barbe

Route de Lorris
Nevoy
45500 Gien
(Loiret)
Tel. 38 67 59 53
Mme Annie Le Lay

Open all year on request. **Rooms** 1 with bath and WC, and 1 studio (5 pers.) in annexe with shower
room and 2 WC. **Price** 250F (1 pers.), 300F (2 pers.) +50F (extra pers.), studio 800F (5 pers. per
weekend). **Meals** breakfast incl., evening meals preferably (separate tables) 75F (wine not incl.)
Pets dogs allowed in kennels. **Facilities** lounge, tennis, loose boxes, fishing. **Nearby** riding,
shooting (on request), golf. **Spoken** English.

Surrounded by woods and fields, this old house hides a superb guest-bedroom, decorated in exceptionally good taste, behind its deceptively simple appearance. You will be made very welcome and there is a lounge for guests' use. The furniture, much of it 18th-century, a Chesterfield sofa, and numerous objects connected with hunting and shooting, make this a place full of character. Breakfasts and good dinners are served in the beautiful dining room. A great success.

How to get there (Map 17): 5km north west of Gien via D44.

172
Château d'Etoges

51270 Etoges par Montmort
(Marne)
Tel. 26 59 30 08
Fax 26 59 35 57
Mme Anne Filliette-Neuville

Closed 31 Jan. – 15 Feb. **Rooms** 17 rooms and 3 suites (3 pers.) with bath, WC and telephone (TV on request). **Price** 480-620F (2 pers.) +80F (extra pers.), suite 950F (3 pers.) **Meals** breakfast 45F, evening meals (separate tables) 160-180F (wine not incl.) **Facilities** lounges, fishing, billiards, piano. **Credit cards** Visa. **Pets** dogs allowed on request (+40F). **Nearby** riding, tennis, golf. **Spoken** English.

It would be difficult not to fall in love with this gorgeous 17th-century château. After crossing the main courtyard you will find a double aspect interior lit from east and west. The view from the bedrooms is unique, and their decor is traditional and cheerful – a model of good taste. Excellent bathrooms with lovely tiles. Beautiful antique furniture and delicate colours throughout. Very kind welcome, and a lovely place.

How to get there (Map 10): 22km south of Epernay via D51 to Montmort, then D18: signposted.

173
Château du Ru Jacquier

51700 Igny Comblizy
(Marne)
Tel. 26 57 10 84
Fax 26 57 11 85
M. Granger

Open all year. **Rooms** 5 with bath and WC, 1 with shower and WC. **Price** 350-400F (2 pers.) +100F (extra pers.) **Meals** breakfast incl., evening meals 150F (wine not incl.) **Facilities** lounge, fishing, horse-drawn carriage, trout. **Pets** dogs allowed (+30F). **Nearby** mountain bikes, 18-hole golf (6km), champagne route, cellar visits, château de Montmort, Condé en Brie.

The turrets of this well-renovated château rise above a park where horses, deer and llamas wander. A fine wooden staircase leads to the mostly large bedrooms, which are comfortable and prettily decorated with antique or reproduction furniture. Good dinners served in a lovely dining room with well presented tables. In fine weather breakfast is served outside. A lovely and good place.

How to get there (Map 10): 20km south west of Epernay via N3 towards Château-Thierry, then left on D18 towards Dormans for 7km.

174
Manoir de Montflambert

51160 Mutigny
(Marne)
Tel: 26 52 33 21
Mme Rampacek

Closed 2 Jan. – 15 Feb. **Rooms** 6 with bath and WC. **Price** 320-570F (1 pers.), 350-600F (2 pers.) **Meals** breakfast incl., evening meals at separate tables from 170F (wine not incl.) **Facilities** lounge, riding centre, fishing. **Pets** dogs not allowed. **Nearby** swimming pool, tennis, golf, visit to Champagne cellars, Epernay, Rheims.

This 17th-century manor standing on a hilltop is totally peaceful. Rescued from ruin by energetic restoration, it is of a good standard of comfort. The fitted carpets and reproduction furniture are a bit at odds, but the garden, with its ornamental lake, is charming. Breakfast and good evening meals are served in a 19th-century-style dining room. Efficient and very kind reception.

How to get there *(Map 10): 9km north east of Epernay via D221 to Ay, then Mutigny; signposted.*

175
Domaine des Oiseaux

12, Grande Rue
51390 Rosnay
(Marne)
Tel. 26 03 63 07
Mme Legros

Open all year. **Rooms** 2 with bath and WC, 2 sharing bath and WC. **Price** 200F (1 pers.), 260-280F (2 pers.) +70F (extra pers.) **Meals** breakfast incl., no evening meals. **Restaurants** 5 and 7km. **Facilities** lounge, swimming pool. **Pets** dogs allowed on request. **Nearby** tennis, golf (3km), vineyards and cellars of Champagne, Rheims cathedral.

This is a very pretty village house with a pleasant garden and a swimming pool. The bedrooms are under the eaves, and are decorated with lovely fabrics and good taste. They are all very comfortable, but try to get one with its own bathroom. Breakfast is served at a large table in the dining room. The lounge has an open fire. A very friendly welcome awaits you.

How to get there *(Map 10): 12km west of Rheims via N31 towards Soissons, then after Thillois D27 left towards Rosnay; it's in the village.*

176
Domaine de Boulancourt

Boulancourt
52220 Montier-en-Der
(Haute-Marne)
Tel. 25 04 60 18
M. and Mme Viel-Cazal

Open April – 15 Dec. **Rooms** 5 with bath or shower and WC, and 1 suite (3 pers.) with bath and WC. **Price** 200F (2 pers.) **Meals** breakfast 25F, evening meals, on reservation, at communal or separate table 110F (aperitif and wine incl.) **Facilities** lounge, telephone. **Pets** dogs not allowed. **Nearby** tennis (2km), lakes (15km).

Once called "Ferme du Désert", this guest house is set in totally peaceful surroundings, with a very pleasant garden and a 5-hectare lake below. It has been beautifully decorated, using bright colours. The refurbished bedrooms are charming and comfortable. Excellent evening meals often include local game. The fish comes from the nearby lake and the boar is farmed on the property. Natural and warm welcome.

How to get there (Map 11): 48km south west of St-Dizier via D384. At Montier-en-Der head for Troyes; at Ceffonds right on D174 Longueville/Laines. Pass through Longeville/Laines; it's on the left after 1km.

177
Rue du Puits

3, rue du Puits
39100 Gévry
(Jura)
Tel. 84 71 05 93
M. and Mme Picard

Open all year. **Rooms** 3 with bath and WC, 3 with shower and WC. **Price** 150F (1 pers.), 180F (2 pers.) +30F (extra pers.) **Meals** breakfast incl., evening meals at communal table 90F (wine incl.) **Facilities** lounge. **Nearby** tennis, riding, golf, Jura and Burgundy vineyards, forest of Chaux. **Spoken** English, German.

Formerly a village farm, this large house still has its original beams and pillars. The huge sitting room is generously furnished and decorated with regional objects. The bedrooms are nicely done too – our favourite gives directly on to the garden. A cheerful welcome and excellent evening meals, served outside in fine weather.

How to get there *(Map 19): 8km south of Dole via N73 towards Chalon-Beaune, then left on N5 towards Genève; right in the first village.*

178
Ferme-Auberge de la Bergerie

Crenans
39260 Moirans-en-Montagne
(Jura)
Tel. 84 42 00 50
M. and Mme Baron

Closed first few days of September. Half board or full board only. **Rooms** 4 with shower and WC. **Price** half board 195F per pers., full board 260F per pers. in double room. **Meals** auberge on the spot. **Facilities** lounge, equestrian centre, theme tours. **Pets** dogs allowed on request. **Nearby** tennis, lake, Gallo-Roman sites, Château du Pin. **Spoken** English.

Behind the attractive severity of the stone façade lies a very welcoming house. Inside you will find the works of several talented sculptors, pale wooden regional furniture, beams, stone walls, and plenty of kindness. The bedrooms are pleasant and quiet, the cooking wholesome and successful. Off the beaten track, it is an ideal place for keen walkers.

How to get there *(Map 19): 38km south east of Lons-le-Saunier via N78 and D470 towards St Claude-Genève via Moirans; 3km before Moirans, left on D296 towards Crenans; it's in the village.*

179
Château d'Epenoux

Route de Saint-Loup
Epenoux
70000 Vesoul
(Haute-Saône)
Tel. 84 75 19 60
Mme Germaine Gauthier

Open all year. **Rooms** 4 with bath, telephone, WC and TV, 1 with shower, WC and TV. **Price** 250F (1 pers.), 300-360F (2 pers.) **Meals** breakfast incl., half board 650F (2 pers.) evening meals at communal table 200F (wine incl.) **Facilities** lounge. **Credit cards** Amex, Eurocheque. **Nearby** swimming pool, tennis, riding, 18-hole golf, Luxeuil, villages of Montigny and Charriez, Vesoul. **Spoken** English, German.

The small château of Epenoux backs onto a 5-hectare park and is owned by a very charming lady who will welcome you as if you were part of her family. The interior is furnished in 19th-century style and is comfortable and colourful. The large bedrooms are harmoniously decorated, with good furniture and ornaments. In the evening, guests sit at an elegant table sharing an excellent meal.

How to get there *(Map 20): 4km north of Vesoul via D10 towards St-Loup; at the entrance to the village, left opposite the sign.*

180
La Ferme de Vosves

Vosves
77190 Dammarie-les-Lys
(Seine-et-Marne)
Tel. (1) 64 39 22 28/
(1) 64 39 02 26
Mme Lemarchand

Open all year. **Rooms** 1 with bath and WC, 1 with shower and WC, and 1 auxiliary room. **Price** 190F (1 pers.), 210-240F (2 pers.) +180-200F (extra room). **Meals** breakfast incl., no evening meals. **Restaurants** L'Ile aux Truites in Vulaine. **Pets** dogs allowed on request. **Nearby** Château de Vaux-le-Vicomte, forest of Fontainebleau, Barbizon. **Spoken** English, Italian.

This is a working farm situated on the edge of the small village of Vosves. Mme Lemarchand will receive you with great kindness. She is an artist and has decorated her house with excellent taste. For families, the small 'suite' is very pleasant and is decorated in an elegant country style. Otherwise choose 'l'atelier' with its high beams and a large velux window. Excellent breakfasts.

How to get there (Map 9): 15km north west of Fontainebleau (A6 Exit 12). N7 towards Fontainebleau. After Ponthierry, left on N472 for 3km, then right to Vosves.

181
Vivescence

9, place Greffulhe
77810 Thomery
(Seine-et-Marne)
Tel. (1) 60 96 43 96
Fax (1) 60 96 41 13
Mme Brigitte Stacke

Open all year (except Christmas – New Year's Day). **Rooms** 8 with bath, WC and telephone, 1 with shower, WC and telephone. Room cleaning every day, except weekends. **Price** 320F (1 pers.), 370F (2 pers.) +50F (extra pers.) **Meals** breakfast incl., evening meals at communal or separate table 120F (wine and coffee incl.), light lunch in the garden in summer. **Facilities** lounge, covered and heated swimming pool, sauna, massage, yoga, fitness training, bicycle hire (40F per day), loose boxes. **Nearby** golf, riding (3km), fishing, windsurfing, rock climbing, Château of Fontainebleau, Moret-sur-Loing, Rosa Bonheur museum in Thomery. **Spoken** English.

At this unusual place all sorts of fitness activities are available, or you can just enjoy the very well kept grounds and pretty bedrooms (named after spices), all of them light and comfortable. Good bathrooms too.

How to get there (Map 9): 7km east of Fontainebleau via A6 then N7. At the obelisk in Fontainebleau, N6 towards Sens, then left on D301 towards Thomery; it's on the church square.

182
La Ferté

10, rue de la Grange aux Moines
La Ferté, 78460 Choisel
(Yvelines)
Tel. (1) 30 52 05 03
Fax (1) 30 47 12 45
M. and Mme Spaak

Open all year. **Children** on request. **Rooms** 1 suite (2/4 pers.) with bath, WC and TV. Room cleaning on request. **Price** 350F (1 pers.), 450F (2 pers.) +150F (extra pers.) **Meals** breakfast incl., no evening meals. **Restaurants** many close by. **Pets** dogs not allowed. **Nearby** 18-hole golf, riding, tennis, swimming pool, forest of Rambouillet, châteaux of Breteuil and Dampierre, ruins of Port-Royal abbey, Chevreuse valley. **Spoken** English.

This restored farmhouse stands in one of the charming little hamlets of the Chevreuse valley. The guest suite is big and as comfortable as could be, with beautiful, antique furniture, much of it English. Breakfast is served in an equally attractive dining room, except in the summer when the 2-hectare, flower-filled garden is used. Extremely kind welcome.

How to get there (Map 9): 25km south west of Versailles on D906 between Chevreuse and Cernay.

183
Château de Villepreux

78450 Villepreux
(Yvelines)
Tel. (1) 30 56 20 06
Fax (1) 30 56 12 12
Comtesse de Sainte Seine

Open all year. **Rooms** 2 with bath and WC (telephone on request), 5 with bath and shared WCs. **Price** 1000F (1 pers.), 1200F (2 pers.) **Meals** breakfast incl., no evening meals. **Restaurants** 500m. **Facilities** tennis, park. **Pets** dogs allowed on request. **Nearby** golf on weekdays, Versailles, Dompierre, Fontainebleau.

Close to Paris, Villepreux has a wonderful 18th-century façade and stands on the edge of a 200-hectare park. This is a splendid house: the magnificent rooms are decorated in the purest Empire style. Don't expect the bathrooms to be smart or luxurious – they are small and old-fashioned, part of the charm of the place. Many of the bedrooms have their original period wallpaper. A place for purists who are more interested in history than comfort.

How to get there (Map 9): 20km west of Paris via A12 exit Versailles-Ouest, then N307 towards Bailly and Villepreux.

184
Le Rocher Pointu

Plan-de-Dève
30390 Aramon
(Gard)
Tel. 66 57 41 87
Fax 66 57 01 77
Annie and André Malek

Open 15 March – 5 Nov. **Rooms** 1 with bath and WC, 3 with shower and WC. **Price** 280-310F (1 pers.), 300-380F (2 pers.) +80-100F (extra pers.). **Meals** breakfast incl., no evening meals. **Restaurants** in Aramon. **Facilities** lounge, telephone, swimming pool with barbecue. **Pets** dogs not allowed. **Nearby** riding, golf, fishing, shooting, Avignon, les Baux, Séguret, Uzès, Tarascon, Saint-Rémy, Pont du Gard. **Spoken** English.

This Provençal house, surrounded by greenery, is not far from Avignon, in beautiful hilly countryside. There is a swimming pool, a large reception room with sitting areas, and very pleasant small bedrooms. The decor is natural: wood, stone, pretty fabrics. Breakfast is a mini-brunch served outside at green-laquered tables; there is also a barbecue. Pleasant welcome.

How to get there (Map 33): 12km west of Avignon; from Avignon head for Nîmes, then D2 towards Aramon and D126 towards Saze; signposted.

185
Beth

Hameau de Beth
30580 Lussan
(Gard)
Tel. 66 72 94 80
M. and Mme Schuh

Open all year, 3 nights min. **Rooms** 1 suite (2/5 pers.) with 3 bedrooms, bath and WC. Room cleaning responsibility of guests. **Price** 300F (2 pers.) +100F (extra pers.) **Meals** breakfast incl., no evening meals. **Restaurant** in Vallerargues (5km) and in Méjannes (8km). **Facilities** lounge. swimming pool. **Pets** dogs not allowed. **Nearby** golf (25km), tennis, riding (8km), gorges of the Ardèche, Uzès, Pont du Gard. **Spoken** English, German.

All that remains of the old farmhouse are its stone walls and its roof. The interior has been completely restructured by an architect, who has created a very successful contemporary layout. The lovely suite is on several levels and opens on to a small terrace. Excellent welcome and superb view.

How to get there (Map 32): 20km north of Uzès via D979 . After Lussan take the Malataverne road; in the village, turn right, then in the hamlet of Beth take the road to the menhir; left after 200m.

186
Château de Ribaute

30720 Ribaute-les-Tavernes
(Gard)
Tel. 66 83 01 66
Fax 66 83 86 93
Comte and Comtesse Chamski-
Mandajors

Open all year. **Rooms** 3 with bath and WC, 1 with shower and WC, 1 suite (3 pers.) with bath and WC, 1 studio (2 pers.) with bath, WC and kitchenette. **Price** 350-500F (2 pers.), suite 600F (3 pers.), studio 500F (2 pers.) **Meals** breakfast 40F, evening meals at communal table 150-200F (wine incl.) **Facilities** lounge, swimming pool, equestrian centre. **Credit cards** accepted (except Amex). **Pets** dogs allowed on request (+50F). **Nearby** fishing, tennis, golf, ski-ing on Mont Aigoual, Anduze, Nîmes, Camargue, Cévennes park. **Spoken** English, German.

Surrounded by a garden with a swimming pool, this 17th-century château is classically beautiful and very quiet. The entrance hall is magnificent and has an elegant staircase. The comfortable bedrooms are enormous and superbly furnished. Evening meals are excellent and there is a happy, family atmosphere – strongly recommended.

How to get there *(Map 32): 27km north west of Nîmes via N106. At Pont-de-Ners, take D982 towards Anduze for 5km. It's on the right after crossing N110.*

187
Mas de Casty

Boisson
Allègre
30500 Saint-Ambroix
(Gard)
Tel. 66 24 82 33
M. and Mme Mesnage

Open all year (2 nights min.) **Rooms** 4 and 1 studio (with kitchenette) with shower and WC, and 1 suite (2/4 pers.) with bath, WC, bedroom, lounge and kitchen. **Price** 170-320F (2 pers.), suite 460-500F, studio 280-320F (according to season). **Meals** breakfast 25F, no evening meals. **Restaurant** in Allègre. **Facilities** lounge, swimming pool planned for '93. **Pets** dogs allowed on request (+20F). **Nearby** golf, canoeing, Pont du Gard. **Spoken** English.

For the last 20 years Michèle and Alain Mesnage have been restoring this little piece of paradise in the middle of the country with their own hands. Divided between two houses, the comfortable bedrooms are pretty and have some antique furniture. Breakfast is served on one of the terraces or in the summer dining room surrounded by a rock garden. Very friendly welcome.

How to get there *(Map 32): 48km north west of Pont-du-Gard via D981 towards Uzès, then D979 through Lussan and D37. In Pont d'Auzon, right on D16 towards Rivières.*

188
Mas du Platane

Place du Platane
Collorgues
30190 Saint-Chaptes
(Gard)
Tel. 66 81 29 04
Claude and Claudine Vieillot

Open Easter – All Saints (2 days min.) **Rooms** 1 with shower and WC, 1 studio (2 pers.) with shower, WC and kitchenette (only 1 room heated). **Price** 300F (2 pers.), weekly terms available. **Meals** breakfast incl., evening meals at communal or separate table 100F (wine not incl.), menus 120-150F. **Facilities** swimming pool. **Pets** dogs not allowed. **Nearby** 18-hole golf, tennis, seaside (60km), Cévennes park, Nîmes, the Camargue, Anduze. **Spoken** English.

Le Mas de Platane is first and foremost a restaurant. It is small, elegant and hidden in an enchanting garden full of the perfumes of Provence. There are two very attractive bedrooms, with exposed stonework and lovely modern bathrooms. The bedrooms open directly on to the garden near the swimming pool. Excellent welcome.

How to get there (Map 32): 11km west of Uzès via D982 towards Moussac. After Garrigues right on D114; it's in Collorgues, behind the château.

189
Cruviers

Route de Saint-Ambroix
Cruviers-Larnac
30700 Uzès
(Gard)
Tel. 66 22 10 89
Thérèse Delbos

Open March – Dec. **Rooms** 4 with shower and WC. **Price** 230F (1/2 pers.) +30F (extra pers.) **Meals** breakfast 20F, half board 215F per pers., full board 295F per pers. in double room, lunch and evening meals (separate tables) 95 and 135F. **Facilities** lounge. **Credit cards** MasterCard, Eurocard. **Pets** dogs allowed on request. **Nearby** 9-hole golf, swimming pool, tennis, riding (4km), Uzès, Pont du Gard, Gardon gorges, Nîmes, Anduze, Avignon.

There are four guestrooms in this old, well renovated inn. All face south. They are comfortable and have mezzanines, making them ideal for families. It's a pity the bedrooms don't have the delightful Provençal fabrics used in the charming small restaurant, where authentic and good food is served. A pleasant welcome from a young owner.

How to get there (Map 33): 5km north of Uzès towards Lussan (autoroute: Remoulins-Pont-du-Gard exit).

190
Domaine de la Redonde

Montels
34310 Capestang
(Hérault)
Tel. 67 93 31 82
M. and Mme Hughes de Rodez
Bénavent

Open all year. **Rooms** 1 studio (4 pers.) and 1 suite (2 pers.) with bath and WC. Room cleaning on request. **Price** suite 400F- 500F , studio 430F-500F (according to season). **Meals** breakfast incl., no evening meals. **Restaurants** nearby. **Facilities** lounge, swimming pool. **Pets** small dogs allowed on request. **Nearby** tennis, riding , golf, barge trips on the Midi canal, Narbonne, Carcassonne, Fontfroide abbey, Minerve. **Spoken** English, Spanish.

This small château stands alone in the vineyards. Its young owners are very welcoming and have just completed one guest bedroom and one apartment. The rooms are large, the furniture is good quality and their taste has made the overall effect successful. A shady path leads to the swimming pool from where you can enjoy the classic elegance of the château. A very good address where you will be independent and comfortable.

How to get there (Maps 31 and 32): 21km south west of Beziers. Take D11 towards Capestang. South of Capestang on D16.

191
Les Prunus

9, rue des Prunus
34230 Plaissan
(Hérault)
Tel. 67 96 81 16
M. and Mme Colin

Open all year. **Rooms** 3 with shower and WC, 1 suite (2/3 pers.) with lounge, bath and WC. **Price** 180-240F (2 pers.) +50F (extra pers.), suite 280F. **Meals** breakfast incl., no evening meals. **Restaurant** Le Beaulieu in Plaissan. **Facilities** lounge. **Pets** dogs allowed on request. **Nearby** golf, seaside, tennis, riding, canoeing, swimming pool, Salagou lake, St Guilhem-le-Désert, the Midi canal. **Spoken** a little English.

The house once belonged to vineyard owners. It is in a small village but has a large garden. The theme in the bedrooms is the 1930s: ornaments, furniture, murals. Comfort is not neglected, especially in the small but delightful bathrooms. The welcome, the good breakfasts (served outside in fine weather), and the very reasonable prices make Les Prunus an excellent address.

How to get there (Map 32): 32km south east of Montpellier (autoroute: Sète exit); take D2 to Poussan, then Villeveyrac: signposted.

192
Mas Cammas
66300 Caixas
(Pyrénées-Orientales)
Tel. 68 38 82 27
M. Vissenaeken-Vaes

Closed Nov. (except All Saints) and Jan. **Rooms** 3 and 3 suites (4/5 pers.) with shower and WC.
Price 300-400F (according to season), suites 460-560F (4 pers.) **Meals** breakfast 35F, half
board (2 days min.) 250-300F per pers. Lunch and evening meals at separate tables in the
auberge 110F-150F (wine not incl.) **Facilities** lounge, telephone, swimming pool. **Pets** dogs not
allowed. **Nearby** sea, mountains, Collioure. **Spoken** English, German.

Clinging to the hillside at a height of 400m, Cammas dominates the
Roussillon plain with the sea in the distance. The small bedrooms are
all white, charming and sparsely furnished and overlook the valley. Light
lunches and excellent evening meals are served in the dining room, which
is full of character. You can stroll on the hills, or relax by the swimming
pool and on the terrace with its panoramic views. Friendly atmosphere.

How to get there *(Map 31): about 25km south west of Perpignan via D612A and
D615. At Fourques, left on D2 towards Caixas through Montauriol.*

193
Château de Camon

Camon
09500 Mirepoix
(Ariège)
Tel. 61 68 14 05
Fax 61 68 81 56
M. du Pont

Open March – end Nov. **Rooms** 7 with bath or shower and WC. **Price** 500-1000F (2 pers.) **Meals** breakfast incl., evening meals at communal table, on reservation 300F (wine incl.) **Facilities** swimming pool, fishing. **Credit cards** accepted. **Pets** dogs not allowed. **Nearby** tennis, riding, prehistoric caves. **Spoken** English.

This 12th-century château and its park are in the middle of one of the most beautiful villages of the region. Inside, a big stone staircase leads to a wide gallery which serves the bedrooms. They are all comfortable and different, with fine antiques and shimmering fabrics. The dining room and lounge have an attractive atmosphere. Good breakfasts and dinners. There is a swimming pool in the grounds.

How to get there (Map 31): 36km south east of Pamiers via D119. At Mirepoix take D7 towards Chalabre.

194
Domaine de Montagnac

09500 Saint-Félix-de-Tournegat
(Ariège)
Tel. 61 68 72 75
Fax 61 67 44 84
Mme Jean Bertolino

Open all year. **Rooms** 4 with bath and WC, 4 with shower and WC, 2 children's rooms. **Price** 220-300F (2 pers.) **Meals** breakfast incl., half board 195-235F per pers. in double room, lunch and evening meals at communal or separate table 85F (wine incl.) **Facilities** lounge, telephone, swimming pool, equestrian centre, billiards. **Pets** dogs allowed on request. **Nearby** tennis, golf, skiing. **Spoken** English, Italian.

A character house in a flowery setting standing alone in a magnificent landscape typical of the Ariège. The bedrooms are pleasant with a very beautiful view. The decor is simple and rustic: wooden floors, old furniture. The bathrooms are pleasant. Excellent breakfasts and evening meals. Friendly lounge with billiard table.

How to get there (Map 31): 66km south east of Toulouse via N20. At Pamiers head for Mirepoix; at Pujols turn left for St-Amadou, then right for Saint-Félix-de-Tournegat.

195
Le Poulsieu

Cautirac
09000 Serres-sur-Arget
(Ariège)
Tel. 61 02 77 72
Jenny and Bob Brogneaux

Open all year. **Rooms** 2 with shower and WC, 2 with basin sharing shower and WC. **Price** 150-170F (1 pers.), 180-200F (2 pers.) +50F (extra pers.) **Meals** breakfast incl., half board (4 days min.) 145-155F per pers. in double room, evening meals at communal table 65F (wine incl.) At lunchtime there is a kitchenette for guests' use. **Facilities** lounge, riding, off-road driving. **Pets** dogs allowed. **Nearby** golf (18km), swimming pool, tennis, caves. **Spoken** Dutch, English, German, Spanish.

Having travelled the world, Jenny and Bob Brogneaux have come to rest here in an isolated mountain village where they now welcome travellers into their home. The white-walled bedrooms are fresh and simple. Evening meals have a relaxed atmosphere. The cooking, more "European" than French, is not spectacular. Friendly welcome.

How to get there (Map 30): 12km west of Foix; in Foix head for St Girons, then D17 towards Col de Marrons to La Mouline; left opposite the bar; signposted.

196
Baudeigne

La Rives
09120 Varilhes
(Ariège)
Tel. 61 60 73 42
Fax 61 60 78 76
M. and Mme Jean Baudeigne

Open all year. **Rooms** 4 with shower, WC and telephone, and 1 with shower, telephone and shared WC. Room cleaning on request. **Price** 180F (1 pers.), 240F (2 pers.) +40F (extra pers.) **Meals** breakfast incl., no evening meals. **Facilities** swimming pool, tennis, fishing. **Pets** dogs allowed in kennel. **Nearby** golf, ski slopes (50km), Romanesque churches, caves. **Spoken** English.

A beautiful country house very close to the Pyrenees. The very well-kept grounds have a tennis court, a swimming pool and a stretch of water for fishing. The bedrooms are decorated with floral wallpaper and antique furniture and all have views over the garden. Breakfast is served on the terrace or in a handsome dining room. The guests' lounge is pleasant. Discreet and friendly welcome.

How to get there (Map 31): At Foix take N20 towards Toulouse until Varilhes; signposted.

197
Ferme-Auberge de Quiers

Compeyre
12520 Aguessac
(Aveyron)
Tel. 65 59 85 10
M. and Mme Lombard Pratmarty

Open Easter – All Saints. **Rooms** 2 with bath and WC, 4 with shower and WC (of which 1 for 4/6 pers. with mezzanine). Room cleaning once a week. **Price** 200F (2 pers.), mezzanine bedroom 300F (4 pers.) **Meals** breakfast 25F, half board 193F per pers. in double room (3 days min.), evening meals (separate tables) 80-100F (wine not incl.) **Credit cards** Visa. **Nearby** riding, fishing.

Not far from the medieval village of Compeyre, the Ferme-Auberge de Quiers overlooks a hilly landscape. The bedrooms are in an old barn and open directly on to the grounds. They are pleasant and charming: white walls, natural wood furniture and a few splashes of pink or blue. Breakfast and good regional evening meals are served in the two rustic dining-rooms of the farm.

How to get there *(Maps 31 and 32): At Millau take N9 towards Severac. At Aguessac, take D907 to Compeyre; signposted.*

198
Château de Croisillat

31460 Caraman
(Haute-Garonne)
Tel. 61 83 10 09
M. Guérin

Open 15 March – 15 Nov. **Rooms** 1 with bath and WC, 4 with bath or shower and shared WCs. **Price** 350-500F (1 pers.), 450-600F (2 pers.) **Meals** breakfast incl., no evening meals. **Restaurant** La Ferme d'En Bouyssou (10km). **Facilities** lounge, swimming pool, loose boxes, fishing. **Pets** dogs allowed on request. **Nearby** golf, Albi, Castres. **Spoken** English, German.

This very old house is covered in Virginia creeper and surrounded by terraces. The reception rooms and bedrooms are cluttered with an entertaining mixture of antiques and curios which makes them charming and old fashioned. Ask for the Empire or Louis XV bedrooms. Green surroundings and good welcome.

How to get there *(Map 31): 23km east of Toulouse via N126. At Montauriol take D1. Leaving Caraman follow D1 towards Revel; after 2.5km on the right there's an avenue of plane trees and a sign board.*

199
Château de Larra

Larra
31330 Grenade-sur-Garonne
(Haute-Garonne)
Tel. 61 82 62 51
Baronne de Carrière

Open Easter – All Saints. **Rooms** 2 with shower and WC, and 2 suites with bath and WC. **Price** 350-400F (2 pers.), suite 500F (4 pers.) **Meals** breakfast incl., evening meals at communal table 100-120F (wine not incl.) **Facilities** lounge. **Pets** dogs allowed on request. **Nearby** riding, golf, Belleperche abbey, Caumont, Pibrac, Montauban, Toulouse.

The 18th-century ambience of the Château de Larra remains intact. Louis XVth furniture and painted fabrics in the drawing room, plasterwork in the dining room, and an impressive staircase with unusual wrought-iron bannisters. The bedrooms and the suites are large and pleasant, a little old fashioned, but charming. Good breakfasts and dinners. Mme de Carrière is kind and energetic.

How to get there (Map 30): 30km north west of Toulouse. On A62 exit 10, then N20 towards Grisolles, Ondes, Grenade. At Grenade, signposted. It's on D87.

200
Domaine de Menaut

Auzas
31360 Saint-Martory
(Haute-Garonne)
Tel. 61 90 21 51
(at meal times)
Mme Jander

Open all year. Children under 10 not accepted. **Rooms** 2 with bath and WC, and 1 suite (4 pers.) with bath and WC. **Price** 300F (1 pers.), 350F (2 pers.), suite (3/4 pers.) 600F. **Meals** breakfast incl., lunch and evening meals at communal or separate tables from 70F (wine incl.) **Facilities** lounge, lakes, fishing, bathing, walking. **Pets** no animals allowed. **Nearby** tennis, ski-ing, museums. **Spoken** English, German.

This 90-hectare estate, with its three small lakes, is far from civilisation, and the house enjoys absolute peace. The interior is tasteful, restrained and well looked after, with elegant reproduction furniture in the dining room and lounge. Comfortable bedrooms with good bathrooms, and a sunny terrace for summer breakfasts. A place for nature lovers – food lovers too.

How to get there (Map 30): About 20km east of St Gaudens. Leave N117 at Boussens in direction of Mancioux, then D33; 5km before D52 (St-Martory/Aurignac) go right and follow the fence.

201
Ferme de Mounet

32800 Eauze
(Gers)
Tel. 62 09 82 85
M. and Mme Molas

Open Easter – All Saints. **Rooms** 2 with shower and WC. **Price** 220F (1 pers.), 240F (2 pers.)
Meals breakfast incl., half board 220F per pers. in double room (200F for more than three days).,
evening meals at communal table 90F, gastronomic menu 170F (wine incl.) **Facilities** lounge,
bicycles. **Credit cards** Visa. **Pets** dogs allowed (except in the bedrooms). **Nearby** swimming
pool, tennis, riding, 18-hole golf. **Spoken** English.

Amid the Armagnac vineyards, Mounet is the centre for another local speciality: foie gras. You will be greeted by the geese. In this handsome house the bedrooms are comfortable and well renovated but, sadly, overlook an agricultural building. Excellent evening meals are served in the large dining room and are sometimes enlivened by the friendly owners.

How to get there (Map 29): 39km north east of Aire-sur-l'Adour via N124 towards Nogaro. At Manciet, left on D931 to Eauze; signposted 'Foie Gras'.

202
Le Vieux Pradoulin

32700 Lectoure
(Gers)
Tel. 62 68 71 24
Mme Martine Vetter

Open all year. **Rooms** 3 sharing 1 bath and WC. **Price** 180F (1 pers.), 220F (2 pers.) **Meals**
breakfast incl., no evening meals. **Restaurant** Le Bastard (1km). **Facilities** lounge, telephone.
Pets dogs not allowed. **Nearby** swimming pool, tennis, fishing, riding, golf, Cistercian abbey,
cloisters, châteaux. **Spoken** a little English.

Once you have arrived you can forget the road because within the walls of this house tranquillity reigns. Built on a Gallo-Roman site, it contains some ancient treasures including oil lamps and terracotta fragments. The bedrooms are lovingly arranged and overlook the garden. The beds are old and comfortable, but the bathroom is shared. You will be received as friends. Charming and unconventional atmosphere.

How to get there (Map 30): North of Auch via N21 towards Agen. Just before Lectoure, crossroads; take the road to Condom, turn left after 500m.

203
Le Pigeonnier

32380 Pessoulens
(Gers)
Tel. 62 66 49 25
M. and Mme Jeangrand

Open all year. **Rooms** 1 with bath and WC, and 1 for children. **Price** 220F (2 pers.) **Meals** breakfast incl. **Restaurant** auberge Jouars (1km). **Facilities** lounge, telephone. **Nearby** swimming pool, tennis, lake fishing. **Spoken** Italian.

Y ou will immediately feel as if you have been adopted by M. and Mme Jeangrand, two former teachers who have opened their pretty village house to guests. There is only one bedroom and it is very comfortable. 'Chocolate box' decor in pale pink and white. The lounge–dining room opens into a pretty garden. Breakfast is a feast (cakes, jams, baked apples...).

How to get there (Map 30): North east of Toulouse via D2 and D3. At Beaumont-de-Lomagne take D928 towards Auch, then D18 towards St-Clar; it's in the village.

204
En Bigorre

32380 Tournecoupe
(Gers)
Tel. 62 66 42 47
Jean and Jacqueline Marqué

Open all year. **Rooms** 5 with shower and WC. Room cleaning on request. **Price** 150F (2 pers.) **Meals** breakfast 25F, half board 170F per pers. (for a couple), evening meals at communal table 70F (all incl.) **Facilities** lounge, telephone, swimming pool, loose boxes, fishing. **Nearby** tennis, golf, St-Clar, Cologne, Avezan, Solomiac.

A recently built village house in regional style, with a spacious garden ensuring tranquillity. The bedrooms are pleasant, panelled or painted white. Breakfast and dinner are served in a pretty dining room or under a canopy equipped with a barbecue beside the swimming pool. Good regional cooking and very reasonable prices. Warm welcome.

How to get there (Map 30): 40km south of Agen via N21 towards Lectoure, then left on D27. Before Lectoure follow signs for St-Clar and Tournecoupe.

205
Château de Cousserans

46140 Belaye
(Lot)
Tel. 65 36 25 77
Fax 65 36 29 48
M. and Mme Georges Mougin

Open Easter – All Saints. **Rooms** 4 with bath and WC. **Price** 700-800F. **Meals** breakfast incl.,
no evening meals. **Restaurants** in Lascabanes and St-Médaud-Catus. **Facilities** lounge, fishing.
Nearby Lauzerte, Montcuq, prehistoric sites. **Spoken** English, Spanish.

The château is glimpsed through the trees as you approach it. Its medieval
appearance is austere and contrasts with its comfortable interior. A lift
takes you to the bedrooms. They are vast, completely renovated, very
comfortable and contain antique mahogany furniture. Very inviting lounge;
breakfast served in a light, vaulted dining room, or on the terrace in summer.

*How to get there (Map 30): 30km from Cahors via D911. At Castelfranc, left towards
Anglars, then D45 towards Montcuq.*

206
Moulin de Fresquet

46500 Gramat
(Lot)
Tel. 65 38 70 60
M. and Mme Ramelot

Open all year. **No smoking** in the bedrooms. **Rooms** 5 with shower and WC (TV on request).
Price 220-320F (2 pers.) +70F (extra pers.) **Meals** breakfast incl., evening meals at communal
table 100F (wine incl.) **Facilities** lounge, fishing, boating, footpath. **Pets** dogs not allowed.
Nearby riding, swimming pool, tennis, mountain biking, potholing, Rocamadour, Padirac,
Loubressac. **Spoken** English, German.

This old mill is in a peaceful setting close to Gramat, with greenery all
around. It has been beautifully restored throughout. We loved the
bedrooms (two of which overlook the water) and the lounge-library. Claude
and Michel will greet you warmly. The evening meal is remarkably good
and so is the 'aperitif-foie gras'. An excellent place which we strongly
recommend.

*How to get there (Map 24): 800m south west of Gramat; in Gramat take N140
towards Figeac and turn left after 500m; the drive is in 300m.*

207
L'Ermitage

46230 Lalbenque
(Lot)
Tel. 65 31 75 91
M. Daniel Pasquier

Open all year. **Children** under 2 not accepted. **Rooms** 2 independent studios with shower, WC and kitchenette. Room cleaning guests' responsibility. **Price** 180F (2 pers.) **Meals** no evening meals. **Restaurant** Chez Bertier in the village. **Nearby** tennis, riding, St-Cirq-Lapopie, Gallic remains. **Spoken** German.

In a forest of oak trees, on whose roots truffles grow, there are three small 'gariotte' houses where you will live like a hermit. Completely circular, spotlessly clean, cool in summer, warm in winter, they have a kitchenette (where you can prepare your breakfast), a shower room and a double bed. They are comfortable but rather small.

How to get there (Map 30): 16km south of Cahors via D6; turn left at sign at the entrance to Lalbenque.

208
Château de Gamot

Gamot
46130 Loubressac
(Lot)
Tel. 65 10 92 03/65 38 58 50
(1) 48 83 01 91
Mme Belières

Open 1st April – 30 Oct. **No smoking. Rooms** 4 of which 2 with basin sharing bath and WC, and 1 apartment and 1 suite (3 pers.) with bath and WC. **Price** 260F (2 pers.), suite 400F (3 pers.), apartment 550F (4 pers.) Room cleaning guests' responsibility. **Meals** breakfast incl., no evening meals. **Restaurant** in Loubressac. **Facilities** swimming pool, except July and August. **Pets** dogs not allowed. **Nearby** tennis, riding, swimming pool, Padirac, Rocamadour.

A fine, homogeneous ensemble, Gamot seems unchanged since it was built in the 17th century. The dining room has exposed stonework and a good smell of open fires. On the first floor, the bedrooms are as comfortable as they can be considering their age. Lovely antique furniture, pleasant bathrooms. Very generous breakfasts. A charming place. The only problem is that the swimming pool is closed to guests in summer!

How to get there (Map 24): At Brétenoux take D14 towards Gramat, then D30.

209
La Petite Auberge

Domaine de Saint Géry
Lascabanes
46800 Montcuq
(Lot)
Tel. 65 31 82 51
M. Patrick Duler

Open 1 March – 31 Dec. **Rooms** 4 and 1 suite (4/6 pers.) with bath and WC. Room cleaning every 2 days. **Price** 250-420F (1/2 pers.), suite 550-630F (4 pers.) **Meals** breakfast 50F, half board 320-380F per pers. in double room, lunch and evening meals (separate tables) 100-320F (wine not incl.) **Pets** dogs allowed on request. **Facilities** swimming pool. **Nearby** tennis, golf (8km), walks, mountain biking, boating on the Lot.

In this wild limestone area of Le Quercy there are some lovely houses, and this is one of them. The bedrooms are in various buildings and are delightful, with white plastered walls or barrel vaulted, pretty antique furniture and quarry tiled floors. Add to that decent bathrooms, excellent regional specialities and a young and cheerful welcome.

How to get there *(Map 30): 18km south west of Cahors via N20 towards Toulouse, then right on D653 towards Montcuq and left on D7 to Lascabanes.*

210
Domaine du Barry
Barran

"Le Barry", Duravel
46700 Puy-l'Evêque
(Lot)
Tel. 65 24 63 24
M. and Mme Jean François Nioloux

Open Easter – All Saints. **Rooms** 5 with bath and WC, 1 with shower and WC. **Price** 200-400F (1/3 pers.) **Meals** breakfast incl., evening meals at communal table, on reservation 105F (wine incl.) **Restaurants** La Roseraie in Duravel (3km) and Bellevue in Puy-l'Evêque (3km). **Facilities** lounge, telephone. **Pets** small dogs allowed on request (+10F). **Nearby** riding, swimming pool, tennis, châteaux.

Perched on the edge of a little valley, this beautiful stone house is a good example of the local architecture. The pleasant bedrooms are light, simple and comfortable. Each one has a view of the landscape of meadows and hills. The beds are big, the bathrooms impeccable. The large bedroom has a superb covered terrace. Quality regional cooking. Relaxed atmosphere.

How to get there *(Maps 23 and 30): D911 between Cahors and Villeneuve-sur-Lot; signposted from the hamlet of Girard between Puy-l'Evêque and Duravel.*

211
Domaine de Jean-Pierre

Route de Villeneuve
65300 Pinas
(Hautes-Pyrénées)
Tel. 62 98 15 08
Mme Marie Colombier

Open all year. **Rooms** 3 with bath and WC, 2 without bath (poss. bedrooms en suite). **Price** 200F (1 pers.), 240F (2 pers.) +60F (extra pers.) **Meals** breakfast incl., no evening meals. **Restaurants** Chez Maurette and Le Relais du Castera (5/7km). **Facilities** lounge, loose boxes. **Nearby** swimming pool, tennis, golf, Lourdes, St-Bertrand-de-Comminges. **Spoken** English.

In a peaceful setting on the edge of the village, this beautiful house is covered with Virginia creeper and surrounded by a very well kept garden. The quiet bedrooms look out over greenery. Each one has antique furniture and a colour scheme of its own. Huge modern bathrooms and very tasteful decor throughout. Mme Colombier is very welcoming and prepares excellent breakfasts, served on the terrace in good weather.

How to get there *(Map 30): 30km east of Tarbes via N117 towards Toulouse. At Lannemezan head for Pinas and follow the signs.*

212
Chez Mme Salvador

Place des Arcades
81140 Castelnau-de-Montmiral
(Tarn)
Tel. 63 33 17 44
M. and Mme Salvador

Open 1 April – 1 Nov. **Rooms** 5 with bath and WC, 1 with bath and shared WC, and 2 suites (2/4 pers., 4 days min.) with lounge, kitchen, bath or shower and WC. Room cleaning every 2/3 days or on request. **Price** 150-170F (2 pers.) +30F (extra pers.), suite 220F (2 pers.), 280F (4 pers.) **Meals** breakfast 20F, no evening meals. **Restaurants** in the village. **Facilities** lounge. **Pets** small dogs allowed. **Nearby** swimming pool, fishing, tennis, riding, golf, walled towns.

The house is located on the main square of Castelnau, a perfect small medieval town, and is easily recognisable by its two large mullioned windows. The bedrooms are simply furnished in country style and comfortable. The lounge has an extraordinary Louis XIII fireplace. Breakfast is served either in the ground floor dining-sitting room or outside under the arcades. Kind welcome.

How to get there *(Map 31): 30km west of Albi in the Gaillac direction, then in Gaillac take the Caussade road.*

213
Château de Garrevaques

81700 Garrevaques
(Tarn)
Tel. 63 75 04 54/61 52 01 47
Fax 63 70 26 44
Mme Barande and Mme Combes

Open all year, on reservation only. **Rooms** 7 (2/3 pers.) and 2 suites with bath and WC. **Price** 650F (2 pers.), suite 1000F (3/4 pers.) **Meals** breakfast incl., half board 450F per pers. in double room (3 days min.), evening meal at communal table, on reservation 170F (wine incl.) **Facilities** lounge, telephone, swimming pool, tennis, billiards. **Credit cards** Visa, Amex. **Pets** small dogs allowed on request. **Nearby** golf, excursions, antiquities. **Spoken** English, Spanish.

Burned down in the Revolution and restored at the beginning of the 19th century, Garrevaques stands in a large park with a swimming pool and a tennis court. The beautiful suite of reception rooms is furnished with Empire and Napoleon III pieces. We recommend the first floor bedrooms and suites: big, well furnished and comfortable. In the evening the owners join their guests for a traditional dinner. Pleasant, professional welcome.

How to get there (Map 31): 50 km south east of Toulouse via D1. At Revel turn on to D79 (opposite the police station) for 5km.

214
Taverne de la Dame du Plô

5, rue Père-Colin
81500 Lavaur
(Tarn)
Tel. 63 41 38 77
M. Fèvre

Open all year. **Rooms** 4 with shower and shared WC. **Price** 170F (1 pers.), 200F (2 pers.) **Meals** breakfast incl. **Restaurant** snacks in the evening in the piano-bar until 2am from 30F (wine not incl.) **Facilities** lounge. **Nearby** golf, river, old town of Lavaur. **Spoken** English, Italian, Spanish.

In the history of the Catharists, Lavaur is a hallowed place and has a heroine, La Dame du Plô. Bernard Fèvre will tell you the story. Entirely renovated, his ancient house has four small bedrooms which are pretty and comfortable. You can be completely independent here. In the basement there is an intimate piano-bar, open to the public, serving food until late in the evening. Every morning breakfast is laid ready in the sitting room – all you have to do is heat the tea, coffee or chocolate.

How to get there (Map 31): 37km east of Toulouse via D112.

215
Montpeyroux

81700 Lempaut
(Tarn)
Tel. 63 75 51 17
M. and Mme Adolphe Sallier

Open 1 April – 1 Nov. **Rooms** 1 with bath (slipper bath) and WC, 2 with shower and WC, 2 sharing bath (slipper bath) and WC. Room cleaning twice a week, or on request. **Price** 200-300F (1/2 pers.) **Meals** breakfast incl., evening meals at communal table 100-120F (wine not incl.), or a simple lunch 60F. **Facilities** lounge, swimming pool, tennis. **Pets** dogs not allowed. **Nearby** riding, golf, St Féréol lake, Albi, Toulouse, Carcassonne.

A very peaceful old house in a green setting. Beautiful antique furniture – 18th and early 19th century – is the theme for the very successful decor in the lounge as well as the comfortable bedrooms, some of which have bathrooms. Quality evening meals and breakfasts, served, in fine weather, under a small canopy. Kind and unaffected welcome.

How to get there (Map 31): 12km north east of Revel via D622 towards Castres for 9km, then left on D12. At Lempaut left on D46 towards Blan.

216
Villa Les Pins

81700 Lempaut
(Tarn)
Tel. 63 75 51 01
Mme Delbreil

Open 1 April – end Nov. **Rooms** 5 with bath and WC and 2 small rooms sharing shower and WC. Room cleaning twice weekly. **Price** 180-400F (1/2 pers.) **Meals** breakfast incl., evening meals at communal table on request 100F (wine incl.) **Facilities** lounge, fishing. **Pets** dogs not allowed. **Nearby** 18-hole golf (30km), tennis, riding, lake (12km), Montagne Noire, Castres. **Spoken** English.

This lovely Italian–style villa was built at the beginning of the last century by Madame Debreil's grandfather and has been completely renovated with excellent taste and attention to detail. The bedrooms are charming and bright, with flowered wallpaper, and have good family furniture. The largest has a pleasant semi-circular balcony. Friendly, family welcome.

How to get there (Map 31): 12km north east of Revel via D622 towards Castres for 9km, then left on D12. At Lempaut, left on D46 towards Blan, then take 2nd turn left.

217
Domaine équestre des Juliannes

Les Juliannes
81250 Paulinet
(Tarn)
Tel. 63 55 94 38
M. and Mme Choucavy

Open March – Dec. Weekly bookings for July/August and school holidays. **Rooms** 3 and 3 suites (4/5 pers.) with bath and WC. **Price** 300F (2 pers.), suite 450F (2 pers.) +70F (extra pers.) **Meals** breakfast incl., half board from 230F per pers. in double room, lunch (cold buffet) and evening meal (65-100f) at communal table, on reservation (wine not incl.) **Facilities** lounge, swimming pool, equestrian centre, fishing. **Credit cards** Visa. **Pets** dogs allowed on request. **Spoken** English.

This old farm has been very well restored and offers total peace and a beautiful view. The bedrooms are large and comfortable, and are decorated with an elegant simplicity that emphasises the pale wood floors, stone walls and pretty quilts on the beds. Quality evening meals. Pleasant lounge. Weekly bookings only in school holidays. First class equestrian centre and good swimming pool.

How to get there *(Map 31): 37km south east of Albi via D999 towards Millau. Before Alban right on D86 towards Réalmont, then 2nd road on the left; signposted.*

218
Château d'En-Haut

59144 Jenlain
(Nord)
Tel. 27 49 71 80
M. and Mme Demarcq

Open all year. **Rooms** 2 with bath and WC, 4 with shower and WC (possible suite). **Price** 230-300F (2 pers.) +100F (extra pers.) **Meals** breakfast incl., no evening meals. **Restaurants** close by. **Facilities** lounge. **Dogs** allowed in kennel. **Nearby** golf, forest of Mormal. **Spoken** English.

Jenlain, with its rows of red brick houses, is not a particularly seductive place, so discovering this delightful château far from the road comes as a lovely surprise. Inside it is extremely comfortable, with fitted carpets, rugs, antique furniture brought to life by a very successful use of colours in the decor. Very pleasant bedrooms. Breakfast is served in one of three dining rooms. A friendly welcome, and very good value for money.

How to get there (Map 3): 8km south east of Valenciennes via N49 towards Maubeuge.

219
La Maison de la Houve

62179 Audinghen
(Pas-de-Calais)
Tel. 21 32 97 06/21 83 29 95
Mme Danel

Open all year. **Rooms** 3 with bath and WC, 2 with shower and WC, 2 with basin. **Price** 100-140F (1 pers.) 125-165F (2 pers.) **Meals** breakfast incl., no evening meals. **Facilities** lounge, telephone, botanical garden, rose garden. **Credit cards** Visa. **Nearby** tennis, riding, golf, seaside, fishing, château and museum in Boulogne-sur-Mer, museum of the sea. **Spoken** English.

This unusual and pleasing house occupies an open site with views of the côte d'Opale. The house is comfortable and fabulously decorated and furnished – everything has been done to make guests happy. Excellent breakfasts are served on porcelain at tables which have a panoramic view of the countryside. Mme Danel is exceptionally kind, and you will be sad to leave!

How to get there (Map 1): Between Calais and Boulogne, 5.5km from Cap Gris-Nez on D191 towards Marquise; at Onglevert.

220
La Gacogne

La Gacogne
62310 Azincourt
(Pas-de-Calais)
Tel. 21 04 45 61
Marie-José and Patrick Fenet

Open all year. **Rooms** 3 with shower and WC, 1 with basin and WC. **Price** 220F (2 pers.) **Meals** breakfast incl., no evening meals. **Restaurants** in Azincourt, Hesdin and Fruges. **Facilities** lounge, water-colour and oil painting courses, carriage rides. **Pets** dogs not allowed. **Nearby** seaside, tennis, riding, fishing. **Spoken** English.

This welcoming house is on the historical site of Agincourt, on the place where the English camp once stood. The bedrooms are in a small separate building which has a lounge, kitchen and fireplace. They are all charming and unusual. Breakfast is served at a communal table in an attractively decorated room, and the atmosphere here is convivial.

How to get there *(Map 2): 41km north east of Abbeville via D928 towards Fruges. Before Ruisseauville, right on D71 towards Azincourt, then towards Tramecourt; signposted.*

221
Château d'Asnières-en-Bessin

14710 Asnières-en-Bessin
(Calvados)
Tel. 31 22 41 16
M. and Mme Heldt

Open all year. **Children** under 11 not accepted. **Rooms** 2 with bath and WC. **Price** 350F (2 pers.) **Meals** breakfast incl., no evening meal. **Restaurants** beside the sea. **Pets** dogs not allowed. **Nearby** tennis, riding, seaside, Normandy landing beaches, Bayeux, Château de Bessin, Balleroy forest. **Spoken** English and German (a little).

You can see Asnières reflected in the round ornamental pond in front of the house. Inside the decor is tasteful and authentic. The bedrooms are very big, comfortable, and furnished with antiques. They have polished wood floors and good bathrooms. Breakfast is served at a large table in the Louis XV dining room. The welcome is refined and natural. Very reasonable prices.

How to get there (Map 7): 20km north west of Bayeux via N13 towards Isigny-sur-Mer. In Normaville, before Deux Jumeaux, right on D198 towards Asnières.

223
Le Castel

7, rue de la Cambette
14400 Bayeux
(Calvados)
Tel. 31 92 05 86
Fax 31 92 55 64
Baronne A. de Ville d'Avray

Open 15 March to 1 Oct. (on request in high season). **Rooms** 1 with bath and WC, 1 with shower and WC, 1 suite (4/5 pers.) with bath and WC. **Price** 490-520 (2 pers.) +80F (extra pers.), suite 820F (4/5 pers.). **Meals** breakfast incl., no evening meal. **Restaurants** in Bayeux. **Facilities** lounge, telephone. **Nearby** swimming pool, riding, golf, seaside, Bayeux Tapestry, cathedrals, Suisse Normande. **Spoken** English.

It is a surprise to find a garden hidden behind the little courtyard of this fine old house. The welcome is cheerful and natural. The dining room is at garden level and the 18th-century lounge is very well furnished. The bedrooms are quiet and each has its own colour scheme and overlooks the gardens, where breakfast is served. A good place to stay in Bayeux.

How to get there (Map 7): on the ring road south of Bayeux, opposite the St-Lô crossroads.

223
Château de Vaulaville

Tour-en-Bessin
14400 Bayeux
(Calvados)
Tel. 31 92 52 62
Mme Corblet de Fallerans

Open Easter – All Saints. **Rooms** 1 with bath and WC, 1 suite (3 pers. and 2 children) of 3 bedrooms with bath and WC. **Price** 350F (1 pers.), 480F (2 pers.), suite 700F (3 pers.) **Meals** breakfast incl., evening meals on reservation (separate tables) 150-200F (wine incl.) **Facilities** lounge. **Pets** dogs allowed on request. **Nearby** golf, seaside, Bayeux, Memorial museum, Normandy landing beaches. **Spoken** English.

A small, perfectly proportioned 18th-century château. The bedrooms are superb. In one you actually experience 'la vie en rose' because it has pink for a main colour, blending subtly with the antique furniture. Breakfasts and excellent dinners are served in a magnificent circular room.

How to get there (Map 7): 7km west of Bayeux via N13 towards Tour-en-Bessin; signposted.

224
Chez M. and Mme Rogoff

Le Bourg
Ranchy
14400 Bayeux (Calvados)
Tel. 31 92 36 42
Monique and Guy Rogoff

Open 1 April – All Saints. **Rooms** 1 with bath and WC, 1 with shower and WC. **Price** 130F (1 pers.), 180F (2 pers.) +80F (extra pers.) +100F (2 extra pers.) **Meals** breakfast incl., no evening meals. **Restaurants** in Bayeux. **Facilities** lounge. **Pets** dogs not allowed. **Nearby** swimming pool, tennis, riding, 9- and 18-hole golf, châteaux, manors, fortified farms.

A few minutes from Bayeux, this house is set in a pleasant and peaceful garden. Guests may choose between two good-sized bedrooms, simply decorated but charming. Each has its own bathroom but the bedroom on the ground floor has its bathroom next door. Breakfast is served in the large kitchen, or on the terrace if it is fine. Thanks to Mme Rogoff's spontaneous welcome you will feel quite at home.

How to get there (Map 7): 3km south west of Bayeux via D5 towards Le Molay-Littry, then D169; turn left before the church.

225
Château des Riffets

14680 Bretteville-sur-Laize
(Calvados)
Tel. 31 23 53 21/31 95 62 14
Alain and Anne-Marie Cantel

Open all year. **Rooms** 2 with bath and WC, and 2 suites (2/3 pers.) of which 1 with spa-bath and WC and 1 with multijet shower and WC. **Price** 400F (2 pers.), suite 500F +100F (extra pers.) **Meals** breakfast incl., evening meals at communal or separate tables 100-200F (wine not incl.) **Facilities** lounge, swimming pool, loose boxes. **Pets** dogs not allowed. **Nearby** 18-hole golf (5km), Beauvron-en-Auge, Beaumont, Deauville, Cabourg, Houlgate. **Spoken** English, German.

After a long, flat stretch the road enters rolling countryside. This château stands in beautiful grounds, with a swimming pool, and is completely peaceful. The bedrooms are large and comfortable. We preferred the 'rose' suite and the 'baldaquin' (canopy) bedroom. Small lounge furnished in period style, and excellent evening meals in a friendly atmosphere.

How to get there (Map 7): 10km south of Caen via N158 towards Falaise. At La Jalousie, D23 and D235 before the village; signposted.

226
Manoir des Tourpes

Chemin de l'Eglise
14670 Bures-sur-Dives
(Calvados)
Tel. 31 23 63 47
Mme Landon and M. Cassady

Open all year. **Rooms** 2 with bath and WC, 1 with shower and WC. **Price** 210-300F (2 pers.) +60F (extra pers.) **Meals** breakfast incl., no evening meals. **Facilities** lounge. **Pets** dogs not allowed. **Nearby** 18-hole golf (10km), tennis, swimming pool, riding, sailing, Caen, the Auge region, marshes. **Spoken** English.

This elegant manor house lies between the church and the river, overlooking a landscape of meadows. The beautiful bedrooms are well kept and comfortable, with co-ordinating wallpaper and curtains which set off the pieces of antique furniture. Pleasant lounge-dining room for fireside breakfasts, and attractive garden. A very charming, welcoming place.

How to get there (Map 7): 15km east of Caen via N175, then left on D95 towards Bures-sur-Dives; it's beside the church.

227
Ferme de la Piquoterie

La Cambe
14320 La Cambe
(Calvados)
Tel. 31 92 09 82
Jean–Gabriel Laloy

Open 15 April – 15 Oct. (or on request). **No smoking** in the bedrooms. **Rooms** 2 with bath and WC, 1 with shower and WC, 1 cottage (2 pers. + 1 child). **Price** 450F (2 pers.), cottage 400F per night or weekly rates. **Meals** breakfast incl., no evening meals. **Restaurants** auberges nearby. **Facilities** lounge. **Pets** dogs not allowed. **Nearby** golf, tennis, seaside. **Spoken** English, German, Italian.

This farm comes as a pleasant surprise. Jean–Gabriel Laloy is an artist and has created an unusual home in resolutely contemporary style but without coldness, thanks to the use of the original materials. The place deserves a feature in an interior design magazine: restrained, with pure lines, beautiful objects, paintings and sculptures. The bedrooms are large and comfortable and the bathrooms are a dream. The welcome is young and friendly, the delightful garden is full of rare plants... A discovery.

How to get there (Map 7): 21km west of Bayeux via N13. After the sign for La Cambe, take 1st road on the right; signposted.

228
Ferme Savigny

14230 La Cambe
(Calvados)
Tel. 31 22 70 06
M. and Mme Maurice Le Devin

Open all year. **Rooms** 3 with bath and WC. **Price** 150F (1 pers.), 250F (2 pers.) **Meals** breakfast incl. no evening meals. **Restaurants** La Marée and La Belle Marinière (3km). **Pets** dogs not allowed. **Nearby** tennis, riding, 27-hole golf, seaside, Normandy landing beaches, Bayeux (Tapestry, museum, cathedral), marshland park of Cotentin.

In the Bessin region of Normandy, under the changing colours of a Virginia creeper, this farmhouse reflects its owners' friendliness. A stone staircase leads to good bedrooms, furnished with care, and their very pleasant bathrooms. Breakfast is served downstairs in a large room with stone walls and red and white patterned curtains and table linen. A charming place.

How to get there (Map 7): 25km west of Bayeux via N13 to La Cambe, then at the wayside shrine take D113 towards Grandcamp-Maisy; signposted.

229
Le Relais

19, rue Thiers
14240 Caumont-l'Eventé
(Calvados)
Tel. 31 77 47 85
M. and Mme Boullot

Open all year. **Children** under 3 not allowed. **Rooms** 1 with bath and WC, 1 with shower and WC, and 2 extra bedrooms. Room cleaning twice weekly. **Price** 240F (2 pers.) **Meals** breakfast incl., evening meals at communal table 100F (wine incl.) **Facilities** lounge, swimming pool, riding (+60F). **Pets** small dogs allowed (+20F). **Nearby** tennis, golf, Mont-St-Michel, château de Balleroy. **Spoken** English.

Y ou will be delighted the minute you arrive at Le Relais with its leafy surroundings. The interior is pleasingly countrified and the bedrooms are pretty, with antique furniture and many personal details. Breakfast and dinner are served in a welcoming room with a corner bar, and there is a delightful lounge overlooking the swimming pool. Cheerful and lively welcome. Very good value.

How to get there (Map 7): 23km east of St Lô via D11 and D71. At Caumont-l'Éventé, left on D28 towards Balleroy; signposted.

230
La Ferme du Vey

Le Vey
14570 Clecy le Vey
(Calvados)
Tel. 31 69 71 02
M. and Mme Leboucher-Brisset

Open all year. **Rooms** 3 with shower and WC. **Price** 190F (2 pers.), 240F (3 pers.), 260F (4 pers.) **Meals** breakfast incl., no evening meals. **Facilities** fishing. **Pets** small dogs allowed on request. **Nearby** swimming pool, tennis, riding, canoeing, hang-gliding, 18-hole golf, rock climbing, park of Château du Thury, Château de Pontécoulan. **Spoken** English.

T his old farmhouse is in the Suisse Normande, not far from a cliff popular with devotees of rock climbing and hang gliding. The three bedrooms are charming, comfortable, and decorated in country style. Two of them overlook a pretty orchard bordered by a river. Young and natural welcome.

How to get there (Map 7): 37km south of Caen via D562 towards Flers. At Clecy go left towards Le Vey for 1.5km.

231
Chez Mme Hamelin

Le Bourg
Beuvron-en-Auge
14430 Dozulé
(Calvados)
Tel. 31 39 00 62
Mme Hamelin

Open Easter – All Saints. **Rooms** 1 with shower and WC. **Price** 190F (2 pers.) +60F (extra pers.)
Possibility of one extra room for 2 pers. **Meals** breakfast incl., no evening meals. **Restaurants**
La Boule d'Or, Le Pavé d'Auge in Beuvron-en-Auge and the Crêperie La Galère. **Pets** small dogs
allowed. **Nearby** 18-hole golf, pretty villages. **Spoken** English.

Beauvron-en-Auge is a splendid Normandy village with flowery
balconies and timbered houses. This house is no exception. It is L-
shaped, with a little courtyard garden and a view towards the meadows.
The bedroom is at garden level and charming, with a bathroom decorated
with trellis work. Pretty dining room for breakfast. Friendly and natural
welcome.

*How to get there (Map 7): 27km east of Caen via N175, then D49; it's at the entrance
to the village opposite the manor.*

232
Haras de Bouttemont

Victot-Pontfol
14430 Dozulé
(Calvados)
Tel. 31 63 00 41
Fax 31 63 18 55
M. and Mme P. and B. Aumont

Open all year. **Rooms** 1 with bath and WC, 3 with shower and WC. **Price** 390-400F (2 pers.)
Meals breakfast incl., evening meals on reservation (separate tables) 180F (wine not incl.)
Facilities lounge, golf practice, fishing. **Pets** dogs not allowed. **Nearby** 18-hole golf. **Spoken**
English.

Bouttemont was once a successful stud farm, though now the horses have
gone. For five generations the owners saw their horses winning the
greatest races. You will be unaffectedly received. The bedrooms are
comfortable and full of charm: old tiled floors, painted panelling and views
over the fields. Breakfast and dinner are served in a smart dining room, with
embroidered table linen and lovely china.

*How to get there (Map 7): 30km east of Caen via N13; at the St-Jean crossroads take
D16 for 3.2km and it's on the left.*

233
L'Hermerel

14230 Géfosse-Fontenay
(Calvados)
Tel. 31 22 64 12
M. and Mme François and Agnès
Lemarié

Open all year. **Rooms** 4 with shower and WC. **Price** 160-200F (1 pers.), 190-250F (2 pers.) +60-70F (extra pers.) **Meals** breakfast incl., evening meals at communal table, on reservation 85F (cider incl.) **Facilities** lounge. **Pets** dogs not allowed. **Nearby** tennis, golf, sailing, fishing, Bayeux, châteaux, manors. **Spoken** English.

This fine 17th-century farmhouse is almost a château. The pleasant bedrooms have high ceilings and are comfortable (the one under the roof with a mezzanine is extraordinary). Breakfast is served in a large and attractive room. What used to be the chapel is now the lounge. Mme Lemarié is very welcoming and will advise you on touring the area.

How to get there *(Map 7): 7km north of Isigny-sur-Mer via RN13. In Osmanville, D514 towards Grandcamp-Maisy then left on D199; 2nd road on the right.*

234
Château de Vouilly

Vouilly
14230 Isigny-sur-Mer
(Calvados)
Tel. 31 22 08 59
M. and Mme James Hamel

Open March – Nov. **Rooms** 4 with bath and WC. **Price** 200F (1 pers.), 250F (2 pers.) +50F (extra pers.) **Meals** breakfast incl., no evening meals. **Restaurants** Auberges de la Rivière and La Piquenotiére, and restaurants beside the sea. **Facilities** lounge, fishing, ponies. **Pets** dogs allowed on request. **Nearby** tennis, golf, regional marshland park of Contentin and Bessin, Bayeux (Tapestry, cathedral). **Spoken** English.

Close to the village yet very quiet, Vouilly is a lovely small château of great charm surrounded by a moat. The bedrooms are large and comfortable with fine furniture and superb floors. Breakfast is served in a dining room which once was the HQ of the American press after the Normandy landings. Pleasant welcome. Excellent value.

How to get there *(Map 7): 8km south east of Isigny-sur-Mer via D5 towards Vouilly; signposted.*

235
Ferme-Auberge de la Rivière

Saint-Germain-du-Pert
14230 Isigny-sur-Mer
(Calvados)
Tel. 31 22 72 92
Paulette and Hervé Marie

Open Easter – All Saints. **Rooms** 2 with shower and WC, 2 with basin sharing bath and WC. Room cleaning every 3 days. **Price** 140F (1 pers.), 180F (2 pers.) **Meals** breakfast incl., auberge for lunch (Saturday and Sunday) and evening meals (separate tables) 45-75F (wine not incl.) **Facilities** lounge, river fishing. **Pets** dogs not allowed. **Nearby** golf, tennis, riding, seaside, marshland paths, Bayeux.

This beautiful fortified farm is set in an unspoilt part of Normandy. Excellent dinners are served in a welcoming dining room beside the fireplace, where an open fire often burns. The bedrooms, in good rustic style, are pleasant and well kept. Three of them overlook the marshes. Good welcome and low prices. Book in advance.

How to get there *(Map 7): 6km north east of Isigny-sur-Mer; leave N13 at La Cambe, take D113 for 1km and D124 towards St-Germain-du-Pert for 1.5km.*

236
Cour l'Epée

14340 Saint-Aubin-Lebizay
(Calvados)
Tel. 31 65 09 45
Bernard and Bernardine Bataille

Open all year. 2 nights min. **Rooms** 2 with bath or shower and WC, 1 with shower and 1 with bath both sharing WC. Room cleaning every 2 days. **Price** 230-280F (2 pers.) +70F (extra pers.) **Meals** breakfast incl., evening meals (min. 3 days) at communal or separate table 45-55F (simple meals, wine not incl.) **Facilities** tennis. **Pets** dogs not allowed. **Nearby** golf, Beuvron-en-Auge, Honfleur, Deauville, Cabourg. **Spoken** English.

Cour L'Epée is like a private hamlet. From its elevated position there is a superb view of the landscape. The bedrooms are idyllic, with simple and good furniture and fabrics. Good taste is to be found everywhere. There is total silence. Excellent breakfasts are served indoors or out. A place close to perfection.

How to get there *(Map 7): 18km east of Cabourg; A13 exit Pont l'Evêque take N175 towards Caen. In Dozulé D85 towards Cambremer. 500m after Forges-de-Clermont, sign, turn left.*

237
La Ferme des Poiriers Roses

14130 Saint-Philbert-des-Champs
(Calvados)
Tel. 31 64 72 14
Fax 31 64 19 55
M. and Mme Lecorneur

Open Easter – 15 Nov. (3 rooms all year). **Rooms** 6 (of which 2 for 4 pers.) and 1 suite with lounge, all with bath and WC. **Price** 300-450F (2 pers.) **Meals** gourmand breakfast 50F, no evening meals. **Restaurant** L'Aigle d'Or in Pont l'Evêque. **Facilities** lounge, bicycles. **Pets** dogs not allowed. **Nearby** 27-hole golf, tennis, riding, man-made lake, tour of manors. **Spoken** English.

The rooms are filled with flowers. The bedrooms rival each other for charm and comfort, a mixture of beautiful fabrics and wood. A particular mention for the one close to the dining room. Breakfasts are 'gourmand feasts' and the welcome is very kind. You can enjoy sitting in the garden or go for a bike ride.

How to get there (Map 8): *A13 exit Pont l'Evêque, then D579 towards Lisieux. In Ouilly, left on D98 through Norolles, then D264; 700m before the village.*

238
Château de Colombières

Colombières
14710 Trévières
(Calvados)
Tel. 31 22 51 65
Comtesse E. de Maupeou

Open June – Sep. **Rooms** 1 with bath and 2 suites (2/4 pers.) with bath and WC. **Price** 800F (1/2 pers.) +200F (extra pers.) **Meals** breakfast 40F, evening meals on request 250F. **Restaurants** nearby. **Facilities** lounge, fishing, loose boxes. **Pets** small dogs allowed on request. **Nearby** 27-hole golf, Bayeux Tapestry, marshland park. **Spoken** English, Spanish.

Chiefly built in the 14th and 15th centuries, this château has a moat with flowery banks. The welcome is refined and relaxed. The bedrooms are really suites: large, quiet, very comfortable, each with a style of its own, from the authentic 15th century (reached by an unusual wooden spiral staircase), to the splendours of the 18th century (the one we preferred). Breakfast is served in a magnificent dining room. Several coastal or marshland walks (starting from the château).

How to get there (Map 7): *20km west of Bayeux via N13 towards Mosles, signposted 'Monument historique'.*

239
Ferme de l'Abbaye

Ecrammeville
14710 Trévières
(Calvados)
Tel. 31 22 52 32
M. and Mme Louis Fauvel

Open all year. **Rooms** 1 suite (4 pers.) with bath and WC, and 1 suite (3 pers.) with shower and WC. **Price** 140F (1 pers.), 180F (2 pers.), 250F (3 pers.), 320F (4 pers.) **Meals** breakfast incl., evening meals at communal table 75F (wine incl.) **Facilities** telephone. **Pets** dogs not allowed. **Nearby** swimming pool, tennis, 27-hole golf, seaside, Normandy landing beaches, Bayeux.

This large farm is in a pretty village and has well-kept grounds. It offers two suites ideal for families. One is in the farmhouse and is prettily arranged with antique furniture; the other occupies a little house of its own and is more soberly decorated. Pleasant bathrooms. The sitting room, where breakfast is served, is a bit on the small side.

How to get there (Map 7): 19km west of Bayeux via N13, leave the dual carriageway at the signs to Ecrammeville on the left, then take D30 on the right.

240
Manoir de L'Hormette

Aignerville
14710 Trévières
(Calvados)
Tel. 31 22 51 79
Fax 31 22 75 99
M. and Mme Yves Corpet

Open 15 March - 31 Dec. **Bedrooms** 3 with bath or shower and WC, 1 studio (2 pers.) with kitchen, shower and WC, and 2 suites (4/5 pers.) of 2 bedrooms with kitchen, bath or shower and WC; TV and small sitting room in each bedroom. **Price** 450-500F (2 pers.), studio 550-600F (2 pers.), suite 800-1000F (4 pers.) **Meals** breakfast 50F, evening meals at communal table 250F (wine incl.) **Facilities** telephone. **Credit cards** Visa, Amex. **Pets** small dogs allowed on request. **Nearby** golf, riding. **Spoken** English, Italian.

In an undulating setting, this beautiful manor is decorated with studied elegance and has a high standard of comfort. Evening meals with M. and Mme Corpet are equally good. Breakfasts are served on silverware, with home-made jams, honey, boiled eggs, fruit and three different sorts of bread.

How to get there (Map 7): 18km west of Bayeux via N13 (dual carriageway) exit Aignerville. Telephone for directions.

241
Chez Régine Bultey

Les Coutances
27210 Beuzeville
(Eure)
Tel. 32 57 75 54
Mme Régine Bultey

Open all year. **Rooms** 2 with bath, 1 with shower, shared WCs. **Price** 160F (1 pers.), 190F (2 pers.) +50F (extra pers.) **Meals** breakfast incl., no evening meals. **Pets** dogs not allowed. **Nearby** Honfleur, le Bec Hellouin, the Vernier marshland. **Spoken** a little English.

This house is surrounded by a delightful garden with a large rose bush which blushes crimson every summer. The inside is also flower-filled, and decorated with good taste and care. The bedrooms are quiet, comfortable, and have a lovely view over the countryside and the little Normandy houses nearby. Friendly atmosphere, young and very cheerful.

How to get there *(Map 8): 1km from Beuzeville in the St-Pierre-du-Val direction; sign in the Place de la République in Beuzeville.*

242
Le Vieux Pressoir

Le Clos Potier
Conteville
27210 Beuzeville
(Eure)
Tel. 32 57 60 79
Mme Anfray

Open all year. **Rooms** 3 with bath or shower and WC, and 1 suite (4 pers.) with shower and WC. **Price** 220F (2 pers.) +100F (extra pers.), suite 400F (4 pers.) **Meals** breakfast incl., evening meals at communal table, on reservation 120F (cider incl.) **Facilities** lounge, visit to the 17th century cider press, bicycle hire. **Pets** small dogs allowed on request. **Nearby** swimming pool, tennis, golf, seaside (12km), Honfleur, abbeys. **Spoken** English.

This farm is as alive as the Normandy countryside around it. In the small lounge, the dining room and bedrooms there are a multitude of charming things: dried flowers, pretty lace, thick quilts on the beds, decorated basins. Madame Anfray's kindness creates a cosy and serene atmosphere.

How to get there *(Map 8): 12km east of Honfleur via D180 towards Pont-Audemer, then left on D312 at Fiquefleur to Conteville; signposted.*

243
Les Ombelles

4, rue du Gué
27720 Dangu
(Eure)
Tel. 32 55 04 95
Fax 32 55 59 87
Mme de Saint-Père

Open 1 March – 15 Dec. **Children** under 3 not accepted. **Rooms** 2 with shower or bath and WC.
Price 260F (2 pers.) + 80F (extra pers.) **Meals** Breakfast incl., half board 230F per pers. in
double room (wine incl.), 2 days min., evening meals at communal table (except Saturday) 130F
(wine incl.) **Facilities** lounge. **Pets** dogs not allowed. **Nearby** golf, Giverny, pays de Bray. **Spoken**
English.

Situated in the village beside the road, this simple house has a sheltered
terrace and a garden bordered by a river. Refined decor. Warm welcome.
The bedroom on the road side is small but charming, with its bed in a recess,
and thanks to double glazing there is no traffic noise. The other bedroom
is really lovely and overlooks the garden.

How to get there *(Map 7): 8km west of Gisors on D181.*

244
Château du Landin

Le Landin
27350 Routot
(Eure)
Tel. 32 42 15 09
M. Patrice Favreau

Open Easter – end Dec. **Rooms** 6 with bath and WC. **Price** 450F (2 pers.) **Meals** breakfast 40F,
evening meals on reservation (separate tables) 150-250F (wine incl.) **Facilities** lounge, loose
boxes for horses. **Pets** dogs allowed on request. **Nearby** golf, stud farms, abbeys. **Spoken** English.

This red brick château lies at the end of a large park planted with splendid
trees. Crossing the pillared entrance hall you see, through the windows
on the other side, a loop of the Seine. All the comfortable bedrooms and
their big bathrooms (except one) share this view. Good overall decoration,
but the bedroom in the rotunda deserves a special mention. Breakfast on
the terrace in fine weather.

How to get there *(Map 8): 4km north of Bourg-Achard on D313; signposted.*

245
Château du Hanoy

Le Hanoy
27250 Rugles
(Eure)
Tel. 32 24 70 50
M. and Mme Delaplace

Open 14 Feb. – 2 Jan. **Rooms** 5 with bath and WC, 1 with shower and shared WC. **Price** 200F (1 pers.), 300-350F (2 pers.) +130F (extra pers.) **Meals** breakfast incl., half board 600F for 2 pers. in double room, full board 800F for 2 pers. in double room. Reduced weekly terms. Lunch and evening meals (not Monday or Tuesday) 200F. **Facilities** lounge. **Credit cards** Visa, Amex, Diners. **Pets** dogs allowed on a lead. **Nearby** 18-hole golf (20km), fishing, equestrian centre, l'Aigle market.

This small, typically Norman 19th-century château is sheltered from the road by its flower-filled park. The bedrooms are light, comfortable, mostly big, and are furnished with antiques. Some even have a balcony. Elegant furniture decorates the lounge and dining-rooms (there is also a small restaurant). They open on to the garden and meals can be taken outside. Friendly and attentive welcome.

How to get there (Map 8): *7km south west of Rugles in the l'Aigle direction.*

246
La Michaumière

72, rue des Canadiens
27370 Tourville-la-Campagne
(Eure)
Tel. 32 35 31 28
Mme Paris

Open all year. **Rooms** 2 with bath or shower and WC, 1 with bath and 2 without bath sharing WC. Room cleaning on request. **Price** 170F (1 pers.), 200F (2 pers.) **Meals** breakfast incl., no evening meals. **Restaurants** nearby. **Facilities** lounge, bicycle hire. **Pets** dogs allowed on request. **Nearby** golf, Harcourt, Giverny. **Spoken** English.

In spite of its proximity to other houses, this thatched house is very quiet. It has three comfortable bedrooms overlooking the garden. In winter breakfast is served beside the fire in a room which contains some slightly jarring ornaments; in summer in a small and light dining room (yoghurts, *brioches*, and home-made jams).

How to get there (Map 8): *33km south of Rouen via N138. At Elbeuf, D840 towards Le Neubourg and D26; signposted.*

247
Manoir d'Arville

Sainte-Geneviève
50760 Barfleur
(Manche)
Tel. 33 54 32 51
Mme Jean Le Bunetel

Open 15 April – All Saints. **Rooms** 4 with bath and WC. **Price** 480F (2 pers.) +150F (extra pers.) **Meals** breakfast incl., no evening meals. **Restaurant** in the Hôtel Moderne in Barfleur. **Facilities** lounge, 16th-century cider press. **Pets** dogs allowed on request. **Nearby** golf courses, tennis, riding, seaside, Barfleur, Tatihou island, Valogne, cap de la Hague, Normandy landing beaches. **Spoken** English.

This charming 16th- and 17th-century manor is in an attractive landscape of market gardens. Each bedroom reflects Mme Le Bunetel's love of beautiful fabrics, silks, ornaments and antique furniture. They are superb and very comfortable. The lounge is very well furnished and has 18th-century panelling. Very good breakfast served in the lounge or outside in summer. A very kind welcome and a truly charming place.

How to get there (Map 7): 2km from Barfleur via D901 towards Cherbourg, then 1st left on D10 towards Ste-Geneviève; signposted.

248
Manoir de Caillemont

Sainte-Georges-de-la-Rivière
50270 Barneville-Carteret
(Manche)
Tel. 33 53 81 16
Mme Eliane Coupechoux

Open May – Oct. (on request out of season). **Rooms** 1 studio (2 pers.) with kitchenette, shower and WC, and 1 suite (2/4 pers.) with shower and WC. **Price** studio 360F, suite 400F (1 pers.), 460F (2 pers.) +100F (extra pers.) **Meals** breakfast incl, no evening meals. **Restaurant** La Marine in Carteret (5km). **Facilities** swimming pool, bicycles. **Pets** dogs allowed on request. **Nearby** golf, Mont-St-Michel, Channel Islands. **Spoken** English.

This old Norman manor has a studio and a suite both consisting of a bedroom and a sitting room which are very comfortable, quiet and well kept. The studio is decorated in country style, the suite is more classic, with dark Louis XV panelling. Breakfast is served in the dining room. For good weather there is a heated swimming pool.

How to get there (Map 6): 35km south of Cherbourg via D904. At Barneville-Carteret head for Coutances. Phone for directions.

249
Le Bel Enault

Sainte-Côme-du-Mont
50500 Carentan
(Manche)
Tel. 33 42 43 27
M. and Mme Gérard Grandin

Open all year. **Rooms** 5 with bath and WC. **Price** 220F (1 pers.), 250F (2 pers.) +60F (extra pers.) **Meals** breakfast 30F, no evening meals. **Facilities** lounge, tennis, lakes, boating. **Pets** dogs not allowed. **Nearby** marshes, footpaths, Normandy landing beaches, museums. **Spoken** English.

Behind this small château, rebuilt in the 19th century, there is an extraordinary, exotic garden with all sorts of strange plants growing around ponds, grottoes and rock gardens... The interior is plainer, but the bedrooms are very well kept, quiet, and prettily arranged. Breakfast is served beside a large fireplace or in the bedrooms.

How to get there *(Map 7): 4km north of Carentan via N13 towards Cherbourg, then D913 towards Ste-Marie-Du-Mont for 1km; signposted.*

250
Château de Coigny

50250 Coigny
(Manche)
Tel 33 42 10 79
Mme Ionckheere

Open 15 April – 15 Nov. (on request out of season). **Rooms** 2 with bath and WC (of which 1 has an extra bed). **Price** 400F (1 pers.), 450F (2 pers.) +100F (extra pers.) **Meals** breakfast 35F, evening meals on reservation 180F (wine not incl.) **Facilities** lounge. **Pets** dogs not allowed. **Nearby** riding, golf, museums, Mont-St-Michel, Carentan.

Built by the ancestor of one of Louis XV's Marshals, Coigny is a beautiful 16th-century château. Inside, the antique furniture has been replaced by reproductions but the ensemble is a success. The bedrooms are comfortable, quiet and have a pretty view onto the courtyard or the moat. Breakfast and dinner are served in a large room with a fabulous Renaissance fireplace, in front of which there is a sitting area.

How to get there *(Map 7): 11km west of Carentan via D903 towards Barneville, then D223; after the sign for 'Coigny' take the first entrance on the left.*

251
Chez Victor et Jeanine Vaugrente

Le Bourg
Bourg de Poilley
50220 Ducey (Manche)
Tel. 33 48 44 41
Victor and Jeanine Vaugrente

Open all year. **Rooms** 1 with bath and WC, 2 (1 with shower) sharing bathroom and WC. **Price** 180-200F (2 pers.) +50F (extra pers.) **Meals** breakfast 16F, no evening meals. **Restaurants** at 4km or Auberge de la Sélune (800m). **Facilities** lounge. **Pets** dogs allowed on request. **Nearby** golf (30km), tennis, canoeing, seaside, Mont-St-Michel, Château de Fougères. **Spoken** English, German.

A good address near Mont-St-Michel: a small village house with a delightful garden. The interior is quiet, light, very comfortable, and pleasantly decorated. On the first floor the two superb bedrooms (very light, with antique furniture and bouquets of dried flowers) share an equally pleasant bathroom. The same comfort on the second floor (with private bathroom). Excellent breakfast, warm welcome and very reasonable prices.

How to get there *(Map 7): 10km south east of Avranches; on the way out of Ducey N176 towards Avranches for 1km, then left towards Poilley.*

252
Château de la Roque

50180 Hébécrevon
(Manche)
Tel. 33 57 33 20
Fax 33 57 51 20
Mireille and Raymond Delisle

Open all year. **Rooms** 10 with bath or shower and WC, 1 suite with shower (4 pers.) **Price** 260F (2 pers.), suite 410F (3 pers.) **Meals** breakfast 25F, half board 225F per pers. in double room, evening meals at communal table 95F (wine incl.) **Facilities** lounge, tennis, bicycle hire. **Credit cards** Visa. **Pets** dogs allowed on request. **Nearby** riding, fishing, golf, Bayeux, Mont-St-Michel. **Spoken** English, German.

This elegant 18th-century château encloses a lovely central garden. The best bedrooms are in the tower but all are comfortable and equipped with telephone and TV. The ground floor lounge and dining room may be used by guests on request. It is so nearly professional that it could be a hotel but the warm welcome and the evening meals give the place personality.

How to get there *(Map 7): 6km north west of St-Lô via D972 towards Coutances. At St-Gilles take D77 towards Pont-Hébert for 3km, then right.*

253
Le Cottage de la Voisinière

Route de Sourdeval
50410 Percy
(Manche)
Tel. 33 61 18 47
Daniel and Maryclaude Duchemin

Open all year. **Rooms** 5 with shower and WC (1 with kitchenette). **Price** 170F (2 pers.), studio 220F +40F (extra pers.) **Meals** breakfast incl., no evening meals. **Restaurants** L'Auberge de la Baleine (10km) and Les Gourmets (1.5km). **Facilities** lounge. **Pets** dogs allowed (+20F). **Nearby** 9-hole golf (30km), tennis, sea (30km), Mont-St-Michel, Ambye abbey, Normandy landing beaches.

Two small, simple and welcoming houses. The bedrooms are well kept and decorated in a pleasantly countrified fashion. We recommend those in the separate wing ('Cyclamen' is very special) where there is also a large room reserved for guests with a cooking area. Breakfast is served in the dining room or outside in wonderful gardens whose blooms regularly win prizes at local flower shows.

How to get there *(Map 7): 30km north of Avranches via N175. At Percy, take the Sourdeval road, then signposted, 1.5km from Percy on the right.*

254
La Fière

Route de Pont-l'Abbé
50480 Saint-Mère-l'Eglise
(Manche)
Tel. 33 41 32 66
M. and Mme Albert Blanchet

Open all year. **Rooms** 1 with shower and shared WC, 2 sharing shower and WC. **Price** 120F (1 pers.), 135-160F (2 pers.) +45F (extra pers.) **Meals** breakfast incl., no evening meals. **Restaurants** and crêperie close by. **Facilities** river fishing, picnic area in the grounds. **Pets** dogs not allowed. **Nearby** golf, swimming pool, seaside, Normandy landing beaches, châteaux, manors, museums.

Monsieur and Mme Blanchet still farm their land and will greet you in a friendly fashion. Inside, the stone walls remain untouched. On the first floor only one bedroom has its own shower. The 1930 furnishings are comfortable and of good quality. A simple family stop.

How to get there *(Map 7): 13km north of Carentan via N13, then D15 towards Pont-l'Abbé; signposted.*

255
La Maurandière

50150 Sourdeval-la-Barre
(Manche)
Tel. 33 59 65 44
Mme Evelyne Dupart

Open all year. **Rooms** 1 with bath and WC, 3 with shower and WC (of which 1 is in a small building in the garden). **Price** 165F (1 pers.), 180F (2 pers.) **Meals** breakfast incl., no evening meals. **Restaurant** La Table de Paulinc (3km). **Facilities** lounge, fishing (with permit). **Pets** dogs allowed on request. **Nearby** riding, climbing, windsurfing, Mont-St-Michel, pottery museum, granite museum.

In rolling countryside, La Maurandière is a lovely house with a well-kept garden. You will find the same attention to detail in the successful decoration of the lounge, dining room and bedrooms. The most secluded bedroom is in a converted outbuilding in the garden. If the weather is fine breakfast is served outside on the terrace.

How to get there (Map 7): 16km south of Vire via D977 towards Mortain; signposted 3km after the village.

256
Le Prieuré Saint-Michel

61120 Crouttes
(Orne)
Tel. 33 39 15 15
Fax 33 36 15 16
M. and Mme Pierre Chahine

Closed Feb. **Rooms** 3 with shower and WC, 2 suites (2 pers.) with bath or shower and WC. **Price** 250-600F (2 pers.), suite 700F (2 pers.) +50F (extra pers.) **Meals** breakfast 50F, evening meals (from June) at communal or separate tables 200F (wine incl.) **Facilities** lounge, art centre, concerts and theatre (September). **Credit cards** Visa. **Pets** dogs not allowed. **Nearby** golf, Honfleur, Deauville, Bagnoles-de-l'Orne. **Spoken** English, German, Spanish.

Once part of Jumièges abbey, this priory is in very beautiful Norman countryside. It is quiet and you will feel quite independent. The half-timbered buildings house comfortable and tastefully decorated bedrooms and are set in landscaped grounds with fountains. In the summer the monumental old cider press is used as a lounge-dining room. Have a look at the chapel and the 12th-century barn.

How to get there (Map 8): 34km south of Lisieux via D579. In Vimoutiers take D916 towards Argentan; signposted 'Monuments historiques'.

257
Le Château

Place de l'église
76750 Bosc-Roger-sur-Buchy
(Seine-Maritime)
Tel. 35 34 29 70
M. and Mme Preterre Rieux

Open 1 March – 31 Jan. **Rooms** 4 with bath or shower and WC. **Price** 220F (1 pers.), 320F (2 pers.), 400F (3 pers.), 450F (4 pers.) **Meals** breakfast incl., no evening meals. **Restaurants** in Buchy (1km). **Facilities** lounges, loose boxes, bicycles. **Pets** dogs allowed on request. **Nearby** tennis, swimming pool, 18-hole golf, Mortemer abbey, park of Forges-les-Eaux. **Spoken** English.

Opposite the church in a tiny village, this small château reveals its soothing atmosphere as soon as you cross the threshold. The reception rooms are prettily decorated, comfortable and fresh. The bedrooms are very pleasant and colourful, with new cane or pale wood furniture, and overlook the grounds. The bathrooms are large. Lively and energetic welcome. Excellent breakfast.

How to get there (Map 8): 27km north east of Rouen via N28 towards Neufchâtel, right on D919 towards Buchy, then right towards Bosc-Roger.

258
Domaine de Champdieu

76590 Gonneville-sur-Scie
(Seine-Maritime)
Tel. 35 32 66 82
Messrs Buquet, Maudit and Vacheron

Open all year. **Children** under 14 not accepted. **Rooms** 3 with shower and WC. Poss. suite with bedroom and sitting room. **Price** 350F (1 pers.), 400F (2 pers.), suite 800F (2 pers.) +150F (extra pers.) **Meals** breakfast incl., evening meal at communal table (poss. separate table) 350F (wine incl.), champagne dinner 650F, game dinner 750F. **Facilities** lounge. **Pets** dogs not allowed. **Nearby** golf, tennis, beaches, château de Miromesnil, gardens of Princess Sturdza and Mme Mallet. **Spoken** English, Spanish.

This pretty house, deep in the countryside, has a magnificent interior; antique furniture, paintings and curios abound. Denis Buquet is an excellent host and his table settings are a work of art. He is also a wonderful cook, and dinner by candlelight in this very special house is a memory to treasure.

How to get there (Map 1): 14km south of Dieppe via N27. After Tôtes, right on D50, then D203; sign for 'Chambres d'hôtes'.

259
La Marette

76260 Melleville
(Seine-Maritime)
Tel. 35 50 81 65
M. and Mme Etienne Garçonnet

Open all year. **Rooms** 1 with bath and WC, 1 with basin and WC (poss. in a suite). Room cleaning once a week. **Price** 130-165F (1 pers.), 160-200F (2 pers.) +65F (extra pers.) **Meals** breakfast incl., no evening meals. **Restaurant** Le Moulin de Becquirel (9km). **Pets** dogs not allowed. **Nearby** swimming pool, tennis, river fishing, forest of Eu, seaside. **Spoken** English, German.

This red brick farmhouse on the edge of the forest is quiet and well kept. The bedrooms can be arranged into a suite for families. They are attractively old-fashioned, with their flowered wallpaper and turn-of-the-century furniture. We recommend the one with its own bathroom. Breakfast is served in a dining room at separate tables. Very kind welcome. A simple and charming place.

How to get there (Map 1): 12km south of Eu via D1314, then left on D78; signposted.

260
Le Clos-Cacheu

76730 Rainfreville
(Seine-Maritime)
Tel. 35 06 10 99
Mme Angela Stewart

Closed 1 Sep. – 15 Oct. and for Christmas and New Year's Day. **Rooms** 2 with bath or shower and WC, 1 studio (2/3 pers.) with shower and WC. Room cleaning guests' responsibility. **Price** 350F (2 pers.) **Meals** breakfast incl., evening meals at communal table 140F (wine not incl.) **Facilities** lounge. **Pets** dogs not allowed. **Nearby** golf, tennis, seaside, parc des Moutiers, abbeys along the Seine. **Spoken** English.

Before entering this delightful house, you should have a look around the well kept garden. Angela and Gilbert will greet you very warmly. The lounge and bedrooms have an elegant country decor. You can also sleep in the restored former bakery at the bottom of the garden. Excellent evening meals and guaranteed peace.

How to get there (Map 1): 23km south west of Dieppe via D925 towards Fécamp. At St-Denis-d'Aclon left on D152, then D2 through Brachy. After Brachy, right on D270.

261
Le Val de la Mer

76400 Senneville-sur-Fécamp
(Seine-Maritime)
Tel. 35 28 41 93
Mme Lethuillier

Closed August. **Rooms** 2 with bath and WC, 1 with basin and WC. **Price** 220F (1 pers.), 250F (2 pers.), 320F (3 pers.) **Meals** breakfast incl., no evening meals. **Restaurants** Le Maritime (3km), Le Relais des Dalles (7km). **Pets** dogs not allowed. **Nearby** 18-hole golf in Etretat (18km).

A pretty house on the edge of a village, a few hundred metres away from the sea and the chalk cliffs. You will be made very welcome and advised on the local tourist attractions. The bedrooms are quiet, comfortable and pretty. The one on the ground floor opens onto the garden. In the morning breakfast is served at a large table in the lounge-dining room.

How to get there *(Map 8): At Fécamp take D925 towards Dieppe; it's in the village close to the church.*

262
La Plauderie

1, rue du Verdelet
44680 Sainte-Pazanne
(Loire-Atlantique)
Tel. 40 02 45 08
Mme Mignen

Open 1 May – 30 Oct. **Rooms** 1 with bath and WC, 2 with shower and WC. Room cleaning every 2 days. **Price** 270-400F (2 pers.) **Meals** breakfast 35F, no evening meals. **Restaurant** Le Col Vert in Fresnay-en-Retz. **Facilities** lounge. **Pets** dogs allowed on request. **Nearby** tennis, seaside, golf, Breton marshes, Noirmoutier island. **Spoken** English.

Right beside the church, this beautiful house is hidden in a delightfully romantic garden. Madame Mignen's welcome is reason enough for us to recommend this place, but you will also find an attractive decor and plenty of comfort. Pleasant bedrooms, where you can make yourself a cup of coffee or tea during the day, and good bathrooms.

How to get there *(Map 14): 28km south west of Nantes via D751 towards Pornic. In Port St Père left on D758 towards Bourgneuf-en-Retz.*

263
Château de la Jaillière

La Chapelle-Saint-Sauveur
44370 Varades
(Loire-Atlantique)
Tel. 40 98 62 54
Comtesse d'Anthenaise

Open 15 May – 15 Oct. **Rooms** 4 and 1 suite (4 pers.) with bath and WC. **Price** 600F (2 pers.), suite 800F (4 pers.) **Meals** breakfast incl., evening meals at communal table 200F (wine incl.) **Facilities** lounge, swimming pool, tennis, fishing. **Pets** dogs not allowed. **Nearby** riding (30km), golf. **Spoken** English, German.

La Jaillière is an immense 19th-century house. Inside there are wooden floors, panelled walls and antique furniture, much of it older than the house. The bedrooms are beautiful and comfortable. Evening meals are served in a château-sized dining room, and Countess d'Anthenaise is a kind and energetic hostess.

How to get there *(Map 15): 30km west of Angers via N23, then D30 before Varades; on the way out of the village of La-Chapelle-Saint-Saveur head for St-Sigismond.*

264
Château des Briottières

49330 Champigné
(Maine-et-Loire)
Tel. 41 42 00 02
Fax 41 42 01 55
Hedwige and François de Valbray

Open all year (on request from 1 Jan. – 1 March). **Rooms** 9 with bath, WC and telephone, 2 with bath, telephone but WC upstairs. **Price** 650-900F (2 pers.) **Meals** breakfast 45F, half board 695F per pers. in double room. Evening meals (except Sunday) at communal table, on reservation 300F (everything incl.) **Facilities** lounge, heated swimming pool, loose boxes, fishing. **Credit cards** Visa. **Pets** dogs allowed on request (+50F). **Nearby** tennis, riding, golf, Solesme abbey, Anjou. **Spoken** English.

The Château des Briottières is magnificent, and the Valbrays' welcome is spontaneous. All the superb reception rooms are available to guests. The generously furnished bedrooms are practically apartments and the bathrooms look down on the park. Evening meals in the large dining room are cleverly lit so that as the evening draws on the lights dim.

How to get there (Map 15): 25km north of Angers towards Laval. At Montreuil-Juigné, right on D768 through Feneu, then Champigné.

265
Beauregard

22, rue Beauregard
Cunault
49350 Chênehutte-les-Tuffeaux
(Maine-et-Loire)
Tel. 41 67 92 93
M. and Mme Tonnelier

Open Easter – All Saints. **Rooms** 1 suite (4 pers.) 2 bedrooms with bath and WC. **Price** 330F (2 pers.), 530F (4 pers.) +100F (extra pers.) **Meals** breakfast incl., no evening meals. **Restaurants** La Toque Blanche, Le Val de Loire, Les Rosiers (5km). **Facilities** fishing. **Pets** small dogs allowed on request. **Nearby** equestrian centre, golf, walks, churches of Trèves-Cunault, Le Thoureil, Montreuil-Bellay, Saumur. **Spoken** English.

You leave Saumur on a small road which follows the line of the river and grows steadily prettier until it reaches the manor, which is situated on a slight rise and has a delightful view. The well decorated bedrooms are very big, pretty, and overlook the Loire. Breakfast is served in the dining room, which has some fine furniture. A pity the lounge is not open to guests.

How to get there (Map 15): 10km north west of Saumur on D751 towards Gennes; it's before the village, beside the Loire.

266
Le Domaine de Mestré
49590 Fontevraud-l'Abbaye
(Maine-et-Loire)
Tel. 41 51 72 32
M. and Mme Dominique Dauge

Open all year. **Rooms** 11 and 1 suite (3 pers.) with bath and WC. **Price** 280F (2 pers.) +65F (extra pers.) **Meals** breakfast 35F, half board 290F per pers. in double room (1 week min.) Lunch and evening meals on reservation (separate tables) 130F (wine not incl.) **Facilities** lounge. **Pets** dogs allowed. **Nearby** tennis, riding, golf, Loire châteaux. **Spoken** English, German.

This beautiful house was once the farm of the monks of Fontevrau abbey. The atmosphere is very tranquil, the bedrooms comfortable, large and done in country style. Excellent dinners are served in a lovely dining room at prettily-laid separate tables. Very kind family welcome and a very good address.

How to get there *(Maps 15 and 16): 12km south east of Saumur via D947 towards Chinon, then head for Fontevraud-l'Abbaye; it's between Montsoreau and Fontevraud.*

267
La Croix d'Etain
2, rue de l'Ecluse
49220 Grez-Neuville
(Maine-et-Loire)
Tel. 41 95 68 49
M. and Mme Bahuaud

Open all year. **Rooms** 4 with bath and WC. **Price** 320-350F (2 pers.) **Meals** breakfast incl., evening meals 100F (wine not incl.) **Restaurants** Le Cheval Bleu and La Batelière. **Facilities** lounge. **Nearby** 18-hole golf, tennis, riding, boat hire, châteaux, vineyards. **Spoken** English.

This distinctive house in old Grez–Neuville has been entirely restored to a very high standard of comfort. Modern in style, the bedrooms are spacious and light, thanks to their corner position, and are tastefully and simply furnished. In good weather you can enjoy the large grounds behind the house or stroll along the banks of the Mayenne, which is only 50m away.

How to get there *(Map 15): 3km south east of Lion d'Angers via N162 and D291. In Grez-Neuville, D291, left on bridge between church and La Mayenne.*

268
Château du Plessis

49220 La Jaille-Yvon
(Maine-et-Loire)
Tel. 41 95 12 75
Fax 41 95 14 41
Paul and Simone Benoist

Open 1 March – 31 Oct. **Rooms** 8 (2 with balcony) with bath and WC. **Price** 700F (2 pers.) **Meals** breakfast incl., half board 610F per pers. in double room. Evening meals (except Sunday) at communal table, on reservation 260F (everything incl.) **Facilities** lounge, telephone, tennis, loose boxes, hot air ballooning. **Credit cards** Visa, Amex, Diners. **Pets** dogs allowed on request. **Spoken** English, Spanish.

Madame Benoist loves flowers and her arrangements follow the different seasons of the year. Here, hospitality, comfort and perfection are your hosts' guiding lights. The bedrooms are very well decorated and the bathrooms irreproachable. Generous evening meals are served in a dining room with 1930s frescos. Everything is aimed at making your visit a success.

How to get there (Map 15): 11km north of Lion-d'Angers via N162. At Fleur-de-Lys take D189; sign at the crossroads.

269
Préfontaine

49430 Lézigné
(Maine-et-Loire)
Tel. 41 76 97 71
Mme O'Neill

Closed Jan. and Feb. **Rooms** 3 and 2 suites (4 pers.) with bath and WC. **Price** 250F (1 pers.), 300-400F (2 pers.), suite 450F (4 pers.) **Meals** breakfast incl., evening meals at communal table 100F (wine incl.) **Facilities** lounge, fishing in the lake. **Pets** dogs allowed. **Nearby** golf, swimming pool, tennis, bathing in the Loir. **Spoken** English.

Préfontaine is a lovely house set in a large well-kept park with many trees. The interior is harmoniously decorated and the furnishings well chosen. The bedrooms are pleasant, bright, and quiet. The road can only be heard outside the house, and then only on holiday weekends. Good evening meals, warm welcome, and an excellent halt.

How to get there (Map 15): 30km north east of Angers on N23 towards Durtal; signposted.

270
Château du Goupillon

49680 Neuillé
(Maine-et-Loire)
Tel. 41 52 51 89
Monique Calot

Open 15 Feb. – 15 Dec. **Rooms** 1 with bath and WC, 1 with shower and WC, and 1 suite (5 pers.) with bath and WC. **Price** 270-380F (2 pers.) +60F (extra pers.), suite 660F (5 pers.) **Meals** breakfast incl., no evening meals. **Restaurants** many in Saumur. **Facilities** lounge. **Pets** dogs allowed on request. **Nearby** swimming pool, tennis, Loire châteaux.

Close to Saumur and surrounded by greenery, this château seems set apart from the modern world. The decor is simple and good: wood, bouquets of dried flowers, etc. The bedrooms are very large, with pleasant bathrooms. The atmosphere is serene and the welcome a model of kindness.

How to get there *(Map 15): 9km north of Saumur in the Longué direction. At the La Ronde roundabout take D767 towards Vernantes for 2km, then left on D129 towards Neuillé. 1km before Neuillé take the Fontaine Suzon road, then signed.*

271
La Croix de la Voulte

Route de Boumois
Sainte-Lambert-des-Levées
49400 Saumur
(Maine-et-Loire)
Tel. 41 38 46 66
M. and Mme Jean-Pierre Minder

Open 15 April – 15 Oct. **Rooms** 4 with bath or shower and WC. **Price** 320-390F (2 pers.) **Meals** breakfast 30F, no evening meals. **Restaurants** Les Chandelles, La Croquière in Saumur (5km) and La Toque Blanche (9km). **Facilities** lounge, swimming pool. **Pets** dogs allowed on request. **Nearby** golf, Saumur, Fontevraud, Langeais, Boumois, Montreuil-Bellay. **Spoken** English, German.

The bedrooms at La Croix de la Voulte are named after the provinces of France. Situated in a wing of the house, they are well decorated and well kept and overlook a small garden. Helga Minder is very friendly. She prepares breakfast, which is served in the dining room. A pleasant place to stay but the lack of a lounge is a pity, especially if the weather is bad.

How to get there *(Map 15): 4km north of Saumur via D952, then D229; signposted after the railway.*

272
Château de la Mazure

53260 Forcé
(Mayenne)
Tel. 43 53 55 63
Fax 43 67 03 49
M. and Mme Le Marié

Open April – June and Sept. – Oct. **Rooms** 3 with bath and WC, 1 with shower and WC (poss. suite). **Price** 620-720F (2 pers.) +120F (extra bed), suite 800F (3 pers.) **Meals** breakfast incl., evening meals at communal table, on reservation 250F (wine incl.) **Credit cards** Visa. **Facilities** language courses for children and adults. **Pets** dogs allowed on request. **Nearby** tennis (4km), riding, golf (18 holes), visit to private châteaux. **Spoken** English, Spanish.

The approach to this large house, flanked by rhododendrons, is through an oak forest. Inside there is an exceptional collection of tapestries in an excellent state of preservation. The bedrooms, lounges and dining rooms are all magnificently decorated and have beautiful views. Natural and lively welcome, and excellent food.

How to get there (Map 15): 9km south east of Laval via D21 towards Tours and La Flèche. At Forcé, right on D565 towards Entrammes for 1km.

273
Villeprouvé

53170 Ruillé-Froid-Fonds
(Mayenne)
Tel. 43 07 71 62
M. and Mme Davenel

Open all year. **Rooms** 1 with bath and WC, 4 with shower and WC. **Price** 140F (1 pers.), 180F (2 pers.) **Meals** breakfast incl., half board 150F per pers. in double room, evening meals at communal table 60F (wine not incl.) **Facilities** lounge, fishing. **Pets** dogs allowed on request. **Nearby** monasteries of Solesmes, La Trappe. **Spoken** English.

This farmhouse is as lovely as the natural surroundings in which it stands. The bedrooms are comfortable and large, with rustic furniture and pretty bathrooms. Home grown farm produce is used in the excellent evening meals, cheerfully served by Mme Davenel, and the 'grog flambé au calvados' is spectacular. A very 'country' atmosphere.

How to get there (Map 15): 25km south of Laval via N162 to Villiers-Charlemagne, then D109; signposted in the village.

274
Le Logis du Ray

53290 Saint-Denis-d'Anjou
(Mayenne)
Tel. 43 70 64 10
Martine and Jacques Lefebvre

Open all year. **Rooms** 1 with bath and WC, 2 with shower and WC. **Price** 300-350F (2 pers.) +40F (extra pers.) **Meals** breakfast incl., gastronomic picnic lunch 90F. **Restaurants** Auberge du Roi René and La Calèche (800m). **Facilities** lounge, riding, bicycles. **Credit cards** Visa, Amex. **Pets** dogs allowed on request. **Nearby** golf, tennis, swimming pool (10km), fishing, Solesmes abbey, châteaux, river trips, medieval villages. **Spoken** English.

Don't be surprised if you find this old restored farmhouse full of good country furniture: M. Lefebvre is a cabinet maker and antique dealer. The bedrooms are very comfortable and have been decorated with a sure touch, especially the one with the canopied bed. In summer M. Lefebvre will invite you for a carriage ride. Sadly there is no lounge for guests yet.

How to get there *(Map 15): 9km south east of Sablé-sur-Sarthe via D27 towards Champigné; 500m after Champigné turn right; signposted.*

275
Le Chêne Vert

Chammes
53270 Sainte-Suzanne
Tel. 43 01 41 12
Fax 43 01 47 18
M. and Mme Morize

Open all year. **Rooms** 6 with shower and WC. Room cleaning every 3 days. **Price** 190F (2 pers.) **Meals** breakfast for two incl., half board 150F per pers. in double room (out of season, 3 days min.), evening meals at communal table 70F (wine not incl.) **Facilities** library, walks. **Pets** dogs allowed on request. **Nearby** golf, Château de Mézanger, Solesmes abbey, medieval village of Ste-Suzanne. **Spoken** English.

Close to the medieval village of Sainte-Suzanne, this former farmhouse has been completely renovated and offers three pretty guestrooms. Colourful, fresh fabrics, good furniture and comfortable shower rooms make them very pleasant. Breakfast and evening meals in a large country-style room with a bar-kitchenette area. Young and friendly welcome.

How to get there *(Map 7): 45km west of Le Mans via A81 towards Laval, exit Vaiges. In Vaiges, left on D125 towards Ste-Suzanne until Chammes.*

276
Château le Grand-Perray

72500 La Bruère
(Sarthe)
Tel. 43 46 72 65
M. and Mme Thibault

Open all year. **Rooms** 6 with bath and WC, 2 with shower and WC. **Price** 320-450F (2 pers.) **Meals** breakfast 30F, evening meals at communal table, price to be agreed. **Facilities** lounge, fishing, golf practice. **Pets** dogs allowed on request. **Nearby** tennis, swimming pool, Loir valley, visit to wine cellars, Château du Lude (son et lumière June – Sept.) **Spoken** English.

This château is part medieval and lies deep in the forest. Most of the lovely bedrooms are very large and all have antique furniture and pretty ornaments and fabrics. Those with a taste for the Middle Ages should ask for the bedroom in the tower. Pleasant lounge, large dining room for breakfast and evening meals. Very kind welcome.

How to get there (Map 16): 40km south of Le Mans via N138 towards Tours, then right on D11 towards La Bruère-sur-Loir until Croix de Bonlieu (5km after Château du Loir); signs on D11.

277
Garencière

72610 Champfleur
(Sarthe)
Tel. 33 31 75 84
Denis and Christine Langlais

Open all year. **Rooms** 5 with bath or shower and WC. **Price** 150F (1 pers.), 220F (2 pers.) **Meals** breakfast incl., half board 200F per pers. in double room. Lunch and evening meal at communal table 90F (wine incl.) **Facilities** lounge, telephone, mountain biking. **Credit cards** Visa. **Pets** dogs allowed on request. **Nearby** swimming pool, riding, fishing, St-Ceneri (listed village). **Spoken** English.

You will be very well looked after in this hillside farmhouse. The bedrooms are pleasant: one has a view of the setting sun over the lovely landscape, another is large with windows at floor level; a third, more rustic, occupies a building to itself. Breakfast and dinner are served in a bright and recently refurbished dining room. Good cooking, using home grown farm produce.

How to get there (Map 8): 5km south east of Alençon via N138 towards Le Mans, then left on D55 towards Champfleur.

278
Manoir du Ronceray

72220 Marigné-Laillé
(Sarthe)
Tel. 43 42 12 05
M. and Mme Madamet

Open 15 April – 15 Nov. **Rooms** 3 with bath, 1 with shower, sharing WC. **Price** 350-380F (2 pers.) **Meals** breakfast incl., no evening meals. **Restaurants** in Jupilles (4km). **Facilities** lounge, loose boxes, fishing. **Pets** dogs not allowed. **Nearby** tennis, golf. **Spoken** English.

Ronceray is the perfect model of a manor house: small, very old, full of character. The vaulted entrance hall is hung with trophies of hunting and ancient battles. The bedrooms are less austere, comfortable and light, with lovely fabrics, antique furniture, beds in alcoves, and round bathrooms in the towers. Breakfast is served in a panelled room. Natural and cheerful hospitality.

How to get there (Map 16): 30km south of Le Mans via N138 to Ecommoy, then Marigné-Laillé and D96 for 2km towards Pruillé-L'Eguillé.

279
Château de Saint-Paterne

72610 Saint-Paterne
(Sarthe)
Tel. 33 27 54 71
Fax 33 29 16 71
Charles-Henry de Valbray

Open 1 March – 15 Dec. (on request out of season). **Rooms** 2 bedrooms and 3 suites (3 pers.) with bath or shower and WC. **Price** 500F (2 pers.), suite 700F (2 pers.) **Meals** breakfast 40F, evening meals at communal table, on reservation 250F (wine incl.) **Facilities** lounge, tennis, loose boxes. **Credit cards** Visa, Amex. **Pets** small dogs allowed on request. **Nearby** swimming pool, riding, Mont-St-Michel. **Spoken** English.

The village of St-Paterne is on the edge of Alençon, but the château is protected by the walls which enclose its grounds. With youthful enthusiasm, the owner has just finished its complete restoration and will welcome you warmly. The lounges and the huge, very comfortable bedrooms are decorated with beautiful antiques and lovely fabrics. Delightful bathrooms. All this and dinner by candlelight make the château a fairytale place.

How to get there (Map 8): 2km south west of Alençon on D311 towards Mamers-Chartres; it's in the middle of St-Paterne.

280
Le Domaine du Grand Gruet

Route de Challes
72440 Volnay
(Sarthe)
Tel. 43 35 68 65/43 89 87 27
Mme Eveno-Sournia

Open 15 March – 15 Nov. (in winter on request). **Rooms** 3 rooms and 2 suites with bath or shower and WC, 2 studios with kitchenette, shower and WC (for longer stays). Room cleaning on request. **Price** 300-550F (2 pers.) +70F (extra pers.) **Meals** breakfast incl., brunch 35F, no evening meals (but ask). **Restaurant** in the village. **Facilities** lounges. **Pets** dogs not allowed. **Nearby** equestrian centre, lakes, tennis, golf, Loir valley. **Spoken** German.

Anne Sournia is a painter and has restored this beautiful house with an expert eye. Everything has been made by her artist friends, from the ashtrays to the enamelled basins. The overall impression is bright, modern and comfortable. No two bedrooms are the same and each has a charm of its own. A lovely, peaceful place where you will be warmly welcomed.

How to get there (Map 16): Chartres autoroute, exit Ferté-Bernard in the Le Mans direction. At Connerré, Grand Lucé direction for 15km. At Volnay take the Challes road. After the village, it's 500m on the left.

281
Manoir de Ponsay

Saint-Mars-des-Prés
85110 Chantonay
(Vendée)
Tel. 51 46 96 71
Fax 51 94 56 12
M. and Mme de Ponsay

Open 1 April – 30 Nov. (on request in winter). **Rooms** 6 with bath and WC, 2 with shower and WC. **Price** 340-520F (2 pers.), suite 470F (2 pers.), 570F (3 pers.) **Meals** breakfast (brunch) 35F. Evening meals at communal or separate table 170F (wine incl.) **Facilities** lounge, telephone. **Nearby** swimming pool, tennis, seaside, golf, île d'Yeu, Poitou marshes. **Spoken** English, German.

Far out in the beautiful rolling countryside, amid pastures where horses and cows graze, you will find this perfect 17th-century manor. Some of the bedrooms are simple, others luxurious, but all are comfortable and have wonderful bathrooms. Excellent breakfasts served in a beautiful dining room. Natural and refined welcome.

How to get there (Map 15): 35km east of La Roche-sur-Yon via D948 and D949 bis to Chantonnay and St-Mars-des-Prés; signposted.

282
Logis de Chalusseau

111, rue de Chalusseau
85200 Doix
(Vendée)
Tel. 51 51 81 12
M. and Mme Gérard Baudry

Open 1 April – 15 Nov. (2 nights min.) **Rooms** 1 with bath and WC, 1 with shower and WC. Room cleaning every three days. **Price** 150F (1 pers.), 200F (2 pers.) +50F (extra pers.) **Meals** breakfast incl., no evening meals. **Facilities** lounge. **Pets** dogs not allowed. **Nearby** swimming pool, tennis, seaside (40km), riding, golf, Poitou marshes, forest of Mervent, Romanesque art, Maillezais abbey, Nieul-sur-L'Autize cloisters.

The vast reception rooms in this lovely 17th-century Vendée house still have their exposed beams and stone fireplaces. The bedrooms are charming large, light, and have regional furniture. Generous breakfasts can be served in the pleasant garden. A precious address in a wonderful position where you will be made exceptionally welcome.

How to get there (Map 15): 9km south of Fontenay-le-Comte via D938 towards La Rochelle, then left on D20 after 4km towards Doix.

283
Chez Mme Bonnet

69, rue de l'Abbaye
85420 Maillezais
(Vendée)
Tel. 51 87 23 00
Mme Liliane Bonnet

Open all year (2 nights min.) **Rooms** 4 with shower and WC. Price 280-300F (2 pers.) **Meals** breakfast incl., no evening meals. **Restaurants** L'Auberge Maraîchère in Mazeau and farmhouse-auberge in St-Michel-de-Cloucq. **Facilities** lounge, children's swimming pool, tennis, fishing, boating trips. **Pets** dogs not allowed. **Nearby** riding, forest of Mervent-Vouvant, Maillezais and Nieul abbeys, Coulon, La Rochelle, île de Ré. **Spoken** English, Spanish.

This elegant Vendée house is hidden in a splendid park bordered by a canal where you will find a boat waiting to take you through the marshes... The comfortable bedrooms are charming, with old furniture and lovely bathrooms. There is also a pretty dining room where excellent breakfasts are served (outside in summer) and a large lounge. Very kind welcome.

How to get there (Map 15): 28km north west of Niort via N148 towards Fontenay-le-Comte, then left on D15 to Maillezais.

284
Le Château

85450 Moreilles
(Vendée)
Tel. 51 56 17 56
Fax 51 56 30 30
Mme Danièle Renard

Open all year (on request Oct. – March). **Rooms** 6 with bath and 2 with shower, WC and telephone. **Price** 350F (1 pers.), 400-450F (2 pers.) **Meals** breakfast 45F, half board 400-450F per pers. in double room, evening meals (separate tables) 175-225F (wine not incl.) **Facilities** swimming pool. **Pets** dogs allowed on request. **Nearby** tennis, riding, fishing, 18-hole golf (25km), La Rochelle, Poitou marshes. **Spoken** English.

In this large welcoming house the bed of 'la Belle Otero', delightfully retro, awaits guests who have taken the trouble to book it in advance. The bedrooms are cosy, but the reception rooms are a bit 'hotel' in style. In the dining-room, breakfast and dinner are served under the benevolent eye of Mme Renard. Pretty garden, a bit of traffic noise on busy days.

How to get there (Map 15): 35km north of La Rochelle via the Nantes road N137; it's on N137 at the entrance to the village on the right.

285
Le Castel du Verger

85670 Saint-Christophe-du-Ligneron
(Vendée)
Tel. 51 93 04 14/51 93 10 62
Telex 700 846 chamco F
M. and Mme H. A. Gouon

Open all year. **Rooms** 6 and 1 suite with bath and WC. **Price** 300-350F (2 pers.) +50F (extra pers.) **Meals** breakfast 35F, half board 600F per couple in a double room (2 days min.), evening meals and lunch at separate tables 120-180F (wine not incl.) **Facilities** lounge, heated swimming pool, fishing in the lakes. **Pets** dogs allowed (extra charge). **Nearby** tennis (500m), riding, golf courses (15km); islands of Noirmoutier and Yeu. **Spoken** English.

This 17th-century château has been furnished and decorated in period style by the owners. The bedrooms are comfortable. We preferred the ones with pink or blue 'toile de Jouy'. M. and Mme Gouon are very welcoming and provide excellent local seasonal food. Reasonably quiet in spite of the proximity of the road.

How to get there (Map 14): 10km south east of Challans on D948; 30km before La Roche-sur-Yon.

286
Le Fief Mignoux

85120 Saint-Maurice-des-Noués
(Vendée)
Tel. 51 00 81 42
M. and Mme Schnepf

Open 1 May – All Saints. **Rooms** 2 sharing bathroom with shower and WC. Room cleaning every three days. **Price** 200F (2 pers.) +50F (extra pers.) **Meals** breakfast incl., no evening meals. **Restaurant** Auberge de Maître Pannetier. **Pets** dogs not allowed. **Nearby** tennis, riding, lake, golf, forest of Mervent, Poitou marshes, Maillezais abbey. **Spoken** English, German.

Charming 17th-century Vendée house, full of light, and surrounded by two gardens full of flowers. The bedroom is huge, very light, and very pleasantly furnished in countrified style. There is a shower room opposite. If there are several of you , it is possible to have the use of a second bedroom which is large and beautiful too. Very good welcome.

How to get there *(Map 15): 25km north east of Fontenay-le-Comte via D938 towards La Châtaigneraie. In L'Alouette take D30 towards Vouvant. After St-Maurice-des-Noués right on D67 towards Puy-de-Serre.*

287
Le Clos

Chérêt
02860 Bruyères-et-Montberault
(Aisne)
Tel. 23 24 80 64
M. and Mme Simonnot

Open 15 April – 15 Oct. **Rooms** 1 with bath and WC, 3 sharing shower and WC, and 1 suite (2/5 pers.) with bath and WC. **Price** 180-220F (2 pers.) +80F (extra pers.) **Meals** breakfast incl., evening meals at communal table 70F (wine incl.) **Facilities** lounge. **Pets** dogs not allowed. **Nearby** tennis, swimming pool, golf, medieval town of Laon, St-Gobain forest.

Le Clos is a 17th-century former vine-grower's house. The atmosphere is friendly, cultured and countrified. Evening meals are cheerful affairs thanks to M. Simonnot and his good sense of humour. The house is furnished throughout with fine antiques. The bedrooms have very comfortable beds and are pleasing and light, but book in advance for the suite and the bedroom with their own bathrooms.

How to get there *(Maps 3 and 10): 8km south of Laon via D967 towards Fismes, then D903; signposted.*

288
Domaine des Jeannes

Rue Dubarle
02290 Vic-sur-Aisne
(Aisne)
Tel. 23 55 57 33
M. and Mme Martner

Open all year. **Rooms** 5 with shower, WC and TV. **Price** 290-320F (2 pers.) according to season. **Meals** breakfast incl., evening meals (separate tables) 80F (wine not incl.). **Facilities** lounge, telephone, swimming pool, tennis. **Credit cards** Visa. **Pets** dogs allowed on request. **Nearby** golf, châteaux of Pierrefond, Compiègne, hunting museum in Senlis. **Spoken** English.

The grounds of the estate begin in the town and stretch right to the river's edge. All the bedrooms overlook the park. They are very comfortable and well decorated, with impeccable bathrooms, and the lounge and dining room are equally pleasing. Excellent evening meals and a very friendly welcome.

How to get there *(Map 10): 16km west of Soissons on N31 towards Compiègne; signposted.*

289
Les Patrus

L'Epine-aux-Bois
02540 Viels-Maisons
(Aisne)
Tel. and Fax 23 69 85 85
Mme Royol

Open all year. **Rooms** 5 with bath or shower and WC, and 1 suite (5 pers.) with shower and WC. **Price** 260-330F (2 pers.), suite 530F (4 pers.) **Meals** breakfast incl., evening meals at communal or separate table 90-150F (wine not incl.) **Facilities** lounge, telephone, loose boxes, fishing in the lakes. **Credit cards** Visa. **Pets** small dogs allowed on request (+50F). **Nearby** golf, Château Thierry. **Spoken** English, German.

This large, well laid out farmhouse is the answer to your dreams of a house in the country. Music room, dining room with a multitude of curios, and comfortable bedrooms, elegantly and simply decorated, leave a warm and lasting impression. Home-made jams for breakfast and good family evening meals. Very pleasant welcome.

How to get there *(Map 10): 10km west of Montmirail via D933 towards La-Ferté-sur-Jouarre. At La Haute-Epine, D863 towards L'Epine-aux-Bois; signposted.*

290
Ferme du Château

02130 Villers Agron
(Aisne)
Tel. 23 71 60 67
Fax 23 69 36 54
Christine and Xavier Ferry

Open all year. **Rooms** 2 with bath and WC, 2 with shower and WC. **Price** 300-350F (2 pers.) **Meals** breakfast incl., evening meals at communal table, on reservation 88F (wine not incl.) **Facilities** lounge, tennis, trout fishing, Champagne golf course (18 holes). **Pets** dogs allowed on request. **Nearby** swimming pool, riding (10km), canoeing, Champagne wine route, forest walks, châteaux and abbeys. **Spoken** English, German.

You will be made welcome in this old (13th-18th century) house whose garden extends on to a golf course divided by a river. The interior is tastefully decorated, charming and comfortable. Delightful bedrooms hung with bright coloured fabrics and furnished in old fashioned style. Game is often served at the good and convivial evening meals. Excellent value for money and a place worth discovering.

How to get there *(Map 10): 30km north east of Château-Thierry. A4, leaving it at Dormans, then D380, then D801 towards 'golf de Champagne'; signposted.*

291
Chez Mme Gittermann

26, rue Nationale
60110 Amblainville
(Oise)
Tel. (16) 44 52 03 22
Mme Gittermann

Open all year. **Rooms** 3 with bath or shower and WC, and 1 extra room without bath. **Price** 170-200F (2 pers.) +80-85F (extra room per pers.) **Meals** breakfast incl., no evening meals. **Restaurants** in Méru (4km). **Facilities** lounge. **Pets** well-behaved dogs allowed. **Nearby** swimming pool, tennis, riding, golf, Auvers-sur-Oise, Beauvais.

Sadly this house is on the roadside, but inside, it has been richly and imaginatively decorated down to the last detail. Good breakfasts are served in an extraordinary lounge which contains an accumulation of sculptures, paintings and exotic plants but is not particularly well kept. There are dogs, parrots, cats and toucans. You will be wonderfully welcomed. A unique and unconventional place.

How to get there *(Map 9): 50km north west of Paris via A15 exit Pontoise, then D27 and D927 towards Amblainville (4km before Méru).*

292
Chez M. and Mme Bernard

4, rue de Gomerfontaine
60240 Chambors
(Oise)
Tel. (16) 44 49 77 28
M. and Mme Jean Bernard

Open all year. **No smoking. Rooms** 1 with bath, WC and child's room for under 5s, and 1 bedroom with shower and WC. **Price** 200F (1 pers.), 250F (2 pers.) +50F (child's room). **Meals** breakfast incl., no evening meals. **Restaurants** many in Gisors (4km). **Pets** dogs not allowed. **Nearby** golf (18 holes), riding (8km), walks, Gerberoy, Giverny, Lyons-la-Forêt, Château-Gallard.

This inviting house is set in a pretty hamlet of old stone walls and brown roofs. A well-kept garden bordered by a stream keeps the noises of the world out. The bedrooms are delightful, with duvets matching the curtains and English wallpapers. Breakfast is served in the guests' dining room (outside in summer). There is a log fire, several different sorts of bread and excellent jams. A very pleasant place.

How to get there *(Map 9): 35km north east of Vernon (A13), then D181 towards Gisors; it's 4km south east of Gisors.*

293
La Bultée

60300 Fontaine-Chaalis
(Oise)
Tel. (16) 44 54 20 63
Annie Ancel

Open all year. **Children** under 7 not allowed. **Rooms** 5 with shower, WC and TV. **Price** 300F (2 pers.) +80F (extra pers.) **Meals** breakfast incl., no evening meals. **Restaurants** 3km. **Facilities** lounge, parking. **Credit cards** Visa. **Pets** dogs not allowed. **Nearby** swimming pool, riding, golf, Chantilly, Compiègne, Pierrefond, Jean-Jacques Rousseau park. **Spoken** a little English.

The inner courtyard of this farm has lots of character. There is a large sitting room with a fireplace where breakfast is served when the weather is not good enough to use the tables outside. The bedrooms are beautiful, comfortable, simple and impeccably well-kept, as are the bathrooms. They all overlook a pretty flower garden. Guaranteed peace. Cheerful and spontaneous welcome.

How to get there (Map 9): 8km south east of Senlis (A1) via D330a towards Nanteuil-le-Haudouin; it's after Borest and before Fontaine-Chaalis.

294
Château des Alleux

Les Alleux
80870 Behen
(Somme)
Tel 22 31 64 88 (after 19.30)
M. and Mme René-François de Fontanges

Open all year. **Rooms** 2 with bath and WC, 1 with shower and WC, 1 without bath or shower for 2 children, and 1 studio (2 pers.) with kitchenette, shower and WC. **Price** 280F (1/2 pers.) +75F (extra pers.), studio 300F (2 pers.) **Meals** evening meals and lunch at communal table 100F (drinks incl.) **Facilities** lounge and kitchen for guests, pony riding, loose boxes, bicycles. **Pets** dogs not allowed. **Nearby** golf, tennis, seaside (20km), Somme bay, Marquenterre park. **Spoken** English, Spanish.

Sheltering in its 12-hectare park, this château offers excellent bedrooms in small annexes (except for the lovely 'Empire' bedroom, which is in the château). They are pleasant and well decorated. Very well-tended and flowery garden, friendly and cheerful atmosphere, excellent evening meals. An attractive place, and reasonably priced.

How to get there (Map 1): 10km south of Abbeville via N28 towards Rouen; signposted.

295
Château de Foucaucort

80140 Oisemont
(Somme)
Tel. 22 25 12 58
Mme Mackay

Open all year. **Rooms** 1 with bath and WC, 2 sharing bath and WC, and 1 suite (4 pers.) with bath and WC. Room cleaning every two days. **Price** 275F (1 pers.), 350F (2 pers.), 700F (4 pers.) **Meals** breakfast incl., lunch and evening meals at communal table 110F (wine not incl.) **Facilities** lounge, telephone, equestrian centre, loose boxes. **Pets** dogs allowed on request. **Nearby** golf, tennis (5km). **Spoken** English.

This brick and stone 18th-century château is outside the village in attractive grounds. The sense of bygone days lingers in the reception rooms. The lounge has a happy mixture of furniture from different periods. The suite is nice, but the price for the two bedrooms sharing a bathroom is a bit high. A friendly, family place, but the quality of the meals is uneven.

How to get there *(Map 1): 25km south of Abbeville via N28 to St-Maxent, then D29 to Oisemont and D25 towards Senarpont.*

296
Le Bois de Bonance

80132 Port-le-Grand
(Somme)
Tel. 22 24 11 97
M. and Mme Jacques Maillard

Closed 25 Dec. – 1 Jan. **Rooms** 3 with bath and WC, and 1 suite of 2 bedrooms (4 pers.) with bath, WC, kitchen and sitting room (except July and Aug.) **Price** 300F (1 pers.), 350F (2 pers.) +100F (extra pers.), suite 400F (2 pers.) **Meals** breakfast incl., no evening meals. **Restaurants** Chez Nicole in St-Valéry-sur-Somme, La Clef des Champs in Favières. **Facilities** lounge, swimming pool, loose boxes. **Pets** small dogs allowed in kennels. **Nearby** golf (5km), seaside (10km). **Spoken** English, German.

Standing alone in the countryside, this fine country house is surrounded by very well kept grounds. The interior is very elegant. Each comfortable bedroom has old furniture (mostly Louis XVI style). Breakfast is served in a very attractively decorated dining room furnished with many ornaments and lyre-backed chairs. There is a small TV-lounge for guests. Friendly welcome.

How to get there *(Map 1): 9km north west of Albertville on D40 towards St-Valéry-sur-Somme; signposted at the entrance to the village.*

297
Ferme du Bois de Bonance

80132 Port-le-Grand
(Somme)
Tel. 22 24 34 97
M. and Mme Benoit Maillard

Open all year. **Rooms** 1 with bath and WC, 1 with shower and WC. **Price** 300F (2 pers.) +100F (extra pers.) **Meals** breakfast incl., no evening meals. **Pets** dogs allowed on request. **Facilities** swimming pool, loose boxes, possibility of riding. **Nearby** golf (5km), Le Crotoy, St- Valéry, Somme bay, Marquenterre park. **Spoken** English.

A large Artois farmhouse with two comfortable and elegant twin-bedded guest bedrooms. The hospitality is relaxed, young and friendly. There is a swimming pool in a beautiful garden and breakfast is served outside in good weather. We recommend a summer visit, as there is no guest lounge.

How to get there (Map 1): 8km north west of Albertville via D40 towards St-Valéry-sur-Somme; sign at the entrance to the village.

298
Abbaye de Valloires

Valloires - Service Accueil
80120 Rue   00 33
(Somme)
Tel 22 29 62 33
Fax 22 29 91 54 24
Association de Valloires

Open all year. **Rooms** 5 (of which 3 with bedroom annexe) with bath, WC and telephone. **Price** 315F (1 pers.), 350F (2 pers.), 440F (3 pers.) +60F (child suppl.) **Meals** breakfast incl., no evening meals. **Restaurants** auberges close by. **Facilities** lounge, tour of the abbey. **Pets** dogs not allowed. **Nearby** 18-hole golf (6km). **Spoken** English.

B uilt in the 17th century, Valloires is an enormous abbey, now managed by a company. A large, somewhat gloomy gallery leads to the five delightful bedrooms, formerly used by the Abbot and his guests. Large, comfortable and prettily decorated in old-fashioned style, most of them have panelling and recessed beds. Lovely view over the gardens. Breakfast is served at separate tables in the vast old refectory. A pity there are often tourist groups staying.

How to get there (Map 1): 31km north of Abbeville via N1 to Nampont-St-Martin, then D192 towards Argoules.

299
Chez Claire Sauvage

22, quai du Romerel
80230 Saint-Valéry-sur-Somme
(Somme)
Tel. 22 60 80 98
Mme Claire Sauvage

Closed Jan. 2 nights minimum stay. **Rooms** 1 with bath and WC, 2 with shower and WC, and 1 studio (4 pers.) with bath, WC and living room. **Price** 270-350F (2 pers.), studio 350F (2 pers.) +100F (extra pers.) **Meals** breakfast incl., no evening meals. **Restaurants** many in the village. **Facilities** lounge. **Pets** well behaved dogs allowed on request. **Nearby** tennis, golf, sailing, water sports, canoeing (200m), Marquenterre park.

The three guest bedrooms of this interesting 19th-century house have wide views of the sea and the marshes. They also have comfortable beds, family furniture, and a friendly atmosphere. Breakfast is served at a large table in the handsome dining room with views of boats sailing past. Beside it is the guests' lounge. Pleasant welcome and excellent value for money.

How to get there *(Map 1): 21km north west of Abbeville via D40 and D940; it's between the Crédit Agricole and the mini-golf.*

300
La Grande Métairie

Oyer
16700 Bioussac–Ruffec
(Charente)
Tel. 45 31 15 67
M. and Mme Moy

Open April – Oct. **Rooms** 1 room and 1 suite (4 pers.) with shower and WC. Room cleaning on request. **Price** 150F (1 pers.), 200F (2 pers.), 260F (3 pers.), 320F (4 pers.) **Meals** breakfast incl., half board 155F per pers. in double room, evening meals at communal table, on reservation 55F (wine incl.) **Restaurant** Le Moulin Enchanté in Condac (3km). **Facilities** lounge, swimming pool, bicycles. **Pets** small well-behaved dogs allowed. **Nearby** tennis, riding, fishing, Nanteuil-en-Vallée, château de Cibioux, Verteuil. **Spoken** English.

In mid-country, this old farmhouse has been well renovated and offers two pleasant guest suites. The one in the main house is very attractive, with flagstones and stone alcoves. The Louis–Philippe beds are very comfortable and the bathrooms have recently been redone. The atmosphere at evening meals is very friendly and produce from the farm takes pride of place. Excellent breakfasts.

How to get there (Map 23): 6km west of Ruffec via D740. At Condac, D197 towards Bioussac then left for Oyer; signs before Oyer.

301
La Breuillerie

Trois-Palis
16730 Fléac
(Charente)
Tel. 45 91 05 37
Mme Bouchard

Open all year. **Rooms** 2 with bath and WC, 2 with basin sharing bath and WC; TV. **Price** 110-170F (1 pers.), 180-220F (2 pers.), 260F (3 pers.) **Meals** breakfast incl., no evening meals. **Restaurant** Le Pont de La Meure 500m. **Facilities** bicycles. **Pets** dogs not allowed. **Nearby** tennis, swimming pool, riding at Angoulême. **Spoken** English.

The outskirts of Angoulême are badly spoilt, but La Breuillerie is far enough away to be in the countryside. The guest bedrooms are comfortable, well kept and prettily decorated. The 'bleue' bedroom is delightfully old-fashioned but has a shared bathroom. The suite is like a small house. Good breakfasts served in a dining room with great character. Pleasant and cordial atmosphere.

How to get there (Map 22): 5km west of Angoulême via D699. At Nersac, D41; signed 'Chambres d'hôtes'.

302
Les Granges

16410 Vouzan
(Charente)
Tel. 45 24 94 61
Mme Lousie Le Mouée

Open all year. **No smoking. Rooms** 1 in separate building (2/3 pers.) and 1 suite (4 pers.) with shower and WC. **Price** 210-230F (1 pers.), 230-250F (2 pers.), 310-320F (3 pers.), 380F (4 pers.) **Meals** breakfast incl., no evening meals. **Restaurants** in the vicinity. **Facilities** lounge, telephone, painting and yoga lessons for beginners. **Pets** dogs allowed on request. **Nearby** swimming pool, tennis, 9-hole and 18-hole golf courses, Brantôme, Périgord vert, Romanesque art, châteaux.

A pretty house between Angoulême and Brantôme surrounded by a well kept garden. Choose the bedroom in the small separate building. Comfortable and well decorated, with antique furniture, it has a sitting area, a mezzanine and a private terrace. You will feel quite at home and can have breakfast outside in the sunshine. Friendly, unintrusive hospitality.

How to get there *(Map 23): 16km south east of Angoulême via D939. At Ste-Catherine, D4. At La Petitie first road on the right after 1.6km.*

303
Le Maurençon

10, rue de Maurençon
Les Moulins
17400 Antezant
(Charente-Maritime)
Tel. 46 59 94 52
Pierre and Marie-Claude Fallelour

Open all year. **Rooms** 1 with bath and WC, 1 with shower and WC, 1 with shower and shared WC, 1 sharing bath and WC. Room cleaning twice a week on longer stays. **Price** 230F (2 pers.) +65F (extra pers.) **Meals** breakfast incl., half board 165F per pers. in double room (3 nights min.) Evening meals at communal table, not Sundays and holidays, 80F. **Restaurant** Farmhouse auberge Antezant (200m). **Facilities** lounge, fishing. **Pets** dogs not allowed. **Nearby** golf, swimming pool, riding, tennis, Saintes, Cognac, Poitou marshes, châteaux, Romanesque churches.

The river Boutonne once drove the mill but now makes a romantic border to the garden. Both Mme Fallelour and her house are very welcoming. The bedrooms contain some antique furniture and are light and pleasant. The lounge has a billiard table. Excellent breakfasts, often served outside.

How to get there *(Map 22): 6km north of St-Jean-d'Angély via D127 towards Dampierre; it's at the entrance to the village.*

304
Le Logis

17610 Dompierre-sur-Charente
(Charente-Maritime)
Tel. 46 91 02 05/46 91 00 53
Mme C. Cocuaud

Open 1 March – 30 Oct. **Rooms** 2 with bath and WC, 2 with bath and shared WC, and 1 child's room. **Price** 420F (2 pers.) **Meals** breakfast 45F, half board 430F per pers. in double room (3 days min.), evening meals at communal table, on reservation 200F (wine incl.) **Restaurants** Hostellerie du Marais (5km), Relais d'Orlac (5km). **Facilities** lounge, telephone. **Pets** dogs not allowed. **Nearby** golf, tennis, fishing, equestrian centre, seaside (30km), Saintes, Cognac, Romanesque churches. **Spoken** English.

Built in the 18th century, on a rise close to the Charente, Le Logis is a truly beautiful house. The principal reception rooms are open to guests and have fine furniture and good proportions. The bedrooms, light, prettily decorated and comfortable, feel more like the guestrooms in friends' houses. Mme Cocuaud enlivens the dinner table and her cooking is excellent.

How to get there (Map 22): 13km south east of Saintes via D24 (through the Charente valley).

305
La Jaquetterie

17250 Plassay
(Charente-Maritime)
Tel. 46 93 91 88
Michelle and Jacques Louradour

Open all year. **Rooms** 1 and 2 suites (4 pers.) with bath or shower and WC. **Price** 195-230F (2 pers.) **Meals** breakfast incl., half board 165-175F per pers. in double room, evening meals at communal table 70F (wine incl.) **Facilities** loose boxes. **Pets** dogs allowed on request. **Nearby** fishing, swimming pool, tennis, riding, golf. **Spoken** German.

La Jacquetterie is a pretty house, rich in character and set a little way from the village. The bedrooms are intimate and have lots of charming personal details. The comfortable beds face lovely 18th-century wardrobes. If the weather permits, breakfast is served outside. Evening meals are prepared with excellent produce from the farm. Very friendly welcome.

How to get there (Map 22): 13km north west of Saintes (A10) via N137 in the Rochefort direction for 11km. Then right on D119 towards Plassay for 2km.

306
Le Logis de l'Epine

17250 Plassay
(Charente-Maritime)
Tel. 46 93 91 66
M. and Mme Charrier

Open all year. **Rooms** 1 with bath and WC, 1 with shower and WC, 2 with basin and shared WC. Price 180-260F (2 pers.) **Meals** breakfast incl., no evening meals. **Restaurants** nearby. **Facilities** lounge. **Pets** dogs allowed on request. **Nearby** swimming pool, tennis, riding, seaside, golf, Romanesque Saintonge. **Spoken** English.

This 18th-century house in its large and shady garden seems sheltered from the modern world. M. and Mme Charrier are really very hospitable. The bedrooms contain antique furniture and wide ship's bunks brightened with pretty fabrics. Some of the bathrooms are not as good as others. Breakfast is served outside under the oak trees, or in a room covered with 19th-century frescos of leafy scrolls and fresh fruit. Authentic and full of charm.

How to get there *(Map 22): 10km north west of Saintes via N137, then D119; it's on the way out of the village.*

307
33, rue Thiers

33, rue Thiers
17000 La Rochelle
(Charente-Maritime)
Tel. 46 41 62 23
Fax 46 41 10 76
Mme Maybelle Iribe

Open all year. **Rooms** 6 with bath or shower and WC. **Price** 380-450F (1 pers.), 450-500F (2 pers.) **Meals** breakfast 34F, evening meals (separate tables) 150F (wine not incl.) **Facilities** lounge, telephone, cookery courses. **Pets** dogs not allowed. **Nearby** sailing, golf, île de Ré, Poitou marshes. **Spoken** English.

This house in the very pretty town of La Rochelle has a pleasant inner garden where breakfast is served in summer. The bedrooms (on 2 floors) are quiet, very comfortable, and remarkably decorated, with pictures and family objects. There is an elegant lounge-library for guests. Don't miss the evening meal – Madame Iribe is a very fine cordon-bleu cook.

How to get there *(Map 22): In La Rochelle follow the 'centre ville' signs and go round the main square; in front of the cathedral at the traffic lights, take first right, rue Gargoulleau, which becomes rue Thiers further on.*

308
Château des Salles

17240 Saint-Fort-sur Gironde
(Charente-Maritime)
Tel. 46 49 95 10
Fax 46 49 02 81
Mme Couillaud

Open Easter – end Sept. **Rooms** 5 with bath or shower and WC. **Price** 300-450F (2 pers.) **Meals** breakfast 45F, half board 300-420F per pers. in double room (3 days min.), evening meals on reservation (separate tables) 160F (wine not incl.) **Facilities** lounge, telephone and Fax. **Credit cards** Visa. **Pets** dogs not allowed. **Nearby** tennis, seaside, Cognac, La Rochelle. **Spoken** English, German.

Built in the 15th century and renovated in the 19th, the château has five pleasant guest bedrooms with views over the grounds. The classical decor is the work of the owners, who even painted the water–colours in some of the rooms. Breakfast is served in the bedrooms or in the dining room (no smoking).

How to get there (Map 22): 14km from the A27 Mirambeau-Royan exit at the crossroads of the D125 to St-Fort-sur-Gironde and the D730 to Royan.

309
Rennebourg

Saint-Denis-du-Pin
17400 Saint-Jean-d'Angely
(Charente-Maritime)
Tel. 46 32 16 07
Michèle and Florence Frappier

Open all year. **Rooms** 3 with bath or shower and WC, and 1 suite of 2 bedrooms (3/4 pers.) with 1 bath and WC. **Price** 250-270F (2 pers.) **Meals** breakfast 25F, evening meals (separate tables) 75-90F (table wine incl.) **Facilities** lounge, swimming pool, equestrian centre, loose boxes. **Pets** dogs not allowed. **Nearby** tennis, golf, La Rochelle. **Spoken** English and German understood.

A dream of a place, in the heart of the countryside, which comes close to perfection. You will be received with care and kindness. Inside, there is Louis XV panelling, fine old provincial furniture and, throughout, antique curios, ornaments and paintings. The very comfortable and tastefully decorated bedrooms have lovely bathrooms. Excellent breakfasts and evening meals. Very lovely wooded grounds.

How to get there (Map 22): 7km north of St-Jean-d'Angély (A10 exit 24), via N150; signposted.

310
Manoir de Bonnemie

49, route départementale
17310 Saint-Pierre-d'Oléron
(Charente-Maritime)
Tel. 46 47 22 57
Mme Chassort

Open all year. **Rooms** 3 with shower and WC, 1 with basin and WC (shared shower). **Price** 160F (1 pers.), 210F (2 pers.) **Meals** breakfast incl., half board 175F per pers. in double room, evening meals (separate tables) 75-80F (wine not incl.) **Pets** cats not allowed. **Nearby** swimming pool, tennis, riding, sea fishing, sailing, golf. **Spoken** English.

The île d'Oléron is paradise out of season and hell in July and August. Though less than ideally located beside the road close to the busy part of town, the manoir is sheltered by its pretty garden. Madame Chassort's heart is in her work, and her house is as well presented as her dinners. Pretty verandah. Comfortable bedrooms with marquetry reproduction furniture and soft red carpet. Outside the summer holiday period it's comfortably quiet.

***How to get there** (Map 22): On the way out of St-Pierre-d'Oléron towards St-Gilles St-Denis.*

311
Le Clos

La Menounière
17310 Saint-Pierre-d'Oléron
(Charente-Maritime)
Tel. 46 47 14 34
Micheline Denieau

Open all year. **Rooms** 3 with shower, WC and mezzanine for children. Room cleaning every week for long stays. **Price** 210F (2 pers.) +40F (extra pers.) **Meals** breakfast incl., no evening meals. **Restaurants** Les Alizées in St Pierre d'Oléron, L'Ecailler in La Cotinière. **Pets** dogs allowed on request. **Nearby** 9-hole golf, fishing, bicycle hire, riding, tennis, seaside (500m), salt marshes, bird sanctuary. **Spoken** English, Spanish.

This small house, surrounded with vines, lies at the entrance to the village and has a flowery garden. The bedrooms are simple, pleasant and well kept. Each has a mezzanine (which will please families) and a small terrace at ground level. A good and economical place to stay.

***How to get there** (Map 22): 4km west of St Pierre d'Oléron via D734; at St Pierre take the left at the traffic lights after the Shell station, then follow signs for La Menounière.*

312
Aguzan

Rue du Château
La Sauzaie
17138 Saint-Xandre
(Charente-Maritime)
Tel. 46 37 22 65
M. and Mme Langer

Open all year. **Rooms** 3 with basin sharing 1 bathroom and WC. **Price** 180F (1 pers.), 220F (2 pers.) +90F (extra pers.) **Meals** breakfast incl., no evening meals. **Restaurant** Auberge du Vieux Noyer in Dompierre-sur-Mer (5km). **Facilities** lounge. **Pets** dogs allowed on request (+30F). **Nearby** riding, seaside, golf, La Rochelle, Poitou marshes, Romanesque Saintonge, île de Ré.

Set among fields in the countryside behind La Rochelle, this house faces south and has very well groomed gardens. The inside is also well kept, and the bedrooms are all very comfortable and traditionally decorated. If the excellent breakfasts are not served in the garden, they are laid in the very attractive lounge. Charming welcome.

How to get there *(Map 22): 9km north east of La Rochelle via D9 towards Luçon through Villedoux. Telephone for directions.*

313
La Treille Marine

8, rue des Rosées
Ile de Ré
17740 Sainte-Marie-de-Ré
(Charente-Maritime)
Tel. 46 30 12 57
Alain and Danielle Fouché

Open all year. 2 nights min. **Rooms** 1 bedroom (3 pers.) with bath, WC and TV. Room cleaning every 2 days. **Price** 250F (1 pers.), 320F (2 pers.), 370F (3 pers.). 15% reduction 1 Oct. – 30 March. **Meals** breakfast incl., evening meal on request, at communal or separate table 70F. **Restaurants** nearby. **Facilities** lounge. **Pets** dogs allowed on request. **Nearby** golf (25km), seawater therapy institute and seawater swimming pool (1km), little harbours of La Flotte and St-Martin-de-Ré.

Peacefully situated in a small, white, flowery village, this former wine store has a delightful guest bedroom. Decorated in blue and white, it is utterly comfortable and charming: old furniture, pretty objects and fabrics, duvets, modern bathroom. Breakfast is served with a smile in a large and handsome dining room. A very good address.

How to get there *(Map 22): on the île de Ré (reached by bridge from La Rochelle), in the middle of the village.*

314
Château de la Roche

79290 Argenton-L'Eglise
(Deux-Sèvres)
Tel. 49 67 02 38
M. and Mme Keufer

Open all year. **Rooms** 8 and 1 suite (4 pers.) of 2 bedrooms with 1 bath and WC. **Price** 250F (1 pers.), 400F (2 pers.) **Meals** breakfast incl., evening meals 150F (wine incl.) **Facilities** lounge, telephone, riding (+suppl.), horse and trap, boating. **Pets** dogs allowed on request. **Nearby** golf. **Spoken** English.

Essentially Renaissance in style, this château is situated in the countryside and has huge, quiet and very well furnished guest bedrooms with exemplary bathrooms. It overlooks Argenton. On the ground floor, charmingly old-fashioned lounges and dining rooms open onto a beautiful terrace. A horse and trap can come to collect you from the station. Relaxed welcome.

How to get there *(Map 15): 35km south of Saumur via N147. At Montreuil-Bellay take D938. At Brion-près Thouet take D162 towards Taizon.*

315
Le Logis de Saint Romans

79500 Saint-Romans-les-Melle
(Deux-Sèvres)
Tel. 49 27 04 15
M. and Mme Rabany

Open all year. **Rooms** 1 with bath and WC, 1 with shower and shared WC, 2 sharing 1 shower and 2 WCs. Room cleaning for long stays. **Price** 250-300F +150F (extra room). **Meals** breakfast incl., evening meals at communal or separate table 100F (wine not incl.) **Facilities** lounge, tennis, fishing, boating. **Pets** dogs allowed on request. **Nearby** golf (40km), lake (15km), riding, swimming pool (4km), Poitou marshes. **Spoken** English, Italian.

This magnificent house dates back to the 15th century, and its flowery grounds are bisected by a small waterway navigable by boat. The bedrooms are comfortable and charmingly old-fashioned. We preferred 'rose' and 'bleue'. There is a lounge-billiard room. In summer dinner is served under an awning in the garden. Good food and very pleasant atmosphere.

How to get there *(Map 22): 30km south east of Niort via D948 towards Limoges, then just before Melle follow signs for St-Romans-les-Melle; it's at the entrance to the village just behind the church.*

316
La Talbardière

86210 Archigny
(Vienne)
Tel. 49 85 32 51/49 85 32 52
M. and Mme Lonhienne

Open all year. **Rooms** 3 with bath or shower and WC, and 1 studio (5 pers.) with bath, WC, kitchen, telephone and TV. **Price** 240F (2 pers.), studio 1050-1575F per week for 5 pers. (depending on the season). **Meals** breakfast incl. (except the studio), no evening meals. **Restaurants** close by. **Facilities** fishing (with permit). **Pets** dogs not allowed. **Nearby** riding, tennis, golf, Chauvigny, Angles-sur-Anglin, St-Savin. **Spoken** English, German, Italian.

It's impossible not to be enchanted by this old fortified house with its lovely proportions. The bedrooms are very big, well furnished and have fine bathrooms. Breakfast of jams and home-baked bread is served on waking. The serene and rolling countryside around is ideal for walks. Friendly welcome.

How to get there *(Map 16): 18km south east of Châtellerault via D9 towards Monthoiron, then D3 towards Pleumartin; signed after 1km.*

317
Château d'Epanvilliers

Epanvilliers
86400 Brux-Civray
(Vienne)
Tel. 49 87 18 43
M. Lorzil

Open all year. **Rooms** 1 with shower and WC, and 2 suites (2 pers.) with bath, WC and 1 child's bed. **Price** 250F (2 pers.), suite 400F (2 pers.) +50F (extra pers.) **Meals** breakfast incl., no evening meals. **Restaurant** in Chaunay. **Facilities** lounge, carriage rides (suppl.), tour of the château. **Pets** dogs allowed on request. **Nearby** swimming pool, riding. **Spoken** English.

Monsieur Lorzil is restoring his château with good taste and determination. He will receive you warmly. The bedrooms have lots of character; some have a small museum-room attached and all overlook the park. The bathrooms are not yet fully up to standard. A huge, inviting lounge-library is available to guests, who will take happy memories of this place with them when they leave.

How to get there *(Map 23): 41km south of Poitiers via N10 to Couhé, then D7 towards Civray; signposted.*

318
Moulin de la Dive

Guron
Payré
86700 Couhé
(Vienne)
Tel. 49 42 40 97
M. and Mme Vanverts

Open July and Aug. (on request). **Rooms** 2 with bath or shower and WC. **Price** 300-320F (1 pers.), 340-360F (2 pers.) **Meals** breakfast incl., no evening meals. **Restaurants** in Couhé and Vivonne. **Facilities** lounge, telephone, fishing. **Pets** dogs not allowed. **Nearby** equestrian centre, golf, châteaux (La Roche-Gencay and Epanvilliers).

The Dive meanders through the delightful garden and under several little bridges before being swallowed up underneath the mill. M. and Mme Vanverts will receive you in a fine lounge-dining room, offering you the choice of two comfortable guest bedrooms. The 'Seville' bedroom has old Spanish furniture, and the 'Nohant' bedroom is in memory of George Sand. Breakfast is served in the garden or the lounge.

How to get there *(Map 16): 34km south of Poitiers via N10, then D29 towards Anché.*

319
Le Bois Goulu

86200 Pouant
(Vienne)
Tel. 49 22 52 05
Mme Picard

Open all year. **Rooms** 1 with shower and WC, 1 with bath and shared WC (possible rooms en suite for children). **Price** 200F (2 pers.), suite 250F (2 pers.) **Meals** breakfast incl., no evening meals. **Restaurants** in Pouant and Richelieu. **Facilities** lounge, bicycle hire. **Pets** dogs allowed on request. **Nearby** swimming pool, fishing, golf, shooting, Loire châteaux.

The Bois Goulu is a large farm built around a flowery courtyard. You will be made very welcome. There are two huge bedrooms fitted out in an old-fashioned style; they are light and comfortable and open off a wide corridor with a parquet floor. Breakfast is in the sitting room and includes delicious home-made jams. No evening meals, but there is a restaurant only 1km away.

How to get there *(Map 16): 15km east of Loudun towards Richelieu on D61; it's on the way out of the village in an avenue of lime trees.*

320
Château de la Roche du Maine

86420 Prinçay
(Vienne)
Tel. 49 22 84 09
Fax 49 22 89 57
M. and Mme Neveu

Open 1 April – All Saints. **Rooms** 4 in annexes with shower and WC, 1 in the château with bath and WC. **Price** 380-900F (2 pers.). **Meals** breakfast 45F, half board 440-650F per pers. in double room (3 days min.), evening meals at communal table, on reservation 250F (wine incl.) **Facilities** lounge, swimming pool, gym, tour of the château. **Pets** dogs not allowed. **Nearby** tennis, riding, golf, Loire chateaux, wine route. **Spoken** English.

In this exceptionally beautiful château, guests are assured of every modern comfort. In the annexes the bedrooms are simple and comfortable. The one in the château is exceptional. There is a covered swimming pool, with a lounge and a well-equipped gym. Evening meals are served in the superb dining room in the company of M. and Mme Neveu.

How to get there (Map 16): 33km south of Chinon via D49. After Richelieu, towards Châtellerault. After 2km right on D22 towards Monts-sur-Guesnes, then D46; signposted.

321
Château de Prémarie

86340 Roches-Prémarie
(Vienne)
Tel. 49 42 50 01
M. and Mme Jean-Pierre de Boysson

Open Easter – All Saints. **Rooms** 3 with bath and WC, 2 with shower and WC. 4 bedrooms heated in winter. **Price** 350-450F (2 pers.) **Meals** breakfast incl., no evening meals. **Restaurant** in St-Benoit (8km). **Facilities** lounge, swimming pool, tennis. **Pets** dogs not allowed. **Nearby** equestrian centre (12km), 18-hole golf (10km), Romanesque art. **Spoken** English.

Once an English fortress, this small château is inviting and comfortable. It has plenty of charm and authenticity but it is also cheerful and well equipped, right down to the bathrooms. Everything is admirably well-kept. Excellent breakfasts. The heated swimming pool is open from springtime onwards.

How to get there (Map 16): 14km south of Poitiers via D741 towards La Villedieu/Gençay.

322
Château de Ternay

Ternay
86120 Les Trois-Moutiers
(Vienne)
Tel. 49 22 92 82/49 22 97 54
Marquis and Marquise de Ternay

Open Easter – All Saints. **Rooms** 3 with bath and WC. **Price** 460F (1 pers.), 480-500F (2 pers.) **Meals** breakfast incl., evening meals 100m from the château at communal table 150F (wine incl.) **Facilities** lounge. **Pets** dogs not allowed. **Nearby** golf, Fontevrault abbey, Loire châteaux. **Spoken** English.

Built in the 15th century around an even older Keep, Château de Ternay did not escape some remodelling in the 19th century but retains an impressive character. It has a beautiful inner courtyard and authentically decorated rooms. The bedrooms are quiet, huge, and have beautiful fabrics and antique furniture. Only the bathrooms bring you back into the modern world. Evening meals are in the château's farmhouse and are based on good regional cooking.

How to get there (Map 15): 30km south of Saumur via N147. At Montreuil-Bellay head towards Les Trois-Moutiers, then Ternay.

323
La Malle Post

86260 Vicq-sur-Gartempe
(Vienne)
Tel. 49 86 21 04
Mme de Kriek

Open Easter – All Saints. **Rooms** 3 with bath or shower and WC, and 1 suite (4 pers.) with kitchen, lounge, TV, bath, WC and independent entrance. **Price** 230-330F (2 pers.) +60F (extra bed) – set price for 7 days 1330-1490F (2 pers.) **Meals** breakfast incl., evening meals at communal table 80F (wine incl.) **Facilities** lounge, bicycle hire, boats for fishing. **Nearby** riding, golf. **Spoken** English.

Situated on a small square 50m from a lovely river, this 18th-century former post house is very prettily decorated. The bedrooms are big and comfortable and mostly decorated in Art Deco style, and the lounge has a cosy corner bar. Marion de Kriek takes great care of her guests. She also organises musical evenings. The cooking is very good.

How to get there (Map 16): A10 exit Châtellerault Nord towards La Roche-Posay, then 8km to Vicq-sur-Gartempe.

324
Le Vieux Castel

04500 Roumoules
(Alpes-de-Haute-Provence)
Tel. 92 77 75 42
M. Allègre

Open Easter – All Saints. **Rooms** 4 with bath and WC, 1 with bath and shared WC. Room cleaning guests' responsibility. **Price** 100F (1 pers.), 165F (2 pers.) +50F (extra pers.) **Meals** breakfast incl., half board 150F per pers. in double room, evening meals at communal table 70F (wine incl.) **Facilities** telephone, enclosed parking. **Pets** dogs not allowed. **Nearby** Verdon gorges, lakes of Ste-Croix and Esparron.

L e Vieux Castel presents a slightly austere 17th-century façade. The young proprietors are restoring the building themselves. The bedrooms are on the first floor and their monastic appearance, softened by turn-of-the-century furniture, is not without charm. The beds are comfortable and the small shower rooms have been completely refurbished. A quiet place, except during national holidays. Pleasant welcome.

How to get there *(Map 34): 3km from Riez via D952 towards Moustier: signposted 'Gites de France'.*

325
L'Agapanthe

Le Clos de Sagnes
05400 Manteyer
(Hautes-Alpes)
Tel. 92 57 91 51
Mme Marie-Christine Ratto

Open all year. **Rooms** 1 with bath and WC, 3 with shower and shared WC. Room cleaning on request. **Price** 120F (2 pers.) **Meals** breakfast incl., half board 170F (2 pers. or more), full board 210F (2 pers. or more), lunch and evening meals at communal table 70F (wine incl.) **Facilities** lounge, equestrian centre, fishing. **Pets** dogs allowed in 1 bedroom. **Nearby** ski-ing. mountain biking, climbing, lake of Serre Ponçon. **Spoken** English.

T he lines of this house are reminiscent of a large mountain chalet. The impeccable, completely renovated bedrooms have small shower rooms. The decor is simple, based on pale wood and brightly coloured fabrics. Breakfast and dinner are served in a large vaulted room. Mme Ratto is very obliging and happy to advise on the many sporting facilities available locally.

How to get there *(Map 27): West of Gap via D994 towards Veynes. At La Roche des Arnauds, head for Manteyer; after the camp site left towards Le Clos de Sagnes; 1st farm on the left.*

326
Le Pi-Maï

Hameau de Fréjus
Station de Serre-Chevalier
05240 La Salle-les-Alpes
(Hautes-Alpes)
Tel. 92 24 83 63
M. and Mme Charamel

Open 1 Dec. – 30 April and 15 June – 15 Sept. 3 nights min. **Rooms** 1 with bath and WC, 3 with basin sharing shower and WC. **Meals** breakfast incl., obligatory half board 260-360F per pers. in double room. Lunch and evening meal in the restaurant on the spot. **Pets** dogs not allowed. **Nearby** ski-ing, golf. **Spoken** English.

Alone and clinging to the mountain slopes 2000m up, this modern house is built in the style of a Swiss chalet. The restaurant and its terrace are intimate and charming. The four guest bedrooms are small but pretty and (like the rest of the house) entirely panelled in wood. The largest has a balcony. Sporting but sophisticated atmosphere, and good food.

How to get there *(Map 27): 10km north west of Briançon via N91. At Villeneuve Lasalle, head for Hameau de Fréjus, 7km by road passable except when there is heavy snow; telephone and someone will come and find you.*

327
L'Alpillonne

Sigottier
05700 Serres
(Hautes-Alpes)
Tel. 92 67 08 98
M. and Mme Moynier

Open 10 June – 15 Sept. **Rooms** 3 with bath and WC, 2 sharing bath and WC. **Price** 200-250F (1 pers.), 250-290F (2 pers.) +50F (extra pers.) **Meals** breakfast incl., no evening meals. **Restaurants** in less than 5km. **Facilities,** library and TV, swimming pool, fishing, river bathing. **Nearby** tennis, lake, wind surfing, 18-hole golf (40km). **Spoken** English.

This 17th–18th century house standing at the foot of the mountains is charmingly decorated, with old regional furniture. The bedrooms are pretty, comfortable and light but do not all have bathrooms. Two are ideal for children. Breakfasts are served in a huge vaulted barn housing a bar and places to sit. A very pleasant welcome.

How to get there *(Map 33): 3km north of Serres via N75 towards Grenoble.*

328
La Maison de Poupée aux Volets Verts

Route de Berre-les-Alpes
Le Castellar, 06390 Berre-les-Alpes
(Alpes-Maritimes)
Tel. 93 91 83 51
Mme Vélut

Open 15 March – All Saints. **No smoking. Children** under 7 not accepted. 2/3 nights min. depending on season. **Rooms** 1 with bath and WC, 1 with shower and WC. **Price** 300F (2 pers.), 340F (2 pers.) in July and August. **Meals** breakfast incl., no evening meals. **Restaurants** close by. **Pets** dogs allowed (not in the bedrooms). **Nearby** seaside, mountains, old villages.

Here, the landscape is dotted with little houses surrounded by mimosas, chestnuts and olive trees. There are two very pretty bedrooms with luxurious bathrooms. Mme Vélut, who is always very attentive, offers generous breakfasts served on the terrace under the shade of a pergola. A delightful garden.

How to get there *(Map 35): 20km north of Nice via D2204 towards Sospel, then left on D15 towards Contes. After Contes D615 towards Berre-les-Alpes for 4km.*

329
Le Castel Enchanté

61, route de St-Pierre-de-Féric
06000 Nice
(Alpes-Maritimes)
Tel. 93 97 02 08
Mme Jacqueline Olivier

Open all year. **Rooms** 3 with bath, WC and TV, and 1 extra room. **Price** 400F (2 pers.) +80F (extra bed). **Meals** breakfast (large buffet) incl., no evening meals. **Restaurants** Flo and La Villa de Sienne in Nice. **Facilities** lounge. **Spoken** English, Spanish.

Five minutes from the centre of Nice, the Castel Enchanté clings to the hillside amid a mass of flowers. Inside there is a happy mixture of paintings, ornaments and furniture. The bedrooms are large and very comfortable and in the bathrooms there are lots of toiletries for guests. Two bedrooms have a terrace. A pity the breakfasts are not quite up to standard. Relaxed welcome.

How to get there *(Map 35): 1km north of Nice via expressway, exit Place St-Philippe, then left into Avenue Estienne-d'Orves, after big bend turn left on small private road at the turning on the hill.*

330
Domaine du Paraïs

La Vasta
06380 Sospel
(Alpes-Maritimes)
Tel. 93 04 15 78
Mme Marie Mayer

Open Easter – All Saints. 2 nights min. **Rooms** 4 with shower and WC (2 others being prepared). **Price** 180-300F (1 pers.), 250-380F (2 pers.) +100F (extra pers.) **Meals** breakfast incl., evening meals on reservation, at communal or separate table 150F. **Restaurants** Taverne Toscane and Auberge du Pont Vieux in Sospel (3km). **Facilities** lounge, glazed viewpoint for painting, swimming pool. **Pets** small dogs allowed on request. **Nearby** golf (29km), riding, tennis, footpaths, canoeing, Sospel, valley of la Roya. **Spoken** English, German.

L e Paraïs, home to a family of artists (painter, sculptor and classical musician), is a beautiful 19th-century Italianate house, with comfortable and elegant bedrooms, in a splendid terraced landscape dominated by the mountains of the Mercantour park. Walls and ceilings are painted with murals of intertwined flowers. The welcome is kindness itself.

How to get there *(Map 35): 21km from Menton; in Sospel take the Moulinet road for 1.9km starting from the Mairie, then left on the La Vasta road for 1.3km.*

331
Mas du Barrié

Grand Chemin du Barrié
13440 Cabannes
(Bouches-du-Rhône)
Tel. 90 95 35 39
M. Michel Bruel

Open all year. **No children.** 2 nights min. **Rooms** 2 with shower or bath and WC. Room cleaning every 2 days. **Price** 350F (2 pers.) **Meals** breakfast incl., evening meals at communal table 120F (wine incl.) **Facilities** lounge. **Pets** dogs not allowed. **Nearby** festivals. **Spoken** English.

M ichel Bruel fell in love with this 18th-century Provençal farmhouse, bathed in silence, shaded by two 250-year-old plane trees and surrounded by fruit trees. He has restored it sensitively and tastefully, adding modern comforts to the lovely old rooms. One of the guest rooms is in blue and white, while the other has a canopied bed and a red and white decor. There is also a guest lounge with a fireplace. Breakfast is served in the lounge or in fine weather on the terrace.

How to get there *(Map 33): 12km south east of Avignon A7 exit Noves; N7 towards Orgon then left on D26 towards Cabannes.*

332
La Burlande

Le Paradou
13520 Les Baux de Provence
(Bouches-du-Rhône)
Tel. 90 54 32 32
Mme Fajardo de Livry

Open all year. **Rooms** 1 with bath, WC, patio and TV, 2 with shower, WC, terrace and TV, and 1 suite (2/4 pers.) of 2 bedrooms with bath, WC, terrace and TV. **Price** 260-340F (2 pers.), suite 540F (2 pers.) **Meals** breakfast 45F, evening meals at communal or separate table 135F (wine not incl.), in summer lunch in the garden 100F. **Facilities** lounges, telephone, laundry service, baby sitting, swimming pool. **Pets** dogs allowed on request. **Nearby** tennis, riding, golf, fishing, climbing, bicycle hire. **Spoken** English.

La Burlande stands at the end of a long pebbly road. It is an oasis: the garden is full of flowers and has a beautiful swimming pool. The very quiet bedrooms all look onto the garden. Very friendly welcome with attention to detail and comfort. Excellent breakfasts.

How to get there *(Map 33: 25km south of Avignon towards les Baux and Fontvielle (D78f). Pass the Paradou turning, then follow D78f for 300m and turn left at the sign.*

333
Domaine de la Cride

La Cride
13610 Le Puy-Sainte-Réparade
(Bouches-du-Rhône)
Tel. 42 61 96 96
Fax 42 61 93 28
M. and Mme Chosalland

Open all year (check in winter). **Rooms** 5 with bath and WC. **Price** 400-550F (2 pers.) +50F (extra pers.) **Meals** breakfast 45F, no evening meals. **Restaurants** many in the village and in Aix-en-Provence (15km). **Facilities** lounge, telephone, swimming pool. **Credit cards** Visa, Mastercard. **Nearby** riding, golf. **Spoken** English, German.

Domaine de la Cride is on the wine route and consists of two attractive houses in 2-hectare grounds with a river, terrace, barbecue and swimming pool. The bedrooms are quiet and comfortable. Very colourful decor, walls covered with pictures. In summer breakfast is served in the shade of a large mulberry tree in the garden. Very friendly and professional welcome.

How to get there *(Map 33): 15km north of Aix via D14; it's in the hamlet of La Cride before the village.*

334
Château de Vergières

13310 Saint-Martin-de-Crau
(Bouches-du-Rhône)
Tel. 90 47 17 16
Fax 90 47 38 30
Jean and Marie-Andrée Pincedé

Open 1 March – 15 Nov. **Rooms** 6 with bath and WC. **Price** 750F (1 pers.), 800F (2 pers.) **Meals** breakfast incl., evening meals, on reservation, at communal table 250F (drinks incl.) **Facilities** lounge, telephone. **Credit cards** Visa, Amex. **Pets** dogs not allowed. **Nearby** swimming pool, tennis, golf. **Spoken** English.

The vast plain of the Crau and the closeness of the marshes of the Camargue are enough to draw you to this place, but there is also the late 18th-century elegance of the château, its beautiful old furniture steeped in memories, and the really friendly welcome of M. and Mme Pincedé. The comfortable bedrooms have kept all their character; each has a style of its own, complimenting the fine antique furniture. Excellent Provençal dinners.

How to get there *(Map 33): 17km east of Arles via N113 towards St-Martin-de-Crau, then D24 towards La Dynamite and le mas des Aulnes; signed.*

335
Les Cancades

Chemin de la Fontaine-de-Cinq-
Sous
Les Cancades
83330 Le Beausset (Var)
Tel. 94 98 76 93
Mme Zerbib

Open all year. **Rooms** 1 with bath and WC, 1 with bath, shared WC and terrace, and 1 studio (4 pers.) with shower and WC, made up of 1 large room and 1 small. Room cleaning up to guests. **Price** 300F (2 pers.), studio 400F (1/4 pers.) **Meals** breakfast incl., no evening meals. **Restaurants** in Le Beausset. **Facilities** lounge, swimming pool. **Pets** dogs not allowed.

After passing through a small housing estate, you will discover this large Provençal-style villa standing in a landscape of pines and olive trees. Recently built, and tastefully decorated, it has two good guest bedrooms, one with a private terrace opening onto the garden and the swimming pool; the other, a little smaller, has been prettily redecorated with lovely Provençal fabrics.

How to get there *(Map 34): 20km north west of Toulon via N8 towards Aubagne; opposite Rallye supermarket take the 'Fontaine-de-Cing-Sous' road for 1.3km then dirt track on the left; it's 50 metres after the 90° bend.*

336
L'Ormarine

14, avenue des Grives
L'Eau Blanche
83240 Cavalaire
(Var)
Tel. 94 64 39 45
Heidi and Gérard Léopold

Open 1 May – 20 Dec. **Rooms** 1 suite (2/4 pers.) with bath and WC. **Price** 280F (2 pers.) +100F (extra pers.) – 250F starting from the 2nd night. **Meals** breakfast incl., no evening meals. **Restaurants** Le Solarium, Le Flot Bleu and La Pergola. **Facilities** heated swimming pool, sailing trips (for longs stays). **Pets** dogs allowed on request. **Nearby** golf, sports, St-Tropez, Gassin, Ramatuelle, Verdon gorges, Carthusian monastery of la Verne. **Spoken** German.

L'Ormarine is a Provençal style house built in the residential area of Cavalaire, within the shelter of a magnificent aromatic flower-filled garden. The small guest suite is very simple, with twin beds and white wood furniture, but it has a very comfortable bathroom. Guests have their own terrace to relax on. Thanks to Heidi and Gérard's rare kindness you will feel perfectly at home. Sometimes Gérard will arrange for guests to use the boat for a day's sailing on the sea.

How to get there (Map 34): *telephone for directions.*

337
Château d'Entrecasteaux

83570 Entrecasteaux
(Var)
Tel. 94 04 43 95
Fax 94 04 48 46
M. Lachlan Mc Garvie Munn

Open all year. **Rooms** 2 with bath, WC and telephone. **Price** 850F (2 pers.) +200F (extra pers.) **Meals** breakfast incl., no evening meals. **Restaurants** La Fontaine in Salerne (7km), Chez Bruno in Lorgues (15km). **Facilities** swimming pool, exhibitions. **Credit cards** Amex. **Pets** dogs not allowed. **Spoken** English, Spanish.

Entrecasteaux dominates the village. You may wander through its immense white rooms on your own. The modern paintings and old furniture go together perfectly and the very comfortable bedrooms have an unrivalled view. The most unusual is 'de la marquise' with gold-painted furniture and a splendid marble bathroom with white arches. Generous breakfasts served in a bright dining room.

How to get there (Map 34): *31km west of Draguignan via D562 towards Lorgues, then D31.*

338
Le Mazet des Mûres

Route du Cros d'Entassi
Quartier Les Mûres
83310 Grimaud
(Var)
Tel. 94 56 44 45
Mme B. Godon

Closed 15 Oct. – 15 Dec. and 10 Jan. – 10 Feb. **Rooms** 5 studios (1/4 pers.) with shower, WC, kitchenette and TV. **Price** 380F (2 pers.), 450F (3 pers.) **Meals** breakfast incl., evening meals on request, at communal or separate table 100F max. (wine incl.) **Nearby** beaches, sailing, golf, equestrian centre, tennis, Grimaud, Port-Grimaud, Gassin, St-Tropez. **Spoken** English, German.

Though close to St Tropez, le Mazet des Mûres has surprisingly unspoilt surroundings. Outside the house there are terraces for breakfast in summer. All the bedrooms overlook the garden. They are spruce, prettily decorated (cane furniture, coloured fabrics) and have kitchenettes decorated with tiles from Salerne. Relaxed atmosphere, and reasonable prices.

How to get there *(Map 34): N98 between Ste-Maxime and St-Tropez; at the roundabout, follow 'Les Mûres' signs.*

339
Domaine Espagne

Ginasservis
83560 Rians
(Var)
Tel. 94 80 11 03
Mme Grech

Open all year. **Rooms** 4 with bath and WC. Room cleaning on request. **Price** 260F (2 pers.) +90F (extra pers.) **Meals** breakfast incl., lunch and evening meals on request, at communal table 90F (wine incl.) **Nearby** swimming pool, golf, Verdon gorges, lake of Esparron, mountains of la Sainte-Baume, Luberon park.

A farmhouse surrounded by cultivated fields and close to the Verdon gorges. The bedrooms are in a separate building and all overlook the garden. Simple and fresh decor with pretty fabrics and small pieces of old furniture. Breakfast is served in a day room which has a lounge–cum–library on the mezzanine. Lunch and dinner using produce from the farm. Simple and relaxed atmosphere.

How to get there *(Map 34): In Rians D23 towards Ginasservis, then D30 towards La Verdière; go for 3km, then it's 300m after the grain silos.*

340
La Maurette

83520 Roquebrune-sur-Argens
(Var)
Tel. 94 45 46 81
M. and Mme Rapin

Open 15 March – 1 Nov. **Rooms** 2 with bath and WC, plus 4 bedrooms and 2 studios (2 pers.) with shower and WC. **Price** 320-400F (2 pers.) +100F (extra pers.) **Meals** breakfast 35F, evening meals for residents only (not Sundays and Wednesdays) at communal or separate table on reservation the evening before 100F (wine incl.) **Facilities** lounge, telephone, swimming pool. **Credit cards** Visa. **Pets** dogs not allowed. **Spoken** English, German.

Perched on the top of a small mountain, La Maurette enjoys an exceptional view over the Esterel and Maures mountain ranges. The very comfortable bedrooms have direct access to the garden. Their decor is restrained but pleasing, and their old doors add a rustic touch. Meals are served by the windows in the very large sitting room. There is a swimming pool with a panoramic view. Breakfasts are served outside. Warm welcome.

How to get there *(Map 34): 10km west of Fréjus via N7 between Le Muy and Le Puget-sur-Argens, then D7 towards Roquebrune; signposted.*

341
La Ferme Jamet

Ile de la Barthelasse
84000 Avignon
(Vaucluse)
Tel. 90 86 16 74
Fax 90 86 17 72
Martine and Etienne Jamet

Open 1 March – 1 Nov. (on reservation in winter). **Rooms** 3 with bath and WC, 1 with shower and WC, 3 bungalows and 4 suites (2/4 pers.) with bath or shower, WC, kitchenette or kitchen. **Price** 300-320F (2 pers.), suite 360F (2 pers.), bungalow 290F (2 pers.) +50F (extra pers.) **Meals** breakfast 30F, no evening meals. **Restaurant** La Ferme in 150m. **Facilities** lounge, telephone, swimming pool, tennis. **Credit cards** Visa. **Nearby** golf, Avignon, festivals. **Spoken** English, German.

Jamet farm is very old and occupies an island of green outside Avignon. It is perfect for both touring the district and relaxing. The bedrooms are mostly suites: those in the house have old Provençal furniture. The bungalows are plainer and each has a private terrace. It's all very peaceful and comfortable, and you will get a young and friendly welcome.

How to get there *(Map 33): In Avignon, head for Villeneuve-lès-Avignon via Daladier bridge; signposted.*

342
Château de Saint-Ariès

Route de Saint-Ariès
84500 Bollène
(Vaucluse)
Tel. 90 40 09 17
Fax 90 30 45 62
Michel-Albert de Loye

Open 2 March – 2 Jan. (2 nights min.) **Rooms** 4 with bath, WC and sitting room, and 1 suite with bath, WC and 2 sitting rooms. **Price** 580-710F (2 pers.) +110F (extra pers.), suite 910F (2 pers.), 1010F (3 pers.) **Meals** breakfast 50F, evening meals on request, at communal table 230F (wine incl.) **Restaurants** in Mondragon (4km). **Facilities** phone, swimming pool, equestrian centre, bicycles. **Credit card** Visa, Eurocard. **Pets** small dogs allowed on request. **Nearby** tennis, golf, gorges of the Ardèche, Suze-la-Rousse, Mont Ventoux. **Spoken** English, Italian.

St Ariès, built in 1820 and modelled on the villas of Tuscany, stands in a huge park. The interior is beautiful. From the reception rooms to the bedrooms, family furniture, coloured fabrics and paintings create a marvellously harmonious ensemble. Michel de Loye will greet you as friends and the atmosphere at his excellent table reinforces this impression. A real success.

How to get there *(Map 33): 3km from A7 exit Bollène; town centre, then towards Mondragon. On the way out of Bollène turn left for St Ariès, then go 1.5km.*

343
Bonne Terre

Lacoste
84480 Bonnieux
(Vaucluse)
Tel. 90 75 85 53
M. and Mme Lamy-Gamba

Open 1 March – 30 Oct. 3 nights min. **Rooms** 1 with bath, WC, TV and terrace, 5 with shower, WC, TV and terrace. **Price** 390 and 420F (1 pers.), 450 and 470F (2 pers.) depending on season +120F (extra pers.) **Meals** breakfast incl., no evening meals. **Restaurants** in Lacoste and around (7/8km). **Facilities** telephone, swimming pool. **Credit cards** Visa. **Pets** dogs allowed (+40F). **Nearby** golf, tennis, riding, music festivals, theatre, Luberon villages. **Spoken** English, German and Italian.

At the entrance of the picturesque village of Lacoste, this modern house offers its guests peace and freedom. The bedrooms are prettily decorated, very comfortable, and each opens onto a private terrace where you can have breakfast. The garden is on several levels, with a swimming pool and a beautiful view of Mont Ventoux.

How to get there *(Map 33): East of Cavaillon via N100 towards Apt, then D106 towards Lacoste; opposite the Renault garage.*

344
La Bouquière

Quartier St Pierre
84480 Bonnieux
(Vaucluse)
Tel. 90 75 87 17
Françoise and Angel Escobar

Open all year. **Rooms** 4 with bath or shower, WC and terrace. Room cleaning every 2 days. **Price** 285-325F (2 pers.) +50F (extra pers.) **Meals** breakfast incl, no evening meals. **Restaurants** Le Fournil and Les Cavernes in Bonnieux (3km). **Facilities** lounge and small kitchen. **Pets** dogs allowed. **Nearby** ski-ing (Mont Ventoux), riding, fishing, climbing, tennis, mountain biking, swimming pool, golf (30km). **Spoken** English, Spanish.

Lost in the middle of countryside, La Bouquière enjoys a magnificent view of Mont Ventoux and has four comfortable guest bedrooms, very prettily decorated in Provençal style. Each bedroom has an independent entrance and opens onto a terrace where breakfast can be served. Pleasant welcome from Françoise and Angel Escobar and their little boy.

How to get there *(Map 33): 3km from Bonnieux via D3 towards Apt; signs after 2.5km .*

345
Au Ralenti du Lierre

Les Beaumettes
84220 Gordes
(Vaucluse)
Tel. 90 72 39 22
Mme Deneits

Open 15 March – 1 Nov. **Rooms** 4 with bath and WC, 1 with shower and WC. **Price** 250-500F (2 pers.) +50F (extra pers.) **Meals** breakfast incl., no evening meals. **Restaurants** La Remise and Le Mas des Lavandes. **Facilities** lounge, swimming pool. **Pets** dogs not allowed. **Nearby** golf, walks, fishing, tennis, riding, canoeing, climbing, villages of Gordes, Lacoste and Bonnieux, Senanque abbey.

The interior of this village house is a great success: colours, fabrics and furniture create a lovely harmony throughout the house, including the very comfortable bedrooms. Some of the bedrooms overlook a noisy street, so be careful when booking. For those with a taste for the unusual there is an astonishing suite of two vaulted rooms, one of which is very dark. Pretty garden sloping down the hillside. Excellent breakfast and marvellous welcome.

How to get there *(Map 33): 15km east of L'Isle-sur-Sorgue via N100 towards Apt; in the village of Les Beaumettes.*

346
Relais du Procureur

Rue Basse
Lacoste
84480 Bonnieux
(Vaucluse)
Tel. 90 75 82 28
Fax 90 75 86 94
M. Antoine Court de Gebelin

Open all year (on request in Jan. and Feb.) **Children** under 7 not allowed. 2 nights min. **Rooms** 6 with bath, WC and mini-bar (of which 3 air-conditioned and 3 with TV). **Price** 500-630F. **Meals** breakfast incl., no evening meals. **Restaurants** close by. **Facilities** lounge, telephone, swimming pool. **Credit cards** Visa, Amex. **Pets** dogs not allowed. **Nearby** tennis, riding (and loose boxes), golf, Luberon villages. **Spoken** English.

This very old house lies below the pretty village of Lacoste. Inside it is decorated in medieval style. A lovely stone staircase leads to the bedrooms and, on the second floor, to a... swimming pool! The streets can be a little noisy in summer. Variable welcome.

How to get there (Map 33): From Avignon or Cavaillon via N100 towards Apt, then in Lumières turn right towards Lacoste; in Lacoste keep right.

347
Bois Court

Fontaine-de-Vaucluse
84800 L'Isle-sur-Sorgue
(Vaucluse)
Tel. 90 20 31 93
Mme Douyère

Open all year. **Rooms** 1 with bath, WC and terrace, 2 with shower, WC and terrace. **Price** 240-280F (2 pers.) **Meals** breakfast incl., no evening meals. **Restaurants** close by. **Facilities** lounge. **Pets** not allowed. **Nearby** walks, Ménerbes, Bonnieux, Gordes, Roussillon, Sénanque abbey.

Very near to Fontaine-de-Vaucluse, this house built in 1925 on the side of a hill overlooks a large garden of trees and flowers. The pleasant but rather bare bedrooms have comfortable twin beds. Two of them open onto a private terrace with a view over pine trees. In the morning, lovingly prepared breakfasts await guests in the large, airy lounge.

How to get there (Map 33): From Avignon via N7 and D22 to Petit-Palais, then D24 towards Fontaine-de-Vaucluse; 200m after the La Coutelière camp site at the D24 and D57 intersection.

348
Sous Les Canniers

Route de la Roque
Saumane
84800 L'Isle-sur-Sorgue
(Vaucluse)
Tel. 90 20 20 30
Mme Annie Marquet

Open all year (on reservation in winter). **Rooms** 2 with shower and WC. **Price** 250F (2 pers.) +100F (extra pers.) **Meals** breakfast incl., evening meals at communal table 100F (wine incl.) **Facilities** lounge. **Pets** dogs allowed on request. **Nearby** golf (3km), walks, tennis, swimming pool, riding, abbeys and villages of Luberon. **Spoken** Italian, Spanish.

This is a small Provençal house in a delightful garden. The bedrooms open directly on to the outside. They are pleasant and pretty, with bits and pieces of furniture collected from second-hand shops. One has a mezzanine. Madame Marquet is very welcoming and prepares good evening meals, served at a large table on the terrace. This place has many good qualities.

How to get there (Map 33): 7km east of L'Isle-sur-Sorgue via D938 and D25 towards Fontaine-de-Vaucluse, then left on D57 towards Saumane; signs in the village.

349
Saint–Buc

Route de l'Isle
84800 Lagnes
(Vaucluse)
Tel. 90 20 36 29
Mme Delorme

Open 1 May – 5 Sept. **No children. Rooms** 4 with bath and WC. **Price** 400F (2 pers.) **Meals** breakfast incl., no evening meals. Kitchen for guests' use. **Restaurant** many close by. **Facilities** lounge, telephone, swimming pool, bicycles. **Pets** no dogs allowed. **Nearby** 18-hole golf, Luberon, Gordes, Avignon festival, Fontaine-de-Vaucluse. **Spoken** English.

Saint-Buc is a modern house a few minutes from L'Isle-sur-Sorgue. The comfortable bedrooms are at garden level and pleasantly and plainly decorated; the bathrooms are large and efficient and have sunken baths. Vast lounge, scattered with antique objects. Breakfast is served outside under an awning. There is a swimming pool and a cooking area in the garden for guests. Relaxed atmosphere.

How to get there (Map 33): 23km east of Avignon via N100 towards Apt. At Petit-Palais head for Fontaine-de-Vaucluse. At Lagnes take D99 towards Isle-sur-Sorgue.

350
Domaine de la Lombarde

BP32, 84160 Lourmarin
(Vaucluse)
Tel. 90 08 40 60
Fax 90 08 40 64
M. and Mme Gilbert Lèbre

Open Easter – Oct. **Rooms** 4 with shower, WC, fridge and terrace, and 1 studio (2 pers. + 2 children) with shower, WC, kitchen and terrace. Room cleaning every 3 days. **Price** 280-320F (2 pers.) +120F (extra pers.), studio 2200F weekly. **Meals** breakfast incl. (except studio). No evening meals. **Facilities** swimming pool, bicycles. **Pets** dogs not allowed. **Nearby** tennis, riding, golf, walks, Luberon, many festivals. **Spoken** English, Spanish.

La Lombarde is a lovely Provençal house set among fields and vineyards. Each bedroom has an independent entrance with a wooden canopy over, forming a terrace (with a fridge, very useful in summer). The bedrooms are comfortable and attractively decorated. Good breakfasts served on an old refectory table in a vaulted room. Convivial welcome.

How to get there (Map 33): 30km north of Aix-en-Provence via N556 towards Pertuis, and D973; it's between Cadenet and Lauris; signposted.

351
Villa Saint Louis

35, rue Henri de Savornin
84160 Lourmarin
(Vaucluse)
Tel. 90 68 39 18
Michel and Bernadette Lassallette

Open all year. **Rooms** 1 with bath and WC, 4 with shower and WC. Room cleaning on request. Price 250-350F (2 pers.) +50F (extra pers.) **Meals** breakfast incl., no evening meals. **Restaurants** La Louche à Beurre and La Ferrière. **Facilities** lounge, mountain-bikes. **Nearby** ski-ing, golf (25km), tennis, fishing, riding, canoeing, Luberon nature park, Luberon villages, summer festivals. **Spoken** English.

This beautiful 17th-century house, secluded in its walled garden, is located on the edge of Lourmarin. Created by Michel Lassallette, the interior decoration is an exceptional combination of different periods (18th to 20th centuries) with a profusion of furniture, paintings, ornaments and hangings. Breakfast is served in the lounge-dining-room, sometimes on the terrace. Very comfortable and a marvellous welcome.

How to get there (Map 33): 50km east of Avignon via N7 and D973 towards Cavaillon, then Cadenet and left on D943 towards Lourmarin.

352
Château Unang

Route de Méthamis
84570 Malemort-du-Comtat
(Vaucluse)
Tel. 90 69 71 06
Fax 90 69 92 80
Mme Marie-Hélène Lefer

Open all year (on request in Jan. and Feb.) **Rooms** 4 with bath and WC. **Price** 390-550F (2 pers.) **Meals** breakfast 50F, evening meals at communal or separate table 150F (wine not incl.) **Restaurants** Les Remparts in Vénasque (6km). **Facilities** lounge, swimming pool. **Pets** dogs not allowed. **Nearby** tennis, equestrian centre, golf (15km), ski-ing (30km), Gordes, Senanque abbey, Luberon villages. **Spoken** English, Spanish.

Château Unang is a fine 18th-century house, with a formal French garden, facing the Vaucluse mountains. Inside there is a pleasing blend of different styles. The lounge is very inviting, the bedrooms extremely elegant. We prefer 'Fontaine'; 'Vignes' is equally delightful but the view is not as good. Breakfast served outside when the weather is good. Young and friendly welcome.

How to get there (Map 33): 12km south east of Carpentras via D4 towards Vénasque for 6km, then left for Malemort.

353
Mas de Capelans

84580 Oppède
(Vaucluse)
Tel. 90 76 99 04
Fax 90 76 90 29
Jacqueline and Philippe Poiri

Open 15 Feb. – 15 Nov. 3 nights min. **Rooms** 6 with bath and WC, and 2 suites (4 pers.) with bath and WC., of which 1 with 2 bedrooms and 1 with mezzanine. **Price** 400-800F (2 pers.) +120F (extra pers.), suite 600-900F. **Meals** breakfast 50F, half board 350-500F per pers. in double room, evening meals at communal table 160F (wine not incl.) **Facilities,** lounge, library, TV, heated swimming pool. **Credit cards** Visa, Amex. **Pets** dogs not allowed. **Nearby** golf, tennis, fishing, riding, mountain biking. **Spoken** English, German.

Basking in a sea of lavender, this lovely old house has a pleasant inner courtyard where meals are served in summer. The bedrooms are large, very comfortable, decorated with pale wood and pretty fabrics, and have an exceptionally fine view. The sitting room is high and beamed, with comfortable wooden furniture and painted objects.

How to get there (Map 33): 23km east of Avignon Sud on N100 towards Apt until Coustelet, then 1st road on the right.

354
Mas de Lumière

Campagne Les Talons
84490 Saint-Saturnin-lès-Apt
(Vaucluse)
Tel. 90 05 63 44
M. and Mme Bernard Maître

Open all year. **Rooms** 2 with bath and WC, 1 with shower and WC. **Price** 350-500F (2 pers.) +100F (extra pers.) Special rates for off season. **Meals** breakfast incl., no evening meals. **Restaurants** Ferme de la Huppe and Mas de Tourteron. **Facilities** lounge, swimming pool. **Pets** dogs not allowed. **Nearby** golf (25km), riding, tennis, Luberon villages. **Spoken** English, Spanish.

Standing in a slightly raised position in a tiny hamlet, Mas de Lumière is a great success, both outside and within its cool walls. The bedrooms are luxurious and delightful, with pale decor. Several outside terraces offer guests plenty of room and comfort (the one facing East is ideal for breakfast). Splendid swimming pool overlooking the Luberon plain. Friendly and refined welcome.

How to get there *(Map 33): 10km west of Apt via N100 towards Gordes, and D4 towards Roussillon-Murs, then at the crossroads with D2 go 500m on D4, then turn right at the 'Les Talons' sign.*

355
Le Jardin d'Ansouis

Rue du Petit-Portail
Ansouis
84240 La Tour d'Aigues
(Vaucluse)
Tel. 90 09 89 27
Arlette Rogers

Open all year. **Rooms** 2 with bath and WC. Room cleaning once a week. **Price** 225F (1 pers.), 275F (2 pers.) +50F (extra pers.) **Meals** breakfast incl., lunch 100F (wine incl.) from end March to end Oct., and evening meals 175F (wine incl.) from end Oct. to end March (separate tables). **Restaurant** L'Auberge du Cheval Blanc (12km). **Facilities** lounge. **Pets** dogs allowed. **Nearby** swimming pool (8km), riding, tennis (5km), beach, water sports, château d'Ansouis, Luberon villages, lake la Bonde. **Spoken** English.

Ansouis is a delightful medieval village dominated by an imposing chateau. The house is in a charming little street and has a flower garden where tea is served on summer afternoons. Inside there is a pleasing blend of modern works of art and furniture of various styles. Inviting and comfortable bedrooms. You will be very well looked after.

How to get there *(Map 33): 35km north of Aix-en-Provence via A51, exit Pertuis, then D56.*

356
L'Evêché

Rue de l'Evêché
84110 Vaison-la-Romaine
(Vaucluse)
Tel. 90 36 13 46/90 36 38 30
Fax 90 36 32 43
M. and Mme Verdier

Open all year. **Rooms** 1 with bath and WC, 2 with shower and WC. **Price** 290-330F (1 pers.), 330-370F (2 pers.) **Meals** breakfast incl., no evening meals. **Restaurants** in Vaison. **Facilities** lounge. **Pets** dogs allowed on request. **Nearby** swimming pool, tennis, riding, golf (miniature and practice) in the village, walks, Vaison-la-Romaine.

This former bishop's palace in the medieval part of Vaison-la-Romaine was built in the 17th century and will certainly appeal to you. The austere frontage hides a comfortable, well decorated house, with two terraces (one used for breakfasts) which have a magnificent view. The bedrooms are delightful; the largest is the one with the bath. Pleasant welcome.

How to get there (Map 33): 29km north east of Orange via D975; in Vaison-la-Romaine follow 'ville médiévale' signs.

357
La Fête en Provence

Place du Vieux Marché
Haute Ville
84110 Vaison-la-Romaine
(Vaucluse)
Tel. 90 36 16 05/90 36 36 43
M. and Mme Christiansen

Closed Nov. and Feb. **Rooms** 2 duplex (3/4 pers.) with bath, WC, kitchen area, telephone and TV, 4 studios (2 pers.) with bath or shower, WC, kitchen area, telephone and TV, and 1 apartment (2 pers. and 1 child) with sitting room, kitchenette, bath and WC. **Price** studio 300F (2 pers.), duplex 600-650F (3/4 pers.), apart. 450F. Room cleaning on request. **Meals** breakfast 40F, restaurant for lunch and dinner (except Wednesday and Thursday lunch out of season) 98F and 130F + à la carte (wine not incl.) **Credit cards** Amex, Visa. **Nearby** swimming pool, tennis, 18-hole golf, Merindol les Oliviers. **Spoken** German.

This is one of the loveliest medieval villages in the Midi, and La Fête en Provence is on the market square. A delightful patio leads to the bedrooms. We advise you to take the duplexes, which have a terrace with a beautiful view. They are comfortable and have modern olivewood furniture. Neither a hotel nor a bed and breakfast, this is a charming place.

How to get there (Map 33): 27km north east of Orange via D975.

358
Mastignac

Route de Taulignan
84600 Valréas
(Vaucluse)
Tel. 90 35 01 82
Mme Nicole de Precigout

Open 1 June – 1 Oct. **Rooms** 4 with bath and 1 with shower sharing 3 WCs. **Price** 250-400F (2 pers.) **Meals** breakfast incl., no evening meals. **Restaurants** close by. **Facilities** lounge, swimming pool. **Pets** small dogs allowed. **Nearby** tennis, bathing, golf, festivals. **Spoken** English.

Two kilometres from Valréas you will come upon this big old 18th-century farmhouse. It is well restored and immaculate, with an inner courtyard, an English lawn and a lovely swimming pool. The five tastefully decorated bedrooms are large and light, each with a bathroom but sharing three WCs between them. Breakfast is served outside whenever possible – if not, in the lounge or in the large kitchen. Pleasant and peaceful atmosphere.

How to get there (Map 33): 37km south east of Montélimar via A7, exit Montélimar Sud, then N7 towards Donzère, and D541. In Valréas, left on D47, the Taulignan road; signposted.

359
La Maison aux Volets Bleus

84210 Vénasque
(Vaucluse)
Tel. 90 66 03 04
Mme Martine Maret

Open 15 March – 15 Nov. **Rooms** 5 with bath and WC (of which 1 with shower and bath). **Price** 280-350F (2 pers.) +100F (extra pers.) **Meals** breakfast incl., evening meals (separate tables) 110F (wine not incl.) **Facilities** lounge, telephone. **Nearby** tennis, bicycles, footpaths, Sénanque abbey, Fontaine-de-Vaucluse, Avignon, Luberon. **Spoken** English.

A blue-shuttered house tucked away in the pretty village of Vénasque, perched on top of a rock. The house is stone built and quite delightful, with a small shady courtyard full of flowers. The lounge is large, pleasantly decorated, with antique furniture and dried flower arrangements. The bedrooms are big, comfortable and tastefully done. Beautiful bathrooms. Magnificent, dizzily panoramic view. Pleasant welcome and good food.

How to get there (Map 33): South of Carpentras via D4; signposted.

360
Le Jeu du Mail

07400 Alba-la-Romaine
(Ardèche)
Tel. 75 52 41 59
M. and Mme Maurice Arlaud

Open all year. **Rooms** 1 with bath, WC and fridge, 3 with shower and WC, and 1 suite (4/8 pers.) of two bedrooms (with mezzanine) with 2 showers, 2 WCs and fridge. Room cleaning every 2 days. **Price** 200-290F (2 pers.), suite 480F (4 pers.) **Meals** breakfast incl., no evening meals. **Restaurants** in the village. **Facilities** lounge, swimming pool. **Pets** dogs allowed on request (+30F). **Nearby** tennis, riding, golf, medieval villages, Romanesque churches. **Spoken** English, Italian.

A lba-la-Romaine is a lovely village built of volcanic rock. This old house, just outside the village, has thick walls which keep it cool and quiet. The bedrooms are charming, comfortable, and well decorated, with old furniture and amusing prints. Breakfast is served on the big table in the beautiful sitting room. A place of character, where you will be well looked after.

How to get there *(Map 26): 18km west of Montélimar via N102. At Buis-d'Aps D107 towards Viviers; it's 200m from the château.*

361
Maison Icare

Faugères
07230 Lablachère
(Ardèche)
Tel. 75 39 48 66

Open all year. **Rooms** 2 sharing bath and WC, and 1 suite (2/5 pers.) with shower, WC and kitchen. **Price** 200F (2 pers.) +50F (extra pers.) **Meals** breakfast incl., half board 175F per pers. in double room. Special rates out of season. Evening meals at communal table 75F (wine incl.) **Facilities** lounge, fishing, river bathing. **Pets** dogs not allowed. **Nearby** tennis, swimming pool, footpaths, old villages, gorges of the Ardèche, Romanesque churches, Thines.

A s if in imitation of the surrounding landscape, this very old village house rambles up and down, hither and thither. The bedrooms, full of character, are comfortable and mostly furnished with antiques (except the loft and its sun terrace). Very good evening meals served in different places depending on the season. Magnificent scenery and painless prices.

How to get there *(Map 32): 32km south west of Aubenas via D104 towards Alès. At Lablachère, right on D4 to Planzolles, then right on D250; signposted.*

362
Chez Marcelle and
Jean-Nicholas Goetz

07000 Pourchères
(Ardèche)
Tel. 75 66 81 99/75 66 80 22
M. and Mme Goetz

Closed 1 Jan. – 31 March and 15 days in June and Sept. **No smoking. Rooms** 1 with bath and WC, 3 with shower and WC, and 1 suite (3 pers.) with bath, shower, and WC. Room cleaning every 4 days. **Price** 180-240F (2 pers.), suite 260F (2 pers.) +70F (extra pers.) **Meals** breakfast incl., evening meals at communal table in winter, separate tables in summer 90F (wine incl.) **Pets** well-behaved dogs allowed. **Spoken** English, German.

This rambling old house is built on a lava flow, nowadays alive with flowers. The stone is dark, but the landscape is green. Pleasant bedrooms furnished in regional style, some in a recently converted shepherd's cottage. Good evening meals, served outside in good weather to the accompaniment of a breathtaking view. Only those who love deepest Ardèche will enjoy the austere ambience.

How to get there (Map 26): At Privas head for Les Ollières, at Petit Tournon 2nd left towards Pourchères; signposted.

363
La Croze

07110 Rocles
(Ardèche)
Tel. 75 88 31 43
Myriam and Claude Rouvière

Open all year. **Rooms** 4 with shower and shared WC. Room cleaning on request. **Price** 170F (1 pers.), 220F (2 pers.). **Meals** breakfast incl., half board 165F per pers. in double room, evening meals, on reservation, at communal or separate table 75F (wine incl.). **Facilities** lounge, stabling, bicycles, hacking (suppl.). **Pets** dogs not allowed. **Nearby** fishing, bathing, medieval town of Largentière. **Spoken** English, German, Spanish.

The young and friendly Rouvières live in a large Ardèche farmhouse with a 21-hectare property which keeps them very busy. The guest bedrooms they offer are simple but pleasant and have just been refurbished. Guests are welcome to sit around the big log fire in a room full of interesting things gathered from the four corners of the earth. Cooking with home-grown produce. Informal atmosphere.

How to get there (Map 25): 29km west of Aubenas via D104 towards Joyeuse, then D103 towards Largentière, and D24 towards Valgorge; signposted.

364
Chez Claire

Cros-la-Planche
07310 Saint-Martial-de Valamas
(Ardèche)
Tel. 75 29 27 60
Mme Claire Gélibert

Open all year. **Rooms** 3 with shower and WC. **Price** 205F (2 pers.) +50F (extra pers.) **Meals** breakfast incl., half board 175F per pers. in double room, lunch and evening meals at communal table, on request 75F (wine incl.) **Facilities** lounge fishing, carriage rides. **Nearby** tennis, cross country ski-ing, lake, waterfall of Ray-Pic. **Spoken** English.

In a wild and mountainous part of Ardèche, this house is as inviting as it could possibly be. Claire Gélibert has organised several sweet, small, chalet-type guest bedrooms. There is a profusion of house plants in the skylit lounge. Good evening meals, and a family atmosphere provided by the children of the house.

How to get there *(Map 25): Loriol–La Voulte–Beauchastel–St Sauveur–Le Cheylard–St Martin de Valomas; starting from St Martin de Valomas head for Arcens then towards St Martial; 1km on the left after 'La Chazotte'.*

365
Scarlett's

Bonnemontesse
Beaulieu
07460 Saint-Paul-le-Jeune
(Ardèche)
Tel. 75 39 07 26/75 39 32 49
M. and Mme Munari

Open all year. **Rooms** 1 with bath and WC, 2 with shower and WC (of which 1 has external WC). **Price** 350F (2 pers.) **Meals** breakfast 45F, evening meals (separate tables) 100-120F (wine not incl.) **Facilities** lounge, swimming pool, riding. **Pets** dogs on request. **Nearby** 6- and 18-hole golf courses (3km and 30km), tennis, bicycles, gorges of the Ardèche, Thines, old villages. **Spoken** Italian.

Standing alone on its little hill, this old house and its swimming pool seem to be advancing towards the plain like the prow of a ship. You can see into the far distance. Very comfortable bedrooms (one with a terrace) are well decorated and furnished in old-fashioned style. A charming lounge with a fireplace is reserved for guests. Breakfast and dinner are served beneath a pergola in fine weather. Excellent welcome.

How to get there *(Map 32): 35km south of Aubenas via D104 towards Alès, then left on D111 after Maison-Neuve towards Ruoms, then 1st road on the right; signposted.*

366
Ferme de Prémauré

Route de Lamastre
07240 Vernoux-en-Vivarais
(Ardèche)
Tel. 75 58 16 61
Claudine and Roland Achard

Open Easter – 11 Nov. **Rooms** 1 with bath and WC, 6 with shower and WC. Room cleaning on request. **Price** 200F (2 pers.) +60F (extra pers.) Special rates starting from 4 days. **Meals** breakfast 20F, evening meals at communal or separate table 85F (wine not incl.) **Facilities** lounge, stabling, mountain bike hire. **Pets** dogs not allowed. **Nearby** golf (35km), riding, swimming pool, tennis, botanical trails, châteaux, village of Chalançon. **Spoken** English.

Clinging to the hillside, this ancient farm has an exceptional view over the Ardèche mountains. The welcome is full of kindness and good humour. Pleasant, well-kept bedrooms with antique furniture. Excellent food served in the dining–room cum lounge or on a flowery terrace looking over countryside typical of the Midi.

How to get there *(Map 26): Autoroute exit Valence Nord; 8km south of Lamastre via D2 towards Vernoux-en-Vivarais; signposted.*

367
Grangeon

Saint-Cierge-la-Serre
07800 La Voulte
(Ardèche)
Tel. 75 65 73 86
Mme Paule Valette

Open 1 April – 8 Nov. **Rooms** 2 with bath and WC, 1 with shower and WC, and 2 suites (3/4 pers. and 5 pers.) with bath, shower and WC. **Price** 270-350F (2 pers.) +140F (extra pers.) **Meals** breakfast 35F, half board starting at 270F per pers., evening meals (separate tables) 150F (wine not incl.) **Pets** small well-behaved dogs allowed. **Nearby** golf, Ardèche châteaux. **Spoken** English, Italian.

Grangeon is situated on its own at the end of a long track. The welcome is very pleasant. All the bedrooms are simple, charming, and exceptionally well equipped. Dinner is a delight. Nearly all the produce comes from the property. Outside, the flower-filled terraces overlook a dazzling panorama.

How to get there *(Map 26): 35km south of Valence via A7 exit Loriol, then N104 towards Privas. At 'Fonts-du-Pouzin' right on D265 towards St-Cierge-la-Serre; signposted.*

368
Domaine Saint-Luc

26790 Baume–de–Transit
(Drôme)
Tel. 75 98 11 51
Ludovic and Eliane Cornillon

Open all year. **Rooms** 5 with bath and WC. **Price** 210F (1 pers.), 225F (2 pers.) **Meals** breakfast incl., evening meals at communal table 130F (wine not incl.) **Facilities** lounge, telephone. **Pets** dogs allowed on request (+12F). **Nearby** swimming pool, golf, château de Grignan, villages of St Restitut, La Garde Adhémar. **Spoken** English.

A very pretty, traditional 18th-century southern farmhouse built around a square to give protection against the mistral. Natural materials like stone and wood take pride of place in the very tasteful decor. The comfortable bedrooms are well renovated. Excellent food washed down with wine produced on the property is served at a communal table. Attentive and professional welcome.

How to get there (Map 33): From Bollène head towards Nyons; at Suze-la-Rousse D117 towards Grignan for 5km; it's on the left before Baume-de-Transit.

369
Les Grand' Vignes

Mérindol–les–Oliviers
26170 Buis–les–Baronnies
(Drôme)
Tel. 75 28 70 22
François and Chantal Schlumberger

Open all year. 2 nights min. **Rooms** 1 with shower, WC, TV and fridge, and 1 studio (2 pers.), with bath, WC, TV and fridge. Room cleaning twice weekly. **Price** 190F (1 pers.), 220F (2 pers.), studio 270F (2 pers.). **Meals** breakfast incl., no evening meals. **Restaurant** in 100m. **Facilities** swimming pool. **Pets** small dogs allowed. **Nearby** walks, tennis, riding ski-ing, Vaison-La-Romaine. **Spoken** English.

In rolling country where vineyards and olive groves rub shoulders, this very pretty house reflects the sweetness of life and the goodness of a Provençal welcome. Pleasant and comfortable bedrooms with white walls offset by coloured fabrics. The larger has its own entrance but both are just a few metres from the swimming pool. In good weather breakfast is served outside overlooking the countryside.

How to get there (Map 33): In Vaison D938 towards Nyons then D46 towards Puyméras and D205. In Mérindol D147; 1st house on the right on the Mollans road.

370
Domaine du Grand Lierne

26120 Châteaudouble
(Drôme)
Tel. 75 59 80 71
M. and Mme Charignon-Champel

Open all year. 2 nights min. **Rooms** 3 sharing 1 bath and WC, and 1 suite (2/3 pers.) with private bathroom. **Price** 150F (1 pers.), 200F (2 pers.), 250F (3 pers.), suite 250F (2 pers.) +50F (extra pers.) **Meals** breakfast incl., no evening meals. **Pets** dogs not allowed. **Nearby** tennis, fishing, riding club, golf, cross country ski-ing, clay pigeon shooting, walks, Vercors Bach festival (20 July–15 Aug.) **Spoken** English.

This old stone farmhouse with its square, typically Dauphinois tower is in the plain of Chabeuil. The house is surrounded by fields of maize and has a strongly traditional feel. Three comfortable bedrooms on the first floor share one bathroom. The suite is nicer and opens onto the pretty courtyard. Breakfast served outside in summer, with home-made jams.

How to get there (Map 26): 15km east of Valence via D68 towards Chabeuil; at the roundabout at the entrance to Chabeuil go towards Romans, at the 2nd roundabout 1.5km later right towards Peyrus, 1st house on the left after Les Faucons.

371
Le Balcon de Rosine

Route de Propiac
26170 Mérindol-les-Oliviers
(Drôme)
Tel. 75 28 71 18
Jean and Jacqueline Bouchet

Closed in August. **Rooms** 1 with bath, WC, TV and kitchen, and 1 with shower, WC, TV. Room cleaning twice weekly. **Price** 180F (1 pers.), 220F (2 pers.) **Meals** breakfast incl., no evening meals. **Restaurant** La Gloriette (1km). **Pets** dogs allowed. **Nearby** cross-country ski-ing and ski slopes, tennis, riding, bathing, Vaison-la-Romaine, wine route. **Spoken** English, Italian.

Le Balcon de Rosine has an exceptional position overlooking the plain of Ouvèze, with a view of Mont Ventoux. The old farmhouse has a lovely garden and two simple but pleasant bedrooms with their own entrances (one is in a little building alongside). Breakfast is served outside on the terrace or in the lounge. Relaxed and friendly welcome.

How to get there (Map 33): 10km north east of Vaison-La-Romaine via D938 towards Nyons, then D46 towards 'La Tuillière' for 4km, then left on D205. In Mérindol D147 towards Propiac for 1km.

372
Ferme de Moutas

Saint-Pons
Condorcet
26110 Nyons
(Drôme)
Tel. 75 27 70 13
M. and Mme Taelman

Open 1 June – 30 Sept. **Rooms** 2 with shower, WC and fridge. Room cleaning on request. **Price** 200F (1 pers.), 220F (2 pers.) **Meals** breakfast incl., evening meals once a week at communal table 100F (wine incl.) **Restaurants** in 6km. **Facilities** swimming pool. **Pets** small dogs allowed. **Nearby** fishing, riding, Drôme Provençale. **Spoken** Dutch, English.

The approach to the Ferme de Moutas is down a long narrow road edged with broom. M. and Mme Taelman receive their guests with obvious pleasure. The two large bedrooms have white walls and are comfortable, each with a simply and tastefully decorated sitting area. In summer they are pleasantly cool. Each has a private terrace, lovely for breakfast. A marvellous place.

How to get there *(Map 33): At Nyons, D94 and D70. At Condorcet, D227 towards St-Pons; after St-Pons, take the road on the right after 600m.*

373
Mas de Champelon

Hameau de Saint-Turquois
26790 Suze-la-Rousse
(Drôme)
Tel. 75 98 81 95
Christiane and Michaël Zebbar

Open Easter – All Saints. **Rooms** 4 with bath or shower and WC (1 has private terrace). **Price** 200F (2 pers.) **Meals** breakfast incl., half board 190F per pers. in double room, evening meals at communal table. **Pets** dogs not allowed. **Nearby** gorges of the Ardèche, châteaux of Suze-la-Rousse and Grignan, Vaison-La-Romaine. **Spoken** English, Italian.

This small traditional farmhouse, very peaceful and completely renovated, is set back from the road and hidden between rows of vines and a small wood. The simple, comfortable bedrooms are hung with Provençal fabrics and overlook a flowering garden. Each has a modern bathroom. Breakfast is generally served outside in the shade with a large choice of home-made jams, and the evening meals, based on local recipes, are good.

How to get there *(Map 33): From Bollène head towards Nyons; at Suze-la-Rousse head for St-Paul-Trois-Châteaux and Grignan via D117; the house is at the beginning of St-Turquois.*

374
La Grande Ourse

Bois Barbu
38250 Villard-de-Lans
(Isère)
Tel. 76 95 92 80
Dominique and Agnès Bon

Open all year. **No smoking. Rooms** 3 with shower and WC. **Price** 195F (1 pers.), 230F (2 pers.) +110F (extra pers.) Room cleaning every 2 days. **Meals** breakfast incl., half board 185F per pers. in double room (3 nights min.), evening meals at communal table 90F (wine not incl.) **Facilities** lounge. **Pets** not allowed. **Nearby** ski slopes and cross-country ski pistes, swimming pool, tennis, potholing, mountain biking, golf. **Spoken** English.

This old restored farmhouse, typical of the Vercors area, is surrounded by fields and fir trees, and is right beside the start of the cross-country ski pistes. The bedrooms, intimate, comfortable and prettily decorated, all overlook the landscape. In the evening there are good meals with regional dishes. Very pleasant atmosphere, a well-supplied library and a number of board games.

How to get there *(Map 26): 32km south west of Grenoble via A48 exit Veurey-Voroise, then N532 and D531 towards Villard-de-Lans; it's 3km from Villard in the Bois-Barbu direction.*

375
Château–Auberge de Bobigneux

Bobigneux
42220 Saint-Sauveur-en-Rue
(Loire)
Tel. 77 39 24 33
Mme Danièle Basty

Open Easter – All Saints. **Rooms** 3 with shower and WC, 2 with basin sharing shower and WC. **Price** 140F (2 pers.) +20F (extra pers.) **Meals** breakfast 22F, half board 160F per pers. in double room (2 days min.), evening meals and lunch (separate tables) 60-85F (wine not incl.) **Facilities** telephone. **Credit cards** Visa. **Pets** dogs allowed on request. **Nearby** lake, riding centre, mountain biking, golf (8km), cross-country ski-ing. **Spoken** English.

This small château built of local granite is in the Pilar national park. Madame Basty will greet you with a smile. The bedrooms are simple but sweet, comfortable and quiet. Tables are laid in a beautiful room with 18th-century panelling. Excellent family cooking is served there. You will seldom be alone because this small auberge is very popular locally. Particularly economical for families.

How to get there *(Map 26): 18km north west of Annonay towards Bours-Argental, then D503 towards St-Sauveur; on the left before the village.*

376
Château de Bois-Franc

69640 Jarnioux
(Rhône)
Tel. 74 68 20 91
Fax 74 65 10 03
M. Doat

Open all year. 3 nights min. between 15 Nov. and 15 March. **Rooms** 1 with shower and WC, and 2 suites (3/6 pers.) with bath and WC. **Price** 250F (2 pers.), suites 350-800F. **Meals** breakfast incl., no evening meals. **Restaurants** La Fontaine Bleue in Villefranche (7km) and L'Auberge de Liergues (3km). **Facilities** lounge. **Pets** dogs allowed on request. **Nearby** tennis (1km), riding (6km). **Spoken** English.

Bois-Franc is in the countryside not far from the villages built in golden stone of Beaujolais. Madame Doat will receive you with great kindness. The interior has kept its old-fashioned character. Book the 'chambre jaune' which is the most expensive but absolutely magnificent and beautifully furnished. Avoid the 'Mireille' suite, which is less comfortable. Breakfast served in a pretty dining room. Immense grounds.

How to get there (Map 26): 7km west of Villefranche-sur-Saône via D504 and D19 through Coigny.

377
La Javernière

69910 Villié-Morgon
(Rhône)
Tel. 74 04 22 71
M. François Roux

Open all year. **Rooms** 7 with bath or shower and WC, and 1 suite (4 pers.) of 2 bedrooms with bath or shower and WC each. **Price** 510-550F (2 pers.), suite 920F (4 pers.) **Meals** breakfast 50F, no evening meals. **Restaurants** nearby. **Facilities** lounge, swimming pool, fishing. **Credit cards** Visa, Amex. **Pets** dogs allowed (+30F). **Nearby** riding, golf, Romanesque churches.

All the bedrooms overlook the Beaujolais countryside, with vineyards stretching as far as the eye can see. The interior is elegant and immaculate. In the bedrooms and the lounge there is fine old furniture set off by beautiful curtains and carpets. Some bedrooms have lovely timber beams, and we liked these best. Good breakfasts.

How to get there (Map 26): Take Belleville exit from autoroute, D68 between Morgon and Villié-Morgon; the road is 600m from Morgon.

378
La Revardière

Hameau de Saint-Victor
Trévignin
74100 Aix-les-Bains
(Savoie)
Tel. 79 61 59 12
Madame Jackline Rocagel

Open all year. **No smoking. Rooms** 1 with bath and WC, 2 with shower (sharing WC), sitting room and TV. Room cleaning every 5 days. **Price** 175 and 240F (1 pers.), 265 and 350F (2 pers.) +95F (extra pers.) **Meals** breakfast incl., evening meals at communal table 95F and 110F (wine incl.) **Facilities** lounge. **Pets** dogs allowed on request (+15F). **Nearby** golf, ski slopes and cross-country ski-ing, lake of le Bourget, Hautecombe abbey.

O n the slopes of Mont Revar, this modern chalet overlooks the countryside between the lakes of le Bourget and Annecy. The bedrooms are comfortable, meticulously well kept, have walls clad in wood, and share a pleasant small lounge. Good family cooking and a very kind welcome from Mme Rocagel, who paints (and sells) bottles with scenes of Savoy.

How to get there (Map 27): 7km east of Aix-les-Bains via D913, the Revard road. After Trévignin, turn right; signed close to the stone wayside cross; left on small road towards St-Victor.

379
Chez Mme Gressier

Le Cernix
73590 Crest-Voland
(Savoie)
Tel. 79 31 70 74
Mme Gressier

Open all year, on reservation. **Rooms** 1 with shower and WC, 2 sharing bath, shower and WC. **Price** 150F (1 pers.), 230-250F (2 pers.) **Meals** breakfast incl., no evening meals. **Restaurant** Mont Charvin 100m. **Facilities** lounge, telephone. **Pets** dogs not allowed. **Nearby** Alpine ski-ing (ski-lifts 100m), cross-country ski-ing, walks, bicycle hire, riding, 18-hole golf.

T his modern chalet is in a tranquil Savoy village and has three very comfortable bedrooms, fastidiously well-kept and prettily decorated with attractive wooden furniture, prints, and old mirrors. The bathrooms are equally charming. Breakfast with home-made jams is served in the cosy lounge. Very friendly atmosphere.

How to get there (Map 27): 16km south west of Mégève via N212.

380
Chez M. and Mme Coutin

73210 Peisey-Nancroix
(Savoie)
Tel. 79 07 93 05
M. and Mme Maurice Coutin

Open all year. **Rooms** 2 sharing bath and WC. **Price** 115-125F (1 pers.), 165-185F (2 pers.) +65F (extra pers.) **Meals** breakfast incl., evening meals at communal table 75F (wine incl.) **Facilities** telephone. **Pets** dogs allowed on request. **Nearby** Alpine ski-ing (ski lift 500m, connection with Les Arcs) and cross-country ski-ing, Vanoise national park.

This former farmhouse with its flowery balconies and slate roof is just outside the still unspoilt village of Peisey. It has two guest bedrooms with a shared balcony overlooking the valley and the summit of the Alliet. Breakfasts are served in a large and inviting dining room. Very good hospitality.

How to get there (Map 27): At Moutiers, head towards Bourg-St-Maurice. After Bellentre leave N90 and right on D87 towards Peisey; in front of 'Maison Savoyard', at the top car park, road on the right; signposted.

381
Les Chataîgniers

Rue Maurice Franck
73110 La Rochette
(Savoie)
Tel. 79 25 50 21
Fax 79 25 79 97
Anne Charlotte Rey

Open all year. **Children** under 10 not allowed. **Rooms** 6 (of which 1 apartment) with bath, WC, TV. **Price** 420-900F **Meals** breakfast 55F, lunch and evening meals (separate tables) 98-175F (wine not incl.) **Facilities** lounge, swimming pool. **Credit cards** Visa, Amex, Diners. **Pets** dogs not allowed. **Nearby** golf, tennis, ski-ing, château du Touvet, wine route. **Spoken** English, German, Italian.

A beautiful family house, exquisitely decorated, a captivating hostess, and a poetic menu, are the ingredients which make this place different from others. Here, at guests' request, dinners on 'poetic' themes are organised. The bedrooms are spacious, luxurious and comfortable and mostly overlook the pretty grounds, where there is a swimming pool.

How to get there (Map 27): 30km south east of Chambery via A41 exit Pontcharra, then D925 north to La Rochette.

382
La Girandole
46, chemin de la Persévérance
74400 Chamonix Mont Blanc
(Haute-Savoie)
Tel. 50 53 37 58
M. and Mme Pierre Gazagnes

Open all year. **Rooms** 3 (of which 2 with basin) sharing 1 bath and 1 WC. Price 250F (2 pers.) +30F (extra pers.) **Meals** breakfast incl., no evening meals. **Restaurants** La Tartifle and Le National. **Facilities** lounge. **Pets** dogs allowed on request. **Nearby** golf, all winter sports, all summer sports, Aiguille du Midi, music weeks in summer. **Spoken** English, German.

One could not possibly dream of a better position. Built on the southern slope, this chalet faces the Aiguille du Midi, Mont Blanc and the Bossons glacier. The small, pretty bedrooms and the balcony share this stupendous view. M. and Mme Gazagnes are very obliging; they have an intimate knowledge of the area and their advice will help you to explore it. A good address, and there's even a telescope.

How to get there *(Map 27): At Chamonix sud, head for Bravent téléphérique, then towards Les Moussoux; signposted.*

INDEX

A

B

C

D

E

F

G

M

N

O

P

NOTES